THE FOUNDATIONS OF ARCHITECTURE

DICTIONNAIRE RAISONNÉ

DE

L'ARCHITECTURE

FRANÇAISE

DU XIe AU XVIe SIÈCLE

PAR

M. VIOLLET-LE-DUC

ARCHITECTE DU GOUVERNEMENT

INSPECTEUR-GÉNÉRAL DES ÉDIFICES DIOCÉSAINS

TOME PREMIER.

PARIS

B. BANCE, ÉDITEUR

RUE BONAPARTE, 13.

1854

EUGÈNE-EMMANUEL VIOLLET-LE-DUC

THE FOUNDATIONS OF ARCHITECTURE

Selections from the *Dictionnaire raisonné*

Introduction by Barry Bergdoll
Translation by Kenneth D. Whitehead

GEORGE BRAZILLER
NEW YORK

For information address the publisher:

George Braziller, Inc.
60 Madison Avenue
New York, New York 10010

Library of Congress Cataloging-in-Publication Data:

Viollet-le-Duc, Eugène-Emmanuel, 1814–1879.
[Dictionnaire raisonné de l'architecture française du XIe au XVIe siècle.
Selections. English. 1990]
The foundations of architecture : Selections from the Dictionnaire raisonné of Viollet-le-Duc / introduction by Barry Bergdoll; translations by Kenneth D. Whitehead.
p. cm
Includes bibliographical references.
ISBN 0-8076-1248-C. — ISBN 0-8076-1244-8 (pbk.)
1. Architecture—Dictionaries—French. 2. Architecture—France—Dictionaries.
I. Title.
NA1041.V7413 1990
720′.944—dc20
89-81207
CIP

Designed and manufactured in The United States of America
by Ray Freiman & Company

FIRST EDITION

Table of Contents

The *Dictionnaire raisonné*: Viollet-le-Duc's Encyclopedic Structure for Architecture

> "Examinez tout, ce qui est bon retenez-le"
>
> VIOLLET-LE-DUC'S *ex libris*

> "I believe the 'Raisonné' was the only really sensible book on architecture. . . . That book was enough to keep, in spite of architects, one's faith alive in architecture."
>
> FRANK LLOYD WRIGHT[1]

In both title and form, the *Dictionnaire raisonné de l'architecture française du XIe au XVIe siècle* (1854–68) invokes the doctrine of structural rationalism that is, in the tradition of modern architectural theory, inextricably associated with the name of Eugène-Emmanuel Viollet-le-Duc (1814–79). Indeed the three leading architectural theorists of the mid-nineteenth century found ideal vessels for their visions of architecture in their most famous texts. Ruskin recorded his narrative vision of architecture in the rambling descriptions of his *Stones of Venice* (1853–55); Gottfried Semper outlined, but never completed, his taxonomic sequences of the four generative elements of building in his *Der Stil* (1860–63); and Viollet-le-Duc embedded his conviction that medieval architecture was essentially a rational affair of constructive logic as deeply in the individual articles as in the very structure of his great *Dictionnaire*. Rejecting both the essay and the treatise—the two traditional forms of architectural exposition since the Renaissance—in favor of the seemingly neutral and objectively ordered space of the alphabet, Viollet-le-Duc crafted a theoretical instrument that was *raisonné* in the two senses of the word: it offered a universal explanation, a closed and complete system, and its arguments were throughout based on an unfailing faith in reason and in the rationality of his subject.

The *Dictionnaire* took nearly fifteen years to complete, but as is clear from the cross-references in the first volume, published in 1854, a plan had been established from the start, one that ordered the work even as it evolved from a projected two volumes, with 1,300 figures, to a vast undertaking of ten volumes, totaling over 5,000 pages with 3,367 illustrations intimately linked with the text.[2] In the course of this vast one-man enterprise, Viollet-le-Duc not only honed the theory of structural rationalism, he refined a new form of architectural writing, with text and image integrated. The very composition of this work paralleled his interpretation of Gothic as a scientific, highly ordered architectural system with both the logical structure and the historical complexity of other great systems of form, be they linguistic, anatomical, or geological.

Numerous criticisms of Viollet-le-Duc's decision to subordinate his complex theory to the constraints of a dictionary accompanied the *Dictionnaire*'s publication in installments over the 1850s and 1860s. Its form, to quote the arch-classicist Ernest Beulé, "is quite simply pure chance in alphabetic order."[3] Even Viollet-le-Duc's mentor and loyal friend, Prosper Merimée, wondered aloud, in the pages of the official *Moniteur,* how an argument that was inherently historical could find its exposition in the dispersed, anti-narrative order of a dictionary.[4] But as Hubert Damisch first argued in a now-renowned essay,[5] that form, as much as the text itself, was an integral part of the claims that Viollet-le-Duc made for French Gothic architecture. French medieval architecture was, for him, so rational that, no matter where one began an investigation, or how one dissected the whole, one was inevitably led back to the universal generating principle, the principle of reason.

Wherever one begins, however one excerpts, the principle of the dictionary is inherent in each of its parts, just as the rationality of medieval architecture is, in Viollet-le-Duc's view, to be discerned from its overall organization to its specific forms, such as its most minute molding profiles or joints. The choice, thus, to translate and collect here four of the longest and theoretically most important articles of the *Dictionnaire* does not denature Viollet-le-Duc's agenda. Rather, it suggests one of countless possible readings of this influential text, consulted religiously by architects, archaeologists, and art historians until the early decades of our own century.[6] Nevertheless, these articles are excerpted from the structure in which they take on their full meaning as integral parts of a system of explanation. This introduction intends to resituate the most famous and oft-cited entries, "Architecture," "Construction," "Restoration," and "Style," in the global project of the *Dictionnaire,* a work that occupies a central position in Viollet-le-Duc's relentless effort to hone a comprehensive theory not only of the medieval structures that he restored both in mortar and words, but of the art and science of modern architecture, on the brink, he felt, of a new synthetic flourishing.

Viollet-le-Duc's education and the project of the *Dictionnaire*

The *Dictionnaire* was in many ways the culmination of Viollet-le-Duc's youthful refusal of the French academic establishment, and a milestone in the author's lifelong campaign against the educational philosophy and reputed professional monopoly of the Ecole des Beaux-Arts. In a career better remembered for its literary pursuits than its architectural achievements, the *Dictionnaire* is arguably the best known of the countless textual strategies that Viollet-le-Duc deployed as an architectural theoretician and polemicist. For four decades, he essayed nearly every genre of architectural writing. From early magazine articles in the partisan press in the 1840s, he moved in the 1850s into the newly flourishing professional press,[7] and launched the ambitious project of two great reference works produced simultaneously—the dictionaries of architecture and the lesser known six-volume work on medieval furniture and practical arts.[8] Even before these were complete, he shifted to the more discursive exposition of his ideas in lectures, published as the *Entretiens sur l'architecture.* This, no doubt, is his best-known work for English readers,[9] as it was published in both British and American translations during Viollet-le-Duc's lifetime. Finally, toward the end of his life, Viollet-le-Duc turned to writing books for adolescents, stories on architecture, such as *Histoire d'une cathédrale et d'un hôtel de ville* and *Histoire d'un dessinateur,* intended to reach a larger and more impressionable audience.[10]

After his youthful decision to embrace an architectural career, Viollet-le-Duc set out to construct an alternative reality, a different explanation of the architectural past and a different program for its practice and future; this reality was ultimately described and structured in the *Dictionnaire.* Against the advice of both his family, well placed in the government of the July Monarchy, and his teachers, Viollet-le-Duc steadfastly refused, from the age of sixteen, to enroll as a student in the prestigious state architectural school, the Ecole des Beaux-Arts. Success in its program would have all but guaranteed him access to official commissions. Having studied with Jean Huvé and Achille Leclère, both highly respected practitioners, and given his extraordinary drawing abilities, manifest from his earliest age, it is likely that Viollet-le-Duc would have captured the coveted Prix de Rome, which annually granted one architecture student five years of study at the French Academy in Rome and moreover virtually ensured a secure government position upon his return to Paris. But with characteristic determination, Viollet-le-Duc declared the ateliers of the Ecole so many predictable molds, merely reproducing the masters for the next generation. Viollet-le-Duc opted to chart his own path, though he was certainly influenced by the romantic artists, writers, and critics who frequented the weekly salons both of his father, a minor poet and government official, and of his maternal uncle, the painter and critic Eugène Delécluze, who lived upstairs from the family in the rue Chabanais.[11] Prosper Merimée and Ludovic Vitet, frequent guests at the rue Chabanais, encouraged Viollet-le-Duc's fascination with the romantic renewal of interest in the Middle Ages, and promoted his projects to travel widely to study medieval monuments as legitimate expressions of the French national genius, exemplars in crafting a modern national style.

From the start, Viollet-le-Duc's drawings bear witness to his determination to challenge the standards and conventions of academic architecture, their originality the mark of his refusal to adopt the Ecole's graphic standards as the medium for studying, appropriating, and assimilating a vision of architecture from historical models. Viollet-le-Duc rapidly adopted new modes of depiction, favoring sections, unusual viewpoints, and types of cutaway drawings; they foretold his future insistence that drawing was a way of seeing an essential truth not immediately apparent to the eye. This conviction first came to fruition in the compelling illustrations of the *Dictionnaire,* images that in turn had a dramatic and lasting influence on architectural representation, most notably at the end of the century in the famous axonometric views of Auguste Choisy.[12] It is not surprising that Viollet-le-Duc soon accepted a teaching position at the Ecole de Dessin, a school devoted to honing the practical graphic skills of artisans and commercial artists.

Finally, in 1836–37, Viollet-le-Duc began an extended trip to Italy, again entirely cast on his own terms.[13] The brilliant watercolors and lively sketches that survive from his seventeen months of wandering and studying the monuments there attest to his desire to re-examine the familiar and the canonical from a wholly different point of view. In place of the sanctioned elevations, sections, and plans—all rigorously frontal—and the accompanying proportional analyses of the orders so typical of an academic sketchbook of these years, perspectival drawings and careful studies of construction details filled his portfolios. And like the romantic architects—Duban, Labrouste, Duc, and Vaudoyer—who first posed a challenge to the Academy's official view of classicism a decade earlier, Viollet-le-Duc pushed on to Sicily to examine the rich and eclectic architecture of that oft-conquered crossroads between East and West, a historical laboratory for observing the response of local forms and uses in architecture to new demands, possibilities, and impulses.

Having refused the prestigious *entree* of an Ecole pedigree, Viollet-le-Duc found that his career began, inevitably, somewhat slowly. At the same time that he energetically drew medieval monuments for Baron Taylor's great collection of the *Voyages Pittoresques en France* in the late 1830s, he signed on for a stint in the administration of the Bâtiments Civils that provided a weekly wage. But this slow path to a designing post in the bureaucratic hierarchy of official French architecture came to a quick end when Merimée, who had followed the maverick's early wanderings, took him firmly under the wing of the young government agency for the preservation and restoration of France's architectural heritage, the Commission des Monuments Historiques. Merimée, perhaps better known today as a playwright and dandy, devoted himself to the study of France's medieval past. In 1834, he assumed the administrative responsibilities of crafting the first government agency for the preservation of France's cultural heritage, a post in which he succeeded the historian Ludovic Vitet, whom Guizot had appointed to define the new enterprise and agency in 1830.[14] Confident after his startlingly successful restoration study of the church of the Madeleine at Vezelay in 1840, Viollet-le-Duc proceeded to exploit the bureaucracy of the restoration service as an alternative path for defining both an architectural vision and a program for the profession. In Paris during the same year, he was appointed assistant inspector of the works for the restoration of the Sainte-Chapelle, a position under the direction of Duban and his first inspector, Jean-Baptiste Lassus (1807–57). A pupil of Henri Labrouste, Lassus was a determined rationalist and a pious advocate of Gothic as the only legitimate starting point for a modern French architecture. He honed Viollet-le-Duc's passionate interest in the medieval past, directing him ever more to the contemplation of the meaning of Gothic as a system of structure inherently expressive of the distinctness of Gallic civilization. In partnership, Lassus and Viollet-le-Duc emerged triumphant in the 1844 competition for the restoration and decoration of the most prestigious and venerable of French cathedrals, Notre-Dame of Paris. For the next two decades, Notre-Dame absorbed Viollet-le-Duc's attention. It served as a material and intellectual laboratory for his perceptions on the history of medieval architecture, and even more important, as a school for a generation of disciples who would both perfect a new approach to historical restoration and shape the Gothic Revival as a critique on the received truths of French academic architectural doctrine. As Viollet-le-Duc indicates clearly in the strongly autobiographical overtones of the entry "Restoration" in the *Dictionnaire* (1866), the context of Guizot's *Monuments historiques* was the seedbed for his own intellectual development, as well as for the more general reappreciation of French medieval architecture. Not only did it mark a turning point in the Gothic Revival, a threshold between the early nostalgic cultivation of sensibility for the aesthetic qualities of the medieval and the scientific study of historical development and formal classifications, but it defined an entirely new approach to the past. With the new profession—for as Viollet insisted, "both the word and the thing are new"—was born a new approach, a "scientific" approach, based on new standards of historical research, and a new appreciation of the social and political currents of the eleventh to the fifteenth centuries. Moreover, in the wake of Thierry, Guizot, and finally Michelet, these centuries were viewed increasingly as the vital period during which modern French political and social institutions, as well as the idiom of modern French language, had matured. Viollet-le-Duc acknowledged Vitet, founding father of the commission, as an intellectual inspiration, for it was he "who showed clearly that the architecture of the

Middle Ages was a complete and integral art, possessing its own original laws and its own reasons for doing things the way it did."[15]

This stance was to be the foundation of Viollet-le-Duc's engagement in the growing movement to promote study of the medieval past, a defiant stance against the Academy's conviction that France's cultural mission was to uphold the classical tradition, of which France was the legitimate heir. The mid-1840s were marked by the eruption of the battle over the relevance of Gothic architecture to modern design; Viollet-le-Duc quickly stepped forward as the polemical spokesman for the Gothic. Following the impetus given by Vitet, Viollet-le-Duc argued vigorously that Gothic was not simply a style to be preferred, but an entirely different system of architecture with a set of distinct laws that could not be judged on the same criteria as classical architecture. In a series of nine articles, "De la construction des edifices religieux en France, depuis le commencement du Christianisme jusqu'au XVIe siècle," published in the organ of the Gothic party of the Catholic Revival, Didron's *Annales Archéologiques,* Viollet-le-Duc outlined the essence of his conception of Gothic architecture, which was to remain at the core of his architectural theory for the rest of his career, and which he was to expand with even greater thoroughness and polemical bite in the *Dictionnaire.*[16]

The essence of this theory, laid out in much greater detail a decade later in the entry "Construction" in the *Dictionnaire,*[17] was that "Gothic architecture is above all a construction, . . . its appearance is but the result of its structure." In the historical account serialized in Didron's magazine, Viollet-le-Duc intended to demonstrate that, in a relatively short period, the architects of the cathedrals of the Île-de-France experimented furiously to perfect a structural system in which every element contributed to the dynamic equilibrium of the whole, and in which material was reduced to a daring, but reasoned, minimum. The resulting architecture possessed *style,* for its form and structure were entirely coterminous, identical. Unlike the elements of the classical language learned by rule and rote at the Ecole—elements subject, Viollet-le-Duc maintained, to abstract rules about ideal form—Gothic offered lessons of materiality, of rationality and economy independent of specific forms, and as relevant in the nineteenth century as in the thirteenth. Indeed for him, despite the spiritual dimensions of the Gothic cathedral that he never denied, the spirit of probing rationality, exploration, and progress evident in the great collective experiment of classic Gothic marked the veritable threshold of modern society, a harbinger of the positivist age whose fruition seemed imminent in the industrial nineteenth century.

According to Viollet-le-Duc, the essential "problem," or task, of medieval religious architecture had been posed from the very moment that the wooden roofs of the early medieval church gave way to experiments in vaulting broad spaces capable of containing huge congregations of townspeople. The remaining centuries of trial and error, of variation and refinement, were but necessary extrapolations of the first attempt to respond to the original problem. The groined rib vault marked the development of the principle of directing structural thrusts to specific points of resistance inherent in the pendentive dome of Byzantine construction; this was to remain the generative principle of all Gothic architecture. The rib vault's structure in turn determined the form of the nave elevation. As its form was progressively developed to channel structural forces ever more efficiently to precise points of dynamic resistance, and as its materiality was reduced to the minimal mass necessary to span and cover, the whole system of the classic Gothic cathedral, this carefully calibrated cage of open-work structure, approached perfection. Leaving behind the massive and inert structures of the Romans in favor of an elastic architecture of dynamic thrusts and counterthrusts, French medieval architects devised a system in which every element was equally vital and distinct in the structural diagram. Search as you will, Viollet-le-Duc insisted, "You will not find, among all of the great structures created to contain entire populations, a single unnecessary stone. . . ."[18] The architects, though nameless, of the golden period of medieval architecture in the Île-de-France, that short half century that spans the year 1200, were like modern scientists working frenetically and communally by trial and error to discover fundamental laws of structure and, hence, of architectural form. According to Viollet-le-Duc, this search produced an art that was "profoundly reasoned," and presupposed "an exact knowledge of the forces of materials, a new form, and all of this off in a corner of Europe, there, suddenly, in a quick transition that was so abrupt that one had difficulty fixing it in time."[19]

Moreover, this rationality was not limited to the main lines of the structure; it permeated every detail. Nothing was created that could not be explained by either structural or programmatic necessity. Decorative moldings and stringcourses, analyzed by such pioneer archaeologists of medieval architecture as Arcisse de Caumont, or by his English counterparts, as the signs of workshop style or the evolution of regional styles, were likewise not personal traits for either individual expression or the delight of the eye of a latter-day connoisseur. Rather, all forms were carefully determined by function, either to mark the presence of interior floors or spatial divisions, or more important, to throw rainwater far from the joints of the wall. Even gargoyles were to be understood primarily not as decorative extravagances or even as expressions of a mythical or superstitious religiosity, but simply as carefully reasoned components in an integral system of drainage. Nothing could be left to idle symbolism or taste. From the sculptured finials of the buttresses and window frames, which were carefully calculated as counterweights at key structural junctures and decorated with attention to rational principles of organic decoration, to the quest for ever greater height under the vaults, a functional explanation was always at hand, and indeed determinant. "If twelfth- and thirteenth-century architects created soaring naves, it was with no puerile symbolic intent, but rather to provide air and light to these large, elevated halls in a somber and humid climate; as always, they simply followed the inspiration of their reason."[20] Viollet-le-Duc inveighed against the members of the classical party, who insisted that Gothic was but a barbarous decorative system, as well as against the well-meaning partisans of Gothic who relegated medieval architecture's significance to its expression of national or religious values.

It was not simply to celebrate the past or to underscore the need to preserve the great monuments of the Gothic era that Viollet-le-Duc sought to demonstrate the rationality of what he proclaimed *the* national style of architecture. The Gothic period marked the dawn of the modern age, the youth, essentially, of the present. Inspired by a generation of romantic historians, particularly by Guizot, Thierry, and Rémusat, who are repeatedly cited in the footnotes of the entries in the *Dictionnaire,* Viollet-le-Duc viewed the long period between the fall of the Roman Empire and the creation of the Gothic synthesis as the period of the gestation of modern French society. During this period, the language, social usages, legislative institutions, and artistic forms were all defined, not in relation to an order imposed on a distant province by a remote Roman emperor—a view celebrated in the continual slavish dependence of French academic culture on Italian models—but organically in relation to local conditions, climate, and needs. While the first steps were taken tentatively by the architects who defined the "Romanesque," an architecture of the cloister and the rule of the autocratic church, the rise of Gothic corresponded to the rise of free city-states, a bourgeois commercial class, and most especially the lay artisan. Gothic, if not exclusively the original invention of the lay bourgeois class of the mature Middle Ages, was in every way impregnated with its spirit of searching, uncompromising rationality and economy.

In such historical views Viollet-le-Duc was scarcely original. The vision of the emergence of the third estate in the urban culture of the later Middle Ages was central to the histories of both Guizot and Thierry, and had found its way into a number of architectural histories advanced by architects in these years, most particularly by Reynaud and Vaudoyer.[21] Moreover, the idea of a second golden moment in civilization in the high Middle Ages, one equivalent to the period of Periclean Athens, had been advanced by the followers of Saint-Simon in the 1810s and 1820s. Viollet-le-Duc had certainly come in contact with the ideas of the numerous contributors to the Saint-Simonian publication, the *Globe,* who frequented the weekly salons in his parents' household in the years around 1830. But while the Saint-Simonians held that the nineteenth century was a moment of transition on the brink of a new organic period, of a third, positivist age of human civilization, Viollet-le-Duc argued that the essential French character had been defined for the first time in the Middle Ages and remained immutably valid. All the changes that have occurred since "happily have not altered our old Gaulish character; we have become neither more Greek nor more Roman than we were during the fourteenth century."[22] The rise of the Academy in the late seventeenth century, with its formulation and imposition of a revived classicism, was as unnatural, alien, and destined to failure as would be the attempt to revive the Roman Empire.

This debate over imposed versus organic systems of thought and architectural form was clearly a historical argument masquerading in thin disguise as an attack on Academic doctrine. The Academy was predictably quick to respond. Inspired by the controversies over whether or not a neo-Gothic church, today's church of Ste.-Clotilde, could be erected in the heart of Paris's fashionable

Faubourg St.-Germain, the Academy was eager to silence Viollet-le-Duc's claims. Raoul-Rochette, perpetual secretary to the Académie des Beaux-Arts ever since the staunch classicist Quatremère de Quincy relinquished the post in 1839, took up the challenge. He attacked Viollet-le-Duc's argument point by point in an essay entitled "De Savoir s'il est convenable au XIXe siècle de construire des églises dans le style gothique?" Not only did Raoul-Rochette marginalize Gothic as but one of many styles with which Christianity had expressed its mission during its long history—and even then one exploited only for a short period of time in a particular area—most important, he dismissed the notion that Gothic was anything but an arbitrary style devoid of the underlying proportional laws and compositional principles that rendered classical architecture a universal principle. Viollet-le-Duc responded immediately in a polemical piece, the last he was to contribute to Didron's *Annales Archéologiques.* But his real response came only a decade later, and in much greater detail, in the ten volumes of the *Dictionnaire raisonné de l'architecture française.*

The *Dictionnaire:* a bid for universal authority

If we have retraced the stages of this tale—by now well known to students of the Gothic Revival—of the adamant stances of Viollet-le-Duc's youth and his battle with the Academy over the possibility of reviving medieval forms in the mid-nineteenth century, it is simply to place the *Dictionnaire* in its appropriate polemical context. For in his decision to compose a handbook of an alternative theory of architecture, Viollet-le-Duc continued his campaign on precisely the territory the Academy had up to now reserved as its own, namely the formulation of doctrine through the definition of the language, uses, and appropriate criteria for the judgment and practice of architecture.[23] The Academy itself was at work on a monumental *Dictionnaire de l'Académie des Beaux-Arts,* a massive undertaking destined to fall victim rapidly to disagreements over its format, in particular over whether or not it should include biographical entries (on which Raoul-Rochette was hard at work). Infighting and indecision delayed the publication of the first volume by almost a decade. By the time it appeared in 1858, Viollet-le-Duc had already issued the first four volumes of his pointedly titled *Dictionnaire raisonné de l'architecture française,* a title in which every word counted for its polemical weight.

"*Raisonné*" was clearly a reference back to another enterprise of reason that sought to map out a universal system of knowledge, Diderot and D'Alembert's great *Encyclopédie, ou dictionnaire raisonné des sciences, des arts et des métiers,* that monument of Enlightenment rationality. "*Architecture française*" was a claim to speak for a national principle in architecture, even while the Academy continued to define an official position by rendering France, so Viollet-le-Duc claimed, a cultural outpost of Italy.

Viollet-le-Duc was scarcely the first to undertake a revision of the *Encyclopédie.* A veritable flood of encyclopedias and dictionaries appeared in France during the opening decades of the nineteenth century, nearly all defined as commentaries or updatings of the great work of Diderot and D'Alembert. Many were never brought to completion. Even Viollet-le-Duc's father prepared two volumes—on poetry and on drama—for one of the countless dictionary projects, the *Encyclopédie portative,* launched, but never completed, in these years by enterprising publishers eager to exploit a continually more open publishing market. The small volumes of the "portable encyclopedia" were intended to popularize the fundamentals of a vast range of domains—a volume on architecture to be written by Quatremère de Quincy was planned but, it seems, never completed—and combined a preliminary historical account, an alphabetical reference section, and a glossary of terminology and practical information.[24] Most of these early-nineteenth-century dictionaries and encyclopedias grappled with the thorny problems of organization, particularly the debate between pure alphabetical order and a thematic or scientific order that would underscore the orders and hierarchies of the domains of human inquiry and knowledge, a conflict unresolved since it first preoccupied Diderot in the preface to the *Encyclopédie.*

Already in the famous tree of human knowledge and the highly developed system of cross-references (*renvois*) of the *Encyclopédie,* two other levels or means of reading the text, functioning at counterpoint to the seeming objectivity of the alphabet, were developed to make the encyclopedia not simply a compendium but a real mapping of the domains of human inquiry, divided according to the faculties of reason, imagination, and memory.[25] This conflict had led directly to the publisher Charles Joseph Panckoucke's great enterprise, launched once he had taken over the failing *Encyclopédie,* to restructure this all-encompassing compendium of human knowledge in a more useful way. For a fragmented professionalizing world, he published a score of specialized manuals arranged by discipline. Of all of the components of Panckoucke's *Encyclopédie méthodique,* one had assumed a particularly important role in defining official aesthetic doctrine in early-nineteenth-century France, namely the volumes on architecture. The reputation of this encyclopedia-dictionary, completed only in 1832, grew in authority and reputation with that of its author, the sculptor and theoretician Quatremère de Quincy, who from 1816 to 1839 occupied the powerful position of *secretaire perpetuelle* of the Academy of Fine Arts.[26] This post placed Quatremère de Quincy at the crucial hinge between the instruction of the Ecole des Beaux-Arts, the sanctifying official aesthetic position of the Académie des Beaux-Arts, and the selection of architects to occupy the most important official posts in the far-reaching bureaucracy of the Bâtiments Civils. His *Dictionnaire méthodique de l'architecture,* although begun in 1785, had become by the 1830s a quasi-official compilation of that idealist view of architecture as essentially an imitative art, a view Quatremère had been refining since he first theorized on the nature of imitation in the abstract art of architecture in his 1785 prizewinning essay on Egyptian architecture.[27] For Quatremère, architecture was primarily an ideal form of language that was as capable of expressing ideas as any other art form, written or crafted from material. Its power lay in the aestheticization of form through the abstracting power of imitation, architecture being the highest imitative art because its abstraction from its natural model was the most complete and the least tied to literal representation. While he did not advocate a Greek Revival in any literal way, Quatremère de Quincy remained adamant throughout his career that only the classical *language* of architecture could serve as the framework for the elaboration of modern architectural expression. He increasingly used his political power to enforce this belief in the training and employment of official architects. This type of idealistic description of the genesis and meaning of architectural form served as the foil against which a panorama of theories of architecture took form in the vibrant intellectual circles of Paris in the 1830s and 1840s.

A critique of the Academy's views of architecture, and in particular the theoretical positions of Quatremère de Quincy, had already been outlined in the entries that the young architects Léonce Reynaud and Léon Vaudoyer had supplied to Pierre

Leroux and Jean Reynaud's *Encyclopédie nouvelle* (begun 1833), a vast project intended by this group of Saint-Simonists to popularize their social and historical ideas.[28] In particular, Reynaud, in the entry on "Architecture," had offered a reading of all architectures as a direct reflection of material and social determinants. This reading led to a relativized appreciation of different historical styles, or systems of architecture, in relation to different cultural values, as well as to variously available building materials and techniques and different climates. The architectural entries of the *Encyclopédie nouvelle* were thinly veiled jabs at the views of Quatremère de Quincy, who was repeatedly cast as the principal opposition to new social ideals and relativist historical values in the architectural studies of the young group of reformers known to their contemporaries as Romantics. This group congregated around Labrouste and frequented the fringes of the Saint-Simonian movement in the 1830s, even though today, a century and a half after the vibrant debates, the debt of these young men to Quatremère de Quincy's views is unmistakable. While Reynaud and Vaudoyer's articles remained isolated critiques in a universal reference work, Viollet-le-Duc's encyclopedic enterprise of two decades later was nothing less than a thoroughgoing critique of the famous pundit's dictionary, in which each article was submitted to relentless scrutiny and selection.

Viollet-le-Duc vs. Quatremère de Quincy: an encyclopedic dispute

A comparison of the entries in the dictionaries of Quatremère de Quincy and of Viollet-le-Duc throws the latter's theoretical position immediately into sharp relief. There can be no doubt that many nineteenth-century readers would have experienced this new reference work in precisely this polemical juxtaposition. Such an exercise provides invaluable insights into the architectural debates that rocked the French profession in the 1850s and 1860s, particularly once Viollet-le-Duc began his short-lived and notoriously disastrous stint as professor of history and aesthetics at the reformed Ecole des Beaux-Arts in 1863.[29] It is hardly surprising to find that the countless entries in Quatremère's dictionary defining the terminology of the classical orders of architecture are replaced in Viollet-le-Duc's by entries covering all the constituent parts of medieval architecture. *Astragale* (astragal), *Fronton* (pediment), and the like are thus replaced by *Arête* (rib), *Chaire* (pulpit), *Narthex*—words from the terminology of Gothic architecture, stonecutting, and liturgical practice. Still more revealing is a glance at the longer entries that communicate the bulk of the architectural theory in each dictionary, and that not only occupy the greatest number of pages, but provide a perch for the reader, who is continually sent back to these foundations of the argument by the system of cross-references. Here, a real commentary on the earlier dictionary is manifest. Missing from Viollet-le-Duc's *Dictionnaire* are entries on all the principal categories of classical academic architectural theory and criticism—*Bienséance, Idéal, Imagination, Inspiration, Invention, Licence, Modèle, Pittoresque, Régle*—which occupy key places in Quatremère's dictionary and in his theory of architecture. Missing also is one of the key constructs of his whole theory, the entry on "Type." All such abstract rules of aesthetic judgment, all rules defined externally to the material and structural reality of the architectural object, have now disappeared. In the handful of abstract terms that are granted entries in Viollet-le-Duc's dictionary—few indeed, as though to suggest that theory does not exist *a priori* before building makes it manifest—the debate with Quatremère is taken up explicitly. In such key entries as *Architecture, Chapiteau, Construction, Coupole, Echelle, Goût,* and specifically in *Style* and *Unité,* which appear in the final volumes published in the late 1860s, Viollet-le-Duc either quotes directly or paraphrases the equivalent article penned some thirty years earlier by Quatremère de Quincy, "one of our predecessors, whose writings are justly appreciated,"[30] in order to refute the doctrines of the academic establishment.

If any entry in Quatremère's dictionary was to provide the foil, or the point of departure, for Viollet-le-Duc, it was the entry on Gothic architecture. In it, Quatremère expounds at great length his conviction that, in opposition to classical architecture, whose syntax is elucidated by the linguistic project of Quatremère's dictionary, no orderly grammar of Gothic is possible: "The impossibility of discovering a principle there, that is, a starting point for imitation and a point of view to which she leans, produces a feeling that is at once pained, but inescapable. . . ."[31] Viollet-le-Duc seems to have set out consciously to demonstrate that a similar project could be undertaken for medieval architecture, which in every way lent itself to such a universal and systematic enterprise as a dictionary. At the same time he was keen to insist that architecture was not an imitative art, but rather a logical system equivalent to the workings, rather than the appearances, of nature, one in which forms were the inevitable emanation of universal and natural laws, discernible through observation and objective investigation. Unlike Quatremère de Quincy, who saw architecture as a language, a sort of human invention of ways of creating meaning and expression, Viollet-le-Duc argued for the status of architecture as the result of the interaction of man's imagination with the laws of nature, tempered always by reason. Thus in redefining the terms of the debate through the act of rewriting the *Dictionnaire,* Viollet-le-Duc also sought to create the basis for a new rationalist, scientistic description of man's creation of architectural form.

While the plan of the *Dictionnaire* remained little altered, it seems that Viollet-le-Duc's conception of it evolved along with his theory of architecture during the almost two-decade gestation of the project. The overarching aim remained constant: to lay bare the generative laws of architectural form through a comprehensive investigation of medieval architecture, offered not as a model—the word *model* itself was provocatively dropped from the roster of entries—but as the most appropriate case study for the modern theorist or practitioner in quest of an applicable truth, as he explains in the preface to the *Dictionnaire:*

> Thus if we recommend studying previous centuries before the period when they abandoned their natural path, it is not because we hope to see the houses and palaces of the thirteenth century built during the present era, rather it is because we feel that this study might endow our architects with some of their finesse, that aptitude of applying a principle to everything, that active originality and finally, the independence that comes from our national genius.[32]

By carefully comparing the four entries reprinted here, which span the project from volume one to volume eight, some fourteen years, it is possible to discern a gradual shift in emphasis in Viollet-le-Duc's reasoning from a reliance on historical logic—evident by the numerous references to Guizot and Thierry in the earlier volumes—to increasingly frequent reference to scientific disciplines as models for modern architectural thought. Most notably, in the seminal entry "Style," Viollet-le-Duc shifts from the historical framework, or narrative, that underlies the argument in "Architecture," or in "Construction," to a thoroughly scientistic view based on his readings in geologic, biological, and linguistic research.

In the preface to the first volume (1854), Viollet-le-Duc laid out clearly his reasons for writing a dictionary. Historical narrative is the form most characteristic of an age that has held that any given form is historically determined by a range and constellation of circumstances particular to their time and place; instead the lesson Viollet-le-Duc seeks is one of timeless essence, concerning the universal principles not only of Gothic architectural form, but of the generation of all form, from the sanctified form given to post-and-lintel construction by the Greeks, to the form that might be given to such modern materials as iron. Gothic as a system of particular completeness and unity, and moreover one that flourished on French soil through the means of French materials and French intelligence, was simply the most appropriate starting point for discerning those universal laws of form applicable in every architectural situation. If Viollet-le-Duc put aside the form of historical narrative, which had come increasingly to dominate architectural discourse in the nineteenth century, it was to underscore emphatically the unity of principle everywhere present in Gothic. For practical reasons, the dictionary form made the book more valuable as a reference tool, as it "permits us to present a whole mass of information and examples that could not have found their place in a historical narrative, without, that is, rendering the discussion confusing and nearly unintelligible."[33] With its systems of cross-references, Viollet-le-Duc's great dictionary was meant to offer, from any point of entry selected, a journey of initiation that would lead one rapidly from the particular observation, even of the most casual sort, to the universal system of architectural form, the system of rational structure as the determinant of all form. As he explained in concluding the enterprise, in the preface to the tenth, or index, volume of the *Dictionnaire*—itself an attempt to provide a different menu of entry points into the universe described in the articles—"We would hardly flatter ourselves to find that our *Dictionnaire* was classified among those books that one opens to look up a piece of information, but that one cannot put down, or like one of those rare friends to whom one wants to say only a brief word in a hurry, and who ends up captivating you for hours under the charm of their conversation. Only in these cases do you forgive the time spent reading or listening."[34]

Already in the preface to the first volume, Viollet-le-Duc had proposed a biological analogy for his historical investigation: ". . . the moment has come to study medieval art as one studies the development and the life of an animate being who proceeds from childhood to old age via a series of almost imperceptible transformations, such that it is impossible to pinpoint the day when childhood ended and old age began."[35] It is not a narrative, or chronological historical account, but a scientific probing, which will reveal the true nature of an organic structure, be it animal or architectural. The form of the dictionary, he suggests, is itself a scientific instrument: "It seems to us, precisely for the very multiplicity of examples given, to be more useful to study, and to make better understood the diverse and complicated parts, all rigorously derived from needs, that compose our medieval monuments, because this form obliges us, if we might thus say it, to *dissect* [editor's italics] separately, in describing the functions performed, the use of each of the diverse parts and of the modifications it has experienced."[36] The early entries try to balance a historical account of a particularly accelerated moment of historical change, the period of the maturation of Gothic over several decades in the late eleventh and early twelfth centuries in the Île-de-France, described in an entry such as "Architecture," with a search for the unchanging structure of architectural form in entries such as "Construction." Later volumes turn subtly to a search for underlying principles removed from a historical context, and with them, by implication, a theory applicable to all architecture, not simply French Gothic.

If there is a model for this approach, the key is given by the word *dissection.* The natural sciences became compelling inspirations for Viollet-le-Duc, particularly the highly regarded disciplines of comparative anatomy and historical geology as they had been developed by Georges Cuvier, whose discoveries had far-reaching consequences in mid-nineteenth-century France. Viollet-le-Duc not only became increasingly eager to argue a scientific basis for architectural understanding, but increasingly turned his hand to scientific observations, culminating in the 1870s when he undertook geologic studies of his own in the Swiss Alps. Cuvier's theories had been popularized not only in public lectures and in illustrated books that were widely distributed and translated, but most vividly in the great enterprise of classifying the animal skeletons on display at the natural history museum of Paris's Jardin des Plantes. His controversial notion of classification of biological artifacts by function rather than formal traits had a considerable and long-ranging influence on the writing of the history of art, and on the theory of the decorative arts and architecture in particular. For instance, its impact on Semper's theories of the classification of all the forms of human crafts, not by stylistic traits or even materials but by the functions they performed, has been discussed often.[37] Viollet-le-Duc's notion of structural rationalism in which structural and material considerations, as well as the demands of social and ritual use, are made the determinants of form was likewise to lead to a great sympathy for Cuvier's teachings. In his *Leçons d'anatomie comparée* (Paris, 1800–1805), Cuvier argued that the form of animal skeletons, and thus the whole taxonomy of the animal kingdom, could be understood as the precise response to the functions that different animals were given to perform in the chain of life. For instance, an animal that was to run would have a skeleton whose form was entirely conducive to the maximization of speed. And what was true of the overall skeleton was likewise true of all its individual parts, each of which was perfectly adapted to the specific role it had to fulfill in the overall function that the organism was intended to perform. Characteristic elements and configurations thus revealed relationships determined not by superficial similarities but rather by underlying function. This led to Cuvier's controversial claims that it would be possible to reconstruct—or "to restore," to anticipate the architectural analogy—an animal skeleton, even of a lost species, from a single part of a fragment of a fossil. He demonstrated this experiment, with much-proclaimed results, on a prehistoric pterodactyl.

It is precisely this sequence of dissective analysis and synthesis, this relationship between the part and the organic system, that is at the base of the *Dictionnaire* and of Viollet-le-Duc's conviction that the essence of structural rationalism manifest most perfectly in Gothic structure was equally present in every minute part of a Gothic building, down to the shaping of the individual moldings and the cutting of individual stones. Now, not only could a new theoretical proposition be presented in the fragmented form of the dictionary, but the fragmented form was itself part of the demonstration. Just as all of the elements of the Gothic structure were precisely determined by their position in the whole system, so, too, were their configuration and character the precise tracing of their function according to the universal rules that determined all form. And just as the very nature of the subject demanded the act of dissection in the individual entries of the dictionary, the preliminary step to the act of synthesis was the reading of the dictionary. This act, via the system of cross-references, ultimately returned any detached element to its place with the contingent elements of the system, and led to a key article on the very principles at the root of Gothic form, and indeed of its verbal representation, the *Dictionnaire* and its compelling illustrations.

The innovative drawing style that Viollet-le-Duc rapidly evolved in the 1850s for the *Dictionnaire*'s illustrations was part of the same investigation. The impact of the new drawing types he introduced to architectural illustration remains to this day one of the most dramatic and long-ranging of the *Dictionnaire.* Unusual points of view from above or, occasionally, from below, coupled with perspectival sectional cutaways and other hybrid forms combining the traditional elements of plan, section, and elevation, provide synthesized views of the whole system of Gothic structure. These modes of drawings allowed the reader not only to perceive the whole building at once but also to grasp immediately its fundamental structural principle. They also emphatically avoided the academic practice of the separation of plan and elevation, a distinction against which Viollet-le-Duc rails in the entry "Unité." With the exception of the famous bird's-eye view of an ideal cathedral, from the entry "Cathédrale," itself a historical amalgam of several cathedrals, there are few overall views of complete buildings among the thousands of illustrations in the dictionary. Rather, all the elements are presented individually or as part of the various microsystems into which one might decompose the overall unity of the Gothic system of architecture: vaults, broken down into ribs and the calculations of the profiles of the intermediate webbing; piers, ultimately broken down into individual moldings and even to the individual stones that make up the key structural parts, such as the extraordinary graphic analysis of the springing point of an arch (fig. 1). Here, an exploded perspective drawing clearly delineates the precise function of every stone in the complex stereometric calculations of French Gothic masons. No precedent for these drawings is to be found in the tradition

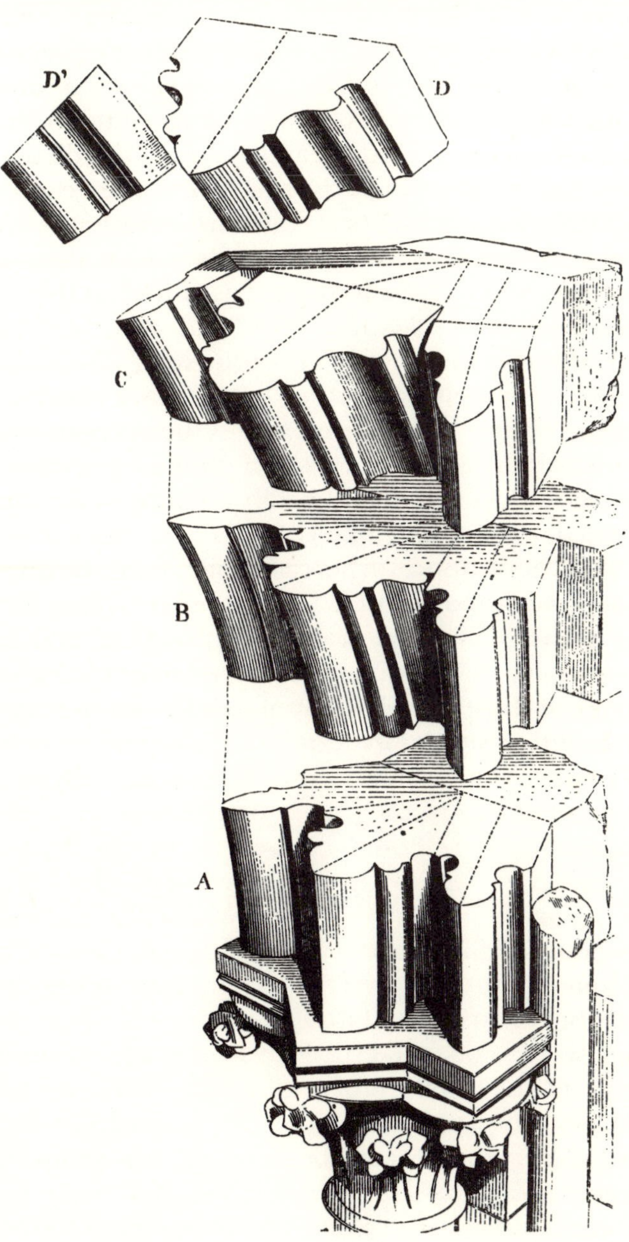

Figure 1

of academic architectural drawing, although Viollet-le-Duc certainly admired the bird's-eye and cavalier perspective drawings of the great châteaux of France in the famous sixteenth-century publications of Androuet Du Cerceau. It seems that Viollet-le-Duc instead took elements from contemporary scientific illustration, in part no doubt from biological and natural history illustration, but most particularly from mechanical drawing such as it was practiced in the engineering and trade schools of Paris. Whether dissecting graphically in the illustrations or analytically in the individual articles, the technique is one based on Cuvier's anatomy, as Viollet-le-Duc makes clear in "Style": ". . . just as in looking at a single leaf, one can deduce the character of the entire plant; the bone of an animal, the entire animal: in the same way, by viewing the profiles, one can determine the architectural members; the architectural members, the monument." Or, as he goes on later in the same entry, ". . . from a logical deduction based on all of the details, rather like that principle observable in the order of all created things, where the part is as complete as the whole, the part composes itself like the whole. The majority of the entries in the *Dictionnaire* make evident the spirit of logic, the unity of principle, that always guided the masters of the Middle Ages." Thus, just as every element of a medieval monument is at once distinct and informed by principles that dominate the whole, so can each entry of the *Dictionnaire* be read separately, as it represents the microcosm of the theory of architecture developed in the whole.

From "Style" to "Unity": a program for modern architecture

That famous definition of style put forth in the eighth volume of the *Dictionnaire* must be situated in the context of Viollet-le-Duc's involvement in the ill-fated reform of the Imperial Ecole des Beaux-Arts in 1863, and especially in the context of the dismal failure of his lectures to the students of the Ecole, who organized disruptions to prevent his message being heard. The frustration of communicating to students both in the institution that had always served as a foil to his own view of architecture and in his own *atelier* not only spurred him on to complete the *Dictionnaire,* with its increasingly lengthy articles of a theoretical and speculative cast, but also gave rise to the project of publishing a series of lectures, the *Entretiens sur l'architecture.* In the mid-1860s, Viollet-le-Duc was in fact writing the second volume of these lectures—

those that move from historical narrative to general issues of architectural theory and questions of contemporary practice—as he finished volumes eight and nine of the *Dictionnaire,* thus effectively writing both historically and analytically in two separate but parallel modes of investigation. The entry "Style" (in Volume 8) is a summary of his theory, as well as the most telling demonstration of his desire to place the description, analysis, and ultimately the practice of architecture on wholly new foundations: namely, those of constructional determinism and structural expression. Taking on, as he does in all the theoretical position papers woven into the *Dictionnaire,* the term itself, Viollet-le-Duc begins by redefining the word *style* and stripping it of all accrued meanings. Purified of the historic "styles," which preoccupy Quatremère in his entry on style, Viollet-le-Duc offers one of the most oft-quoted statements in the *Dictionnaire*: "Style is the manifestation of an ideal based on a principle." Viollet-le-Duc completely turns on its head the traditional definition of style as a handwriting, or a characteristic trait—for Quatremère, it was here that architecture could be equated with other forms of *écriture*—and defines style in relation to the intellectual work that precedes the formal solution. Viollet-le-Duc locates style not in the appearance of the object, but rather in the nexus of relationships that are at the very genesis of form. "Style," he insists, "belongs to men and is independent of objects." Style, then, is the automatic result of the rational process of creation, the making manifest of universal principles in the logical solution to a problem of form. Style is not a trait uniquely of the finished object, one to be categorized *ex post facto,* but rather resides in the act of problem solving, or design, that precedes execution; as he redefines the word further on, style is "the perfect harmony between the result and the means employed to obtain it." Finally, to extend his analogy as universally as possible, Viollet-le-Duc maintains that style is not confined to architecture, or even to objects of man's creation: "From the mountain to the smallest crystal, from the lichen to the oak trees in our forests, from the polyp to man, everything in earthly creation possesses style." Just as Cuvier's studies had taken him from comparative anatomy to geology—the historical matrix for studying the presence of living beings on earth, but also the physical evidence for looking at the primordial forms, the forms of the globe itself—so Viollet-le-Duc moves in the entry "Style" from the study of Gothic architecture to the study of the universal laws that it shares with the structure of the natural world. The only *a priori* he is willing to admit is the existence of geometry, which precedes not only human creation but also natural creation. The perfect equilateral triangle and the perfect circle are irreducible. Man does not invent them, but rather discovers them, as the fundamental act of form making, tellingly illustrated in the vignette on the title page of each of the volumes of the *Dictionnaire,* in which a medieval mason, flanked by the two elite orders of medieval society, the priestly cleric and the aristocratic knight, traces the perfect geometric basis of all form with his compass [*frontispiece*]. Indeed the precise activity that is depicted here is described in words in the entry "Style," attributed not to man *per se,* but rather to the creative activity of Nature herself:

> Nature is at work, her deductions follow one upon the other according to the order of invariable logic. She traces a circle, and in this inscribes the only figure which can't be distorted, one in which the sides and the angles are all equal among themselves, and thus the resistance is the same no matter what side it sits upon, namely the equilateral triangle. She takes a sphere, and in this sphere, by induction, she inscribes a pyramid, whose four faces are each equilateral triangles, that is to say a solid that cannot be distorted and whose properties are the same no matter which one of the sides is used as the base. . . . With this fragment, she will form the solid shell of the incandescent sphere.

In the act of tracing the triangulation that Viollet-le-Duc describes as the geometric underpinings of Gothic architecture in the entry "Echelle," man thus parallels the creative activity of nature. This manifestation of an ideal based on a geometric principle is the beginning of style, the quest for rational form that is gradually inflected by historical conditions and demands.

The entry "Style" thus provides the tale of origins of the world and of all form, that primordial act of creation that is at the core of all powerful theories of architecture from Vitruvius to the Abbé Laugier and Quatremère de Quincy to the mid-nineteenth-century trio evoked at the beginning of this essay: Viollet-le-Duc, Semper, and Ruskin.[38] But if, since Laugier, the irreducible model of architectural form had been the primordial dwelling, the famous primitive hut, now it is simply a geometric configuration that is the basis of all form, both natural and that invented by human intelligence. Geologic science, with its desire to date the evolution of the earth's surface and the various fossils found in differing geologic strata and conditions, was the ideal meeting point of the scientistic and the historicist approaches held at check in Viollet-le-Duc's own study of medieval architecture as a paradigm of architectural creation. In the entry "Style," it is the process of crystallization, or the coming into being of the matter of the earth itself, that is seen as the type of the genesis of form. It can be no mistake that the same year in which the entry "Style" was published, Viollet-le-Duc undertook the first of those extended tours to study the formation of the Alps that were to preoccupy him for the last decade of his life, and to culminate in the grandest of all his "architectural restorations," his study of Mont Blanc, published in 1876.[39] And like the search for architectural form, the mountains proved that the work of geology continued. In turning to the great French Alp, he explained clearly, "In fact our globe is simply a large edifice in which all of the parts have a function; her surface takes on forms ordered by and resulting from a logical order."[40] Through the act of sketching on trips that took him higher and higher into the remotest parts of the glacier landscapes of the Alps, Viollet-le-Duc drew not only a new map of the landscape, presented to the Academy of Sciences in 1874, but also countless studies of rocks to derive the appearances that crystalline formations had taken in giving shape to the earth's architecture. Here, the map was the instrument of analysis and synthesis, just as the dictionary had been for the study of medieval architecture for fifteen years.

At the same time as Viollet-le-Duc sought professional recognition not from the Académie des Beaux-Arts, but rather from the Académie des Sciences, he also sought new audiences among the public for his lessons, seeking now to reach a younger generation with the theory of structural rationalism. Increasingly disheartened by the critical or cool reception to his ideas in the profession, he abandoned the attempt to reach architects through the press, or students at the Ecole through lectures or manuals of architecture, and turned to the uncontaminated minds of the younger generation. In the final years of his life, the dictionaries and historical lectures that had served as media for exploring a logical architectural construct in the 1850s and 1860s were abandoned in favor of fictional tales of discovery aimed at adolescent audiences. Alongside his efforts to promote universal drawing instruction in the schools promoted by the Third Republic, these tales were meant, in emulation of the huge success of Jules Verne, to provide a new rationalist and secular catechism for the upcoming generation. In *Histoire d'un dessinateur, comment on apprendre à dessiner* (1878), Viollet-le-Duc recounts the story of Petit Jean, a young boy whose native talent is the result of his instinctive understanding that drawing is a way of seeing, knowing, and probing, rather than simply of recording. Through instruction in perspective and comparative geometry, the boy gradually comes to realize that drawing is to be understood not simply as an art, but, as Viollet-le-Duc's son said in paraphrasing his father, "as a language." Instruction in comparative anatomy, and a twelve-day trip to the Alps, complete the education of the young draftsman, who finally enters into classes at the Ecole Centrale in preparation for a career in industry—all this in a chapter appropriately entitled "Synthèse." "When drawing is taught properly," he concludes, "it is the best way of developing one's mind and forming judgments, for one learns to see, and to see is to know."[41] Through the new industrial language of drawing, the boy is ready to invent new forms in every way responsive to the needs and means of the age, but derived from principles so fundamental that they govern every form his pencil and eye can dissect, from the mountains to the monuments of his country's past.

Likewise, in the same year that the entry "Style" appeared, Viollet-le-Duc published in the second volume of the *Entretiens* what are no doubt his most famous drawings, the project for a great lecture hall with a ceiling of webbed vaulting supported on an independent iron framework, a framework not surprisingly composed entirely of a skeleton of equilateral triangles (fig. 2). Clustered around the definition of the universal principle of style were the activities of the most primary analysis of formal genesis, and the most speculative of Viollet-le-Duc's proposals for the future applications of the lessons derived through graphic and historical analysis of form. If a new architecture was not formally proposed in the *Dictionnaire*,[42] it is because, as a book of universal principles, it was the prelude and base of invention, not its program.

Figure 2

The entry "Unity" in the closing pages of the final volume of the *Dictionnaire* provides a sort of retrospective definition of the dictionary. The entry opens with a quote from Quatremère de Quincy's entry on "Unity," and proceeds with a lengthy and thoroughgoing critique of the earlier theoretician's position—portrayed as that of the Academy as a whole—that imitation serves as the basis of architecture. Along the way, Viollet-le-Duc offers one of the most cogent summaries of his architectural credo in the years after the debacle of his unsuccessful lectures at the Ecole des Beaux-Arts (1864):

> We are not among those who deny the usefulness of studying earlier arts, inasmuch as no one should forget, or allow to forget, the long chain of past traditions; but what every thinking mind must do when confronted with this mass of materials is to put them in order before even dreaming of using them. What else does one who inherits a rich library do if it is not first to classify the volumes according to a methodical order, so as to make them available for later use. . . . The discoveries in the physical sciences show us every day, with increasing evidence, that if the order of created things manifests an infinite variety in her expressions, it is subject to a number of laws more and more limited to the ways in which we can penetrate the mystery of their movement and of their life; who knows if the final step of these discoveries will not be the recognition of *one* law and *one* atom! In two words: creation is unity; chaos is the absence of unity.
>
> On what could one establish unity in architecture if not on the structure, that is, the means of building?
>
> . . . It cannot be repeated too often that only by following the order that nature herself observes in her creations can one, in the arts, conceive and produce according to the law of unity, which is the essential condition of all creation. . . .[43]

And from this description of a single universal principle that is the act of analysis—synthesized in drawing and in the space of the dictionary—Viollet-le-Duc proceeds to describe, with unsurpassed cogency and conviction, his program for the invention of new form, an architecture for and of the nineteenth century, at once unified with the principles underlying all past form and unmistakably modern. With recourse once again to the natural model, he turns to the origins of the earth's surface, which had preoccupied him in "Style." All known crystals, he explains, result from identical principles of crystallization, notwithstanding the dizzying variety of crystals observable in nature. To respond to a new condition, nature never copies the outward form of a crystal, but rather simply applies once again the universal principle, that of style. Likewise, the same should hold true of architecture:

> Architecture is not a kind of mysterious initiation; it is subject, like all other products of the mind, to principles that are based in human reason. Thus, reason is not multiple, it is *one.* There aren't two ways of being right on any given question. But if the question changes, the conclusion, arrived at by reasoning, is modified. Thus if unity exists in the art of architecture, it is not by applying this or that form, but in seeking the form that is the expression prescribed by reason. Reason alone can establish the connection between the parts, can place each thing accordingly, and can give not only cohesion to the work, but the appearance of cohesion through the true succession of operations that must constitute it. As much as one would like to give credit to the imagination, in order to constitute any form, imagination can only follow the path traced by reason.[44]

And it is this path traced by reason that, for Viollet-le-Duc, will lead the reader through the dictionary, from the detail to the underlying principle, guiding him, by cross-reference and analysis, to the act of synthesis that lies not in the text *per se* but in the act of reading the text. Just as drawing will lead him to see, so the writing of the dictionary is the attempt to find the verbal equivalent of that act of penetration that leads ultimately to the unity of all form. And if he created analogies both verbally and graphically with the procedures of other sciences, it was not simply to break the yoke of academic theory, but to promote architecture itself to the status of a science, a positivist activity ready to face the rigors of the age of science, ready to live in the present through the act of penetration into the past.

—Barry Bergdoll

ARCHITECTURE
the art of construction

ARCHITECTURE, s.f.—the *art of construction*. Architecture consists of two elements, theory and practice. Theory includes the art involved in architecture, properly speaking, rules inspired by taste and traditionally handed down; and the science of architecture, which can be expressed in absolute and unchangeable formulas. Practice is the application of theory to needs; practice adapts both art and science to the nature of the materials employed, to the climate, to the customs of an era, and to the necessities of the moment. When considering the architecture characteristic of the beginning of one civilization succeeding another civilization, we must take into account existing traditions on the one hand, as well as new needs that have arisen on the other. Thus, we will divide the present entry into several parts: the first part will consist of a summary history of the origins of the architecture of the Middle Ages in France; the second will cover architectural developments from the eleventh to the sixteenth centuries, treating the causes of both progress and decline, as well as dealing with the different styles belonging to each province of France; the third will cover religious architecture; the fourth, monastic architecture; the fifth, civil architecture; and the sixth, military architecture.*

The origins of French architecture

At the time of the barbarian incursions into Gaul, Roman construction was everywhere. The indigenous population had long since become accustomed to the Roman way of life; it required some three centuries of disasters before these old traditions were effaced. In the sixth century, there still existed in Gallo-Roman towns a large number of buildings that had been spared from fire and destruction. By the time the barbarians settled down definitively, however, there were no longer any living practitioners of the arts; nobody could say how the Roman buildings had actually been erected. Examples of Roman buildings still stood, but they were puzzles whose solution the new inhabitants could only guess at. Everything that pertained to daily life, to the government of the city, and to language had survived the disaster; but architecture, the art of construction, which requires time, study, and calm in order to flourish, had evidently fallen into oblivion. The few architectural fragments that have come down to us from the sixth and seventh centuries are but pale reflections of Roman art; often they consist of little more than piled-up rubble thrown together by unskilled workers who scarcely knew any longer how to lay bricks or use building stones. No individual character distinguishes these buildings; they appear to mark the decline of a people rather than the beginning of one. What elements of art could the Franks have produced in the midst of the Gallo-Roman population? We see the clergy establishing itself in the basilicas and temples that remained standing; we see kings inhabiting the baths or the ruins of palaces or Roman villas. Once the barbarian storm had subsided, once the new masters of the territory had established themselves, churches or palaces were once again built; but Roman models were simply copied, while the real difficulties of the art of construction were avoided. As far as churches were concerned, the ancient basilica served as the model; with respect to princely dwellings, it was the Gallo-Roman villa that was imitated. Gregory of Tours described some of these religious or civil edifices, although not with any real precision.

*This excerpt covers the first two parts of Viollet-le-Duc's entry "Architecture" from vol. 1, 116–166. [Editor's note]

We should not, however, imagine that all notion of luxurious adornment was excluded from architecture. On the contrary, even though buildings were most often constructed in a barbarous fashion, they were nevertheless decorated inside with paintings, marbles, and mosaics. The same Gregory of Tours, speaking of the church at Clermont-Ferrand built in the fifth century by St. Numatius, the eighth bishop of that diocese, painted a stately picture of this edifice for us:

> He [St. Numatius] had built the church that is still there, the oldest of the churches inside the city. It is one-hundred-fifty feet long, sixty wide, and, inside the nave, fifty feet high up to the ceiling framework. In front is a circular apse, and from each side extend two wings of elegant design. The entire edifice is laid out in the form of a cross; it has forty-two windows, seventy columns and eight doors. . . . The walls of the nave are adorned with marbles adapted to each other. The entire edifice was completed in the space of twelve years. . . .[1]

This is a description of the ancient basilica with its columns and aisles (*ascellae*), and its *camera,* which we believe we have translated correctly here as "ceiling framework," all the more so because this church was completely destroyed by fire when Pepin captured the city of Clermont from the duke of Aquitaine, Eudes. It had to be entirely rebuilt. In other passages of his history, Gregory of Tours speaks of certain princely dwellings with porticoes covered with ceiling frameworks decorated with brightly colored paintings.

The new masters of Gaul preferred to establish themselves in the territories, which they had divided up among themselves. They found there an agglomeration of farmers and slaves accustomed to cultivating the land, and thus a ready source of revenue that could gratify all the desires of a Germanic chieftain. Moreover, the towns had preserved their municipal governments and the barbarians generally respected this. Such remains from an old civilization could only serve to constrain the newcomers, however strong and powerful they might otherwise be. Foreign conquerors do not care to find themselves among a population that, although subdued, is clearly superior to them from the standpoint of customs and civilization. This represented a source of at least moral constraint on men who were otherwise accustomed to a wild and independent life. Their violent pursuits, hunting and war, like their favorite relaxation, orgies, were better suited to country life. Thus, under the dominant race, the *villae* [i.e., villas] were the preferred residences of the new kings and lords of the land; conquerors and conquered inhabited the land together. Their settlements consisted of a number of buildings adapted to a type of agricultural exploitation that resembled more or less our large farms. The Frankish kings held court, and gave themselves up to the pleasure of the hunt. They lived off the products of the land, which were gathered into large storehouses. When their provisions were exhausted, the rulers simply changed residences. Their actual habitations were decorated with a certain elegance, although they were very simple with respect both to construction and to the arrangement of rooms and the like. A royal residence included large porticoes, stables, spacious courts, and large covered spaces where synods of bishops were convoked, or where the Frankish kings presided over assemblies followed by their traditional feasts, which degenerated into orgies. "Around the principal complex of buildings were placed in rank order the habitations of the officers of the palace, whether barbarian or Roman in origin. . . . Other less imposing houses were occupied by a great number of families of which the members, both men and women, carried on all sorts of crafts, such as the goldsmith's or armorer's crafts, or those of the weaver or currier. . . ."[2]

During the Merovingian period only the towns were fortified. The *villae* were open, defended only by palisades and moats. Under the kings of the dominant race, feudalism did not yet exist. The *leudes* were merely large landholders established on Gallo-Roman territory, subject to a central authority, that of the Frankish chieftain; but the authority of the latter became weakened as the memory of the conquest and of the common life of the camp receded. The new landholders lived far apart, separated by forests and empty lands devastated by war; they were able to spread out at their leisure; there were no enemy attacks to repel, nor was there any need to encroach upon the property of their neighbors. Nevertheless, men used to a roving life and to pillage and brigandage of the most unrestrained sort were hardly able to settle down immediately to the peaceful possession as landholders of their share of the conquests. Hence, they threw themselves, as much out of idleness as out of love of gain, on religious establishments or open villages, whenever there was something in them to be taken. Thus, monasteries and Gallo-Roman agglomerations gradually abandoned plains and river valleys, moved to high ground, and fortified themselves. The flat land was abandoned to the incursions of the lords of the land, who, finding in their way only sons or grandsons of their own companions in arms, attacked them and pillaged their *villae* too. Thus, these *villae* came to be surrounded by walls and deep moats as well. However, since they were not well placed for defense, they were soon abandoned to the farmers, and the Frankish chieftains established themselves in fortresses. In the midst of this frightful anarchy, which the Merovingian kings were not in a position to suppress, the bishops and the religious establishments were left to fight on their own: the bishops by means of their patience, of the power of a principle upheld with firmness, and of their exhortations; the religious establishments, having brought within their walls the remains of Roman civilization, by means of their study and their agricultural work.

Charlemagne arose in the middle of all this chaos. By the sheer power of his organizing genius he managed to establish a kind of administrative unity; he picked up the broken threads of ancient civilization and attempted to weave them back together. Charlemagne wanted to bring about a *renaissance.* Contemporary arts were to profit from his supreme effort, not by following the route laid out by the great genius himself but rather by appropriating new elements that he had sought out in the East. Charlemagne understood that mere laws and material force are powerless to impose order on ignorant and barbarous peoples unless some beginning can be made in instructing them. He understood that arts and literacy constituted the most effective antidotes to barbarism. In the West the means to promote them were lacking, however; the lights of the ancient arts had long since been extinguished. The Eastern Empire, though, which had not been overrun by barbarian tribes, had preserved its arts and industries. In the eighth century it was to the Eastern Empire that one had to turn in order to have any effect on the practice of the arts. Charlemagne had had frequent disputes with the Eastern emperors; but he had also maintained contact with Caliph Harun, who in 801 ceded the holy places to him. From 777 on he had maintained a treaty of alliance with the Moorish governments of Saragossa and Huesca. Through these alliances he was in a position to bring the arts and sciences from the countries where they were well developed. In that era, the Moors of Spain, like the Arabs of Syria, were very advanced in the mathematical sciences and in the practice of all the arts; and, although Charlemagne is supposed to have brought grammarians, musicians, and mathematicians from Rome in 787, it is just as likely that he sent geometry professors to visit his allies in Syria and Spain. For we can judge by the remaining Roman monuments that date from that epoch the profound degree of ignorance into which the builders in the capital of the Christian world had fallen.

For Charlemagne, however, everything had to come from Rome as a matter of tradition. He was, first of all, the emperor of the West, and he could not let it be thought that light might possibly come from some other source. Nevertheless, to the primarily Roman renaissance that he wanted to bring about, he added by the sheer force of existing circumstances certain other foreign elements that would cause the arts to deviate from the path on which he thought he had placed them. The emperor could make himself master of the traditions of the Roman government; he could issue ordinances that were wholly Roman; he could put together an administration based on Roman models; but no matter how powerful he might be as emperor, he could not, by decree, establish any art. In order to teach design to his painters or geometry to his architects, he had to bring teachers from Byzantium, Damascus, or Cordova. Yet the planting of such exotic seeds among peoples with their own genius was bound to produce an art that was neither Roman nor Eastern; but which, stemming from both these sources, would eventually produce a tree of its own—a tree so vigorous that it would grow and spread and extend its branches after a few centuries back to the very countries from which its own seed had sprung.

It has been tirelessly repeated that the crusaders exerted great influence on Western architecture. The study of actual monuments, however, is more likely to destroy than it is to confirm this conviction. If the arts and sciences that were preserved and developed by the Moors introduced new elements into Western architecture, it was during the eighth century rather than later that this occurred. Charlemagne must have been impressed by the means employed by the infidels to govern and civilize the peoples they controlled. Already in his time the disciples of Muhammad had founded celebrated schools where all the sciences of that day were taught; these schools, usually located in the shadow of a mosque, could provide him with the models for his own establishments, which became both religious and teaching institutions. The basic idea was of Greek origin, and could well have been transmitted to the Arabs by the Nestorian Christians. However that may be, Charlemagne had more direct relationships with the infidels than he had with the Byzantine court; and if he treated Muslims with greater respect than he accorded, for example, to the Saxons, whom he pounded without respite until they were completely converted, this was because, with the Moors, he found an advanced civilization with cultivated manners and morals and settled habits of order. He profited from these lights in order to achieve the principal goal of his own reign, namely, education. In Spain he found more to take than he himself had to give.

Without wishing to be dogmatic, we nevertheless believe that the reign of Charlemagne can be considered to have introduced into France the arts that we may legitimately style "modern." If we may clarify our idea here by the use of an image, we may say that, from this reign on, even though the cut and the form of the vestment remained Roman, the fabric out of which they both were fashioned became Eastern. It was more specifically in the regions nearer to the seat of the empire, as well as those in which Charlemagne sojourned for long periods of time, that this Eastern influence made itself felt most strongly: it was on the banks of the Rhine, in Languedoc, and along the Pyrenees, that certain imported art forms, foreign to Roman art, were best preserved, even into the thirteenth century.

In spite of his strongly established system of administration, Charlemagne was not everywhere equally able to ensure the teaching of the arts and sciences about which he was so concerned. Even if he could somehow have succeeded by the sheer force of his tenacious genius in imposing an artificial unity on architecture from the banks of the Rhine to the Pyrenees, and this in spite of the differences in nationality, such an accomplishment would undoubtedly not have survived his death. In fact, Charlemagne united under his crown both the spiritual and the temporal powers; it was a question of saving civilization. The sovereign pontiffs, who had watched the emperor save the Church from attacks on it by the Arabs, the Greeks, and the Lombards, had to accord recognition to his unifying of the two powers. Once the emperor was dead, however, the various nationalities that had been united by the power of the genius of a single man once again became divided; the clergy had to take back one step at a time the spiritual power that the successors of Charlemagne also arrogated to themselves—no longer, in their case, in order to preserve it, but, rather, to destroy the liberty of the Church and to traffic in ecclesiastical goods and dignities. The seeds of feudalism, which already existed in the spirit of the Franks, also contributed to the undoing of the combination so laboriously put together by the great prince. Fifty years after his death, each people had resumed its own separate way; art and architecture became fragmented; and the genius of each particular country became evident in the construction of the ninth and tenth centuries. During the eleventh and twelfth centuries, these differences became even more marked. Each province had its own school. The feudal system itself influenced architecture; just as each feudal lord retreated into his own domain, and each diocese isolated itself from the neighboring one, so the art of construction little by little also followed the new political organization. Builders no longer went far and wide in search of valued building materials, nor did they build according to the same plans; they worked in their own territory, employed the materials available to them there, altered their methods in response to the climate where they lived, and modified their methods in accordance with strictly local factors. Only one link united all the efforts that were thus being carried on in isolation: the papacy. The episcopacy, in order to regain its spiritual power, contributed not a little to the fragmentation of the temporal power; since it was itself subject to the Roman court, however, it contributed to directing all these efforts toward the same goal—a goal where they would indeed one day converge. It should be clear how all these isolated efforts served to fertilize the soil of the arts, and how, after so many partial efforts, architecture would undergo an immense development, once unified government, reborn in the thirteenth century, united under itself all the creative spirits molded by long practical experience as well as by many difficulties overcome.

Of all the arts, that of architecture is certainly the one that has the closest affinity with the instincts, ideas, manners, morals, progress, and needs of various peoples; it is therefore difficult to understand the directions that architecture takes or the results at which it arrives, unless the leanings and inclinations as well as the talents of the people among whom it is developed are also understood. Since the seventeenth century the *personality* of the people of France has invariably been absorbed by the *government;* the arts have been *official* arts, no longer subject to violent changes arising out of the domain of art itself, as has been the case with the politics of a number of specific periods. In the twelfth century, however, this was not the case; in the fragmented society that existed then, the despotism of the various feudal lords lacked any unity; morally speaking, it amounted to a kind of freedom not far removed from license. The narrow framework within which we are obliged to work here does not allow us to present a complete political history along with the history of architecture in France from the eighth to the twelfth centuries. That is what ought to be attempted, however, in order to explain the progress of art through the barbaric centuries of the Middle Ages. Nevertheless, we shall limit ourselves to indicating the most salient and general points of political history, which may serve as landmarks along the route we must follow.

As we have already remarked, the political and administrative system that Charlemagne adapted from the Roman tradition was able to check disorder but without abolishing its causes. We have nevertheless noted how this prince was able to reestablish some of the elements of learning in the midst of the general barbarism. During his long reign seeds were planted, which pushed down such deep roots that it became impossible to eradicate them. The clergy became the repository of all intellectual as well as practical knowledge. Going back in spirit to the ninth century, we need to examine for a moment the condition of Gaul and of a large part of western Europe: developing feudalism not yet entirely organized; chronic wars; countrysides covered with forests; lands lying fallow, barely cultivated even near the towns; urban populations lacking both commerce and industry, and subject to decrepit municipal organizations without organic ties to each other; *villae* constantly laid waste, inhabited by farmers or serfs whose condition was roughly the same; the empire fragmented, broken up by the successors of Charlemagne and the possessors of feudal fiefdoms. Everywhere brute, improvident force reigned. In the midst of all this disorder, however, there was a single class of men given neither to bearing arms nor to cultivating the soil; this class owned a notable portion of the land; and this class alone occupied itself with things of the mind, with learning and knowledge. Motivated by an admirable spirit of patience and charity, this class soon acquired by that fact alone a moral dominance against which blind material forces hurled themselves in vain. It was in the bosom of this particular class, in the shelter of the walls of its cloisters, that refined, delicate, and reflective spirits found their refuge. Soon it would be from among these very men, inhabiting as it were a different era, that the feudal era would seek its light. Up until the eleventh century, however, the work that was proceeding along this line was slow and obscure. It seemed that the clergy and the religious establishments were occupied in bringing together the elements of a new future civilization; but nothing was settled yet; nothing was definite. The daily struggle against barbarism almost entirely absorbed the attention of the clerical power that existed; it often appeared to be itself worn down by its constant and piecemeal struggle. The arts suffered the effects of this state of uncertainty; they moved painfully along the path traced out for them by Charlemagne, but without making much progress. The Roman renaissance remained at a standstill, producing nothing either new, bold, or fecund. With few exceptions, of which we will duly take note, architecture too remained tightly wrapped up in its antique shroud. The invasions of the Normans came along to render the situation of the country even more miserable. How could architecture have developed in the middle of such daily ruin? Nevertheless, the obscure work of the cloister continued and would eventually see the light of day.

Development of Architecture in France from the Eleventh to the Sixteenth Centuries—the Causes of its Progress and Decline—the Different Styles Belonging to each Province

With the advent of the eleventh century, a new era began for the arts as well as for politics. As we remarked above, arts, sciences, and literacy had all been confined to the enclosures of the cloisters since the reign of Charlemagne. By the eleventh century, however, the organization of the feudal system had gone about as far as it could go; the land had all been parceled out among lordships and manors, each one the vassal of the one above it, up to the suzerain; the system resembled an arena where each participant would appear on the scene to defend rights of his that had been attacked or to acquire new rights by force of arms. The *written* description of the organization of the feudal system set forth perhaps the only appropriate system of which that particular period was capable, so near was it still to barbarism. In reality, however, the application of the feudal system in practice had little to do with the theory. In practice, the whole thing often amounted to a state of permanent civil war, an uninterrupted series of oppressions and revenges perpetrated by one feudal lord or another; or of constant revolts against the rights of the suzerain. In the midst of such perpetual conflict, we can imagine the state of the people who lived on the land! Even the institution of monasticism, worn down and discouraged, in those times when no one seemed to have any perception of justice or injustice, when the most brutal passions were the only laws heeded, was in a deplorable condition. Monasteries were pillaged and burned by the Normans, forced to pay ransom by secular lords, and taken over by lay abbots. They also saw their regular monastic life singularly relaxed. In the monasteries, among the monks, canons, and even nuns, lay abbots sometimes installed themselves with their wives and children, their armed retainers, and even their own personal gangs.[3] Nevertheless, some religious establishments did still preserve the traditions of Benedictine life. By the beginning of the eleventh century, feudal rights were exercised not only by lay lords but also by bishops and abbots. In this diluting of their power as being a purely spiritual thing, some of the higher clergy lent their authority to the influence that secular feudal lords claimed to be able to exercise with respect to the elections of bishops and abbots; from that time on, in fact, the latter became vassals subject to feudal laws. It was thus that a struggle began in which the two principles of spiritual and temporal authority came into play; the issue was that of the freedom or the vassalage of the Church; and it was the Church, it must be stated, that began the struggle by instituting reforms in her own life.

In the year 909, William, the duke of Aquitaine, founded the Abbey of Cluny. It was to the holy apostles, Peter and Paul, that he gave over all the benefits that were supposed to accompany his foundation.[4] A bull of Pope John XI (March 932) confirmed William's charter, and "freed the monastery from dependence upon any king, bishop, or count whatsoever, including the relatives of William. . . ."[5]

We should not view this intervention by the Roman pontiffs through our modern eyes. We must realize that in the midst of the general anarchy, of the regular encroachments by all existing powers upon the powers of all others, of the frequent unbridled oppressions carried out by brute force, such an acceptance of suzerainty by the chair of St. Peter was the only thing that could interpose a barrier against the prevailing material force, create a spiritual unity, and establish itself as an immense moral force amid all the surrounding barbarism; at any rate, that is what occurred. The entire eleventh century and the first half of the twelfth were marked by a great battle, and in this battle the spiritual power always emerged as the victor. St. Anselm, the archbishop of Canterbury; St. Hugh, abbot of Cluny; and Pope Gregory VII were the great figures who dominated this epoch and who established the spiritual independence of the clergy in the West. As we can imagine, the people at large were not exactly indifferent to these great debates; they still saw an effective refuge from the prevailing oppression in these monasteries, where there was concentrated an elite of intelligent men whose power stemmed from nothing but their own profound convictions, along with the practice of a regular and devout life. So equipped, the monks succeeded in holding at bay all the powers of the age. Public opinion, if we may borrow a modern term, was on their side, and it was not the least of the advantages they enjoyed. The regular clergy alone summed up all the hopes of the lower classes; and we should not be surprised if, during the eleventh century and the beginning of the twelfth, the monasteries became the principal centers of influence, progress, and knowledge. Everywhere the monks established schools where the arts and sciences, as well as philosophy, theology, and letters, were taught. Lanfranc and St. Anselm were priors at the Abbey of Bec and did not disdain the task of instructing young people in the world while, during their vigils, correcting the defective manuscripts of pagan authors, of the Holy Scriptures, and of the Fathers of the Church. At Cluny, extraordinary pains were taken with regard to teaching. Udalric[6] devoted two chapters of his *Customs* to detailing the duties of teachers toward the child or adult pupils committed to them.[7] "The greatest prince was not brought up in the king's palace with any greater care than was the smallest child at Cluny."[8]

From that time forward these communities assumed great importance with regard to the civil populations of the towns; this was because of their resistance to the blind despotism of feudalism, with its spirit of disorder. These monastic communities participated in all kinds of public affairs through the intelligence, knowledge, and capacity of their members. One of the most profound and elegant writers of our own day writes apropos of this as follows, in an excellent book only recently published:[9] "The abbots of those times of austerity and disorder bore little resemblance to the idlers with fat endowments who were later to be mocked in our satiric and bourgeois literature. Their task was laborious; the shepherds' crooks committed into their hands scarcely remained stationary." Both the interior and exterior activities of the monasteries provided an enormous impetus to the arts and, in particular, to architecture. It was within these same abbeys that the masters were formed who, in the eleventh century, would provide the abbeys with a material importance equal to their existing religious and moral predominance. The first architect to lay down the foundations of the vast and admirable monastery of Cluny, today almost entirely destroyed, was himself a Cluniac whose name was Gauzon, former abbot of Baume.[10] The architect who completed the great church was a Fleming who was also a religious, Hezelon, who, before entering Cluny, had taught at Liège. It was the kings of Spain and England who provided the necessary funds for this great work of construction.[11]

Not only were these first great buildings to serve as types for all of the monasteries of the Cluniac rule in France and throughout a great part of western Europe; they also became models for simple parishes and rural constructions as well as for public buildings. All this came about because the monasteries were centers of both wealth and light. In the monasteries, and, indeed, only in the monasteries, were things carried out with prudence and foresight, salubriousness and dignity. In 1009, even before the construction of the Abbey of Cluny under Peter the Venerable,

> Hugh of Farfa sent one of his disciples named John to observe the surroundings and to describe for the use of his monastery "the usages and customs of Cluny." His work, manuscript number 6808 in the Vatican Library,[12] contains information that we would be able to find nowhere else today. There can be no doubt that the dimensions desired for Farfa were those of Cluny in the time of St. Odilon. Even if we should turn out to be wrong about this, it is nevertheless certain that these dimensions were the ones that were given, and the plans too were formulated at Cluny itself. Thus, we are pleasantly surprised to find the glorious Cluniac influence ex-

> tending all the way down into the heart of Italy. . . . "The church must be 140 feet long, 160 glazed windows, two entrance towers, forming a parvis for the laity . . . the dormitory 140 feet long and 34 high, with 92 glazed windows, each one 6 feet high and 2½ feet wide; the refectory, 90 feet in length and 23 feet in height . . . the almonry, 60 feet in length; the atelier of the glassmakers, jewelers, and goldsmiths, 125 feet in length by 25 in width;[13] the stables for the monastery horses and those of visitors, 280 feet in length by 25. . . ."[14]

The religious orders and the bishops who did not accept the vassalage of the Church, with the sovereign pontiff at their head, persisted in their collective struggle against the feudal powers; they wanted to establish a spiritual unity and reform the abuses that had been introduced into the clergy. The people in the towns profited from the enlightenment produced thereby and from the ideas of moral independence that were current around the great monasteries. These people felt the need of a public authority and an internal administration on the model of the unique authority of the Holy See and the internal organization of the monasteries. Thus, the people would eventually come to demand their share of guarantees against the personal power of the secular feudal lords and of the higher clergy.

However, the two movements, monastic and lay, were distinct, and though they proceeded on parallel lines, they were completely independent of one another. The clergy were engaged in teaching youth who were avid to learn what was styled physics and also theology. These same clergy were the first to call the efforts to secure the liberty of the towns "execrable." Meanwhile, the bourgeois who were demanding and obtaining, if necessary by force, rights and immunities to protect industry and commerce were the very ones prepared to accuse and pursue the disciples of Abelard. Such were the strange contradictions of this new era, fecund as it was in other respects. Somehow all the various classes of society seemed to arrive in some mysterious way at a common goal; this was the case even when they were engaged in mutual accusations against each other. They did not seem to notice that they were in fact headed toward the same goal.

Among the abbeys that were dependencies of Cluny, and

which enjoyed the same privileges, was the Abbey of Vézelay. Toward 1119, the counts of Nevers claimed rights of suzerainty over the town, which was a dependency of the monastery.

> They could not stand by without envy watching the great profits that the abbot of Vézelay obtained from the affluence of strangers of all ranks and states of life, as well as from the fairs that took place in the town, especially the fair on the feast of St. Mary Magdalen. In the course of a few days, this fair attracted a vast concourse of merchants both from the kingdom of France and from the *communes* in the Midi. This gave to a town inhabited by only a few thousand souls an importance almost equal to that of the larger cities of the day. Even though they were serfs of the Abbey of St. Mary, the inhabitants of Vézelay had gradually acquired the property of several of the estates located in the vicinity. Their servitude had thus been diminished in the natural course of events, gradually becoming reduced to the payment of taxes and subsidies and to the obligation of having their wheat ground, their bread baked, and their grapes pressed in the common mills, ovens, and winepresses maintained or leased by the abbey. An interminable dispute ensued between the counts of Nevers and the abbots of St. Mary of Vézelay; sometimes it was smoothed over by the intervention of the popes, but it was constantly rekindled under one pretext or another. . . . Count William, who had several times been called upon by papal authority to renounce his claims, instead pressed them with even more tenacity than ever, and, at his death, willed to his son of the same name as himself all his enmity against the monastery.[15]

This count, upon his return from a Crusade, revived the dispute by allying himself with the inhabitants of the town, promising to recognize their *commune*—even entering and swearing fidelity to the bourgeois of the town.

No sooner were the inhabitants of Vézelay emancipated and constituted into a *commune* than they fortified their dwellings.

"They raised up crenellated walls around their houses, each one according to his means; this was the sign and guarantee of their liberty. One of the most important among them, named Simon, laid down the foundations of an enormous square tower. . . ."[16] During the few years before or after this period, Le Mans, Cambrai, Saint-Quentin, Laon, Amiens, Beauvais, Soissons, Orléans, Sens, and Reims all became *communes,* some as a result of violence carried out with arms in hand, others by taking advantage of disputes between bishops and lay lords, each of whom were in possession of some feudal rights over these towns. The long-suppressed Gallo-Roman character of the populations of these towns immediately made itself manifest, although the inhabitants did not, as in our day, overthrow everything all at once that happened to circumscribe their liberty. Nevertheless, through partial and even isolated efforts they did exhibit a spirit of independence, which made them all the more energetic because they had been left to their own devices. This epoch of emancipation of the *communes* marks an important stage in the history of architecture. It amounted to a blow struck at the feudal system whether in its religious or in its secular aspect.[17] From this moment on, the great religious establishments ceased to be the exclusive rulers over the domain of the arts. St. Bernard himself was to contribute to the acceleration of this revolution. As abbot of Clairvaux, he belonged to the strict Cistercian rule. More than once from various pulpits, and, notably, from the pulpit of the church of Vézelay, he inveighed with the passion of an ardent conviction against the luxuriousness that was being displayed in the churches, against the "monstrous and bizarre figures" that, in his view, had nothing Christian about them; yet they were being carved on capitals and friezes and even introduced into the sanctuary of the Lord. The monasteries that were founded under his inspiration, in fact, were marked with an uncommon severity of style; they were devoid of embellishments and bas-reliefs; this was in marked contrast with the excessive richness of the monasteries subject to the rule of Cluny. The influence of these austere structures affected everything else constructed around them.[18] This deviation of religious architecture brought about, in the course of the twelfth century, a kind of indecision in art, which slowed down and even restrained the natural thrust of the monastic schools. The genius of the Gallo-Roman populations, though, ran contrary to the reform that St. Bernard wished to establish; he therefore did not take it into account; and his reform, which momentarily hindered the impetus given to architecture within the great religious establishments, really served to open up a new path of development—new developments that would henceforth belong to the lay corporations. From the end of the twelfth century on, religious architecture, whether monastic or public, made use of all possible resources of sculpture and painting. The establishments founded by St. Bernard stood out as isolated examples of the protest of a single man against the tastes of a whole nation.

In the organization of the lay corporations of the various arts and crafts, the *communes* followed the example that the religious establishments had given them. Since the eighth century, the great abbeys, even the priories, had established around their cloisters and in the enclosures of their domains ateliers of curriers, carpenters, cabinetmakers, ironworkers, cement makers, goldsmiths, sculptors, painters, copyists, etc.[19] These ateliers, composed indifferently of both laymen and clerics, were subject to discipline, and work in them was carried out methodically. Training in all these activities was effected by means of a system of apprenticeship. Each religious establishment was thus a true state in miniature, containing within itself all the means of its own existence, including its own leaders and landed growers, as well as its own industry; each religious establishment depended in fact on its own internal government, under the supremacy of the sovereign pontiff. The example of the abbeys helped the *communes,* which wanted both independence and order at the same time. Even though the center of the activity in the arts was changed, the direction of the arts did not change in any abrupt way. Even though new ateliers were now being organized outside the enclosures of the monasteries, these ateliers were being organized in accordance with the same principles as before; and even though the new secular spirit certainly introduced a very active new element, the ateliers nevertheless continued, in a kind of solidarity, as associations of artisans.

Parallel with the enfranchisement of the towns, a revolution was developing within secular feudalism. In rushing to conquer the holy places in the East, the feudal lords of the day were responding to two demands: in the first place to a religious sentiment; but secondly to a longing for new adventure. The feudal lords yearned to remove themselves from the incessant local conflicts that went on all the time, from powerful overlords who loomed over them, and also, perhaps, from the monotony of an isolated, difficult, and even penurious life. The majority of fief holders among the crusaders left swarms of creditors behind them when they went off to the holy land; they counted on the unforeseen somehow to help extricate them from the many difficulties in which they were generally caught up. It is hardly necessary to add that the kings, the clergy, and the people of the towns discovered certain advantages in the phenomenon of such mass emigration by members of the noble class. Kings could more easily extend their royal power. Religious establishments and bishops found themselves at least temporarily rid of turbulent neighbors, or, if the latter did return, they often did so stripped of everything. This meant opportunities to increase and improve the patrimony of the Church. The people of the cities and towns were able to get charters granted for themselves in return for providing their feudal lords with the sums necessary to finance their lengthy expeditions, for paying their ransoms, or for their maintenance if, as frequently occurred, they came back ruined. Gradually, these kinds of occurrences had the effect of blurring the distinctions between the races, between victors and vanquished, between Franks and Gallo-Romans. They contributed toward the formation of one nationality, united by common interests and by mutual social commitments. Meanwhile, the royal power abandoned its role as head of a class of conquerors in order to become truly national in its scope, destined to protect all classes of citizens without distinction as to race or state; it began to act directly and without intermediaries on the people, not only on lands that were direct royal possessions but on those belonging to its great vassals.

> A feudal lord who granted or sold a charter to a *commune* required the inhabitants of the latter to swear an oath of fidelity to him; for his part he swore to maintain their rights, liberties, and immunities. Several noblemen were required to serve as guarantors of his word; they were obliged to surrender themselves into the hands of the inhabitants of the town if the lord violated any of their rights and to remain prisoners there until the latter rendered justice to them. The king regularly intervened in these agreements in order to confirm and guarantee the charters that were granted. It was impossible to have

> a *commune* without the consent of the king, and thus all the cities and towns came to be considered to be under the direct feudal lordship of the king; he called them "the good towns," a term that was used in various ordinances from the year 1226 on. Later it was required that officials recognize that they held their positions from the king, not in his capacity as another feudal lord and suzerain, but in virtue of his sovereignty as king.[20]

These developments did not take place with complete consistency. Many feudal lords wanted to take back by force charters that they had sold in a moment of distress. The royal intervention, however, leaned toward the *communes,* for the existence of the latter tended to weaken the power of the great feudal lords. The struggle between the clergy and the feudal nobility went on as always, and often feudal lords established *communes* with the single end in view of undermining the power of the bishops. Thus, in the twelfth century, all the powers of the state tended to favor the emergence of the people who had been subjected for several centuries. Becoming conscious of its strength, the third estate recovered its sense of dignity. Among the people alone, in fact, had there been preserved some of the traditions and practices of the old Roman administration: "The charters issued to *communes* in the twelfth and thirteenth centuries seemed to be little more than a confirmation of already existing privileges."[21] Some of the cities of the Midi, such as Toulouse, Bordeaux, Périgueux, and Marseilles, subsisting under a system that was feudal but parceled out and broken up and hence somewhat more liberal, seemed to preserve their municipal institutions almost intact. The rich and populous cities of Flanders were for the most part enfranchised from the tenth century on. A spirit of order is always the result of work and wealth acquired by means of industry and commerce. It is interesting to note the contrast between the developing organization of the *communes* and the anarchy of the feudal system; the *communes* were in effect little republics in which the administrative wheels actually turned even if they were rough and imperfect at first. Later, during the thirteenth century, these *communes* possessed guarantees characteristic of true constitutions. The arts, like commerce and industry, developed rapidly in these centers of relative freedom; the corporations comprising the various arts and crafts attracted all the capable men. What would later become a monopoly that would restrict further development was in this period a source of enlightenment. The influence of the monastic establishments, in architecture and the arts, could only be rivaled by corporations of artists and craftsmen who presented all the same guarantees of order and discipline that the monasteries possessed; they enjoyed the powerful motive that emulation supplied, and they possessed a secular spirit as well. When centers such as Cluny sent out builders, who were monks, to build a priory at some distance from the mother house, they expedited the work by providing them with a fixed and established building program as well as with ready-made plans and patterns or *pounced drawings* (may we be forgiven the use of this latter term!). The architects, who were clerics, could not and must not deviate from these fixed plans. Architecture, thus made subject to a theocratic regime, not only could not entertain new ideas and dispositions, but generally replicated everywhere the same forms, without any attempt to improve upon them. However, when corporations of the laity rose up side by side with the clerical schools, these corporations possessed an innovative spirit resembling that familiar to our modern civilization. Soon the new outlook carried the day, even with the Catholic clergy, who, to do them justice, never rejected progress from whatever source it proceeded, especially when it served to enhance the pomp and magnificence of religious ceremonies. Nevertheless, the spirit of the laity was slow to make itself felt in monastic construction as such. This was natural. But it manifested itself almost immediately in the edifices raised up by the bishops, such as cathedrals and bishops' palaces as well as in feudal castles and manor houses and municipal buildings. In the era currently under consideration, the higher clergy was too enlightened and too closely allied with the powerful men of the day to be unaffected by the spirit of bold and innovative genius that was in the air, and which was the particular possession of lay architects. With the intelligence concerning the affairs of the day that normally characterized it, the higher clergy took over the new spirit and became the most powerful promoter of it.

In the twelfth century, it was not only against the disorder of the great feudal lords and their excesses that the clergy was obliged to deploy its spiritual weapons. For a rival teaching grew up in competition with that of the clergy. This teaching presented itself as every bit as orthodox as that which the clergy taught; at the same time, however, it demanded that the faith be based upon *rationalism.* We have already taken note of how a select few, having taken refuge in the great religious establishments, studied, commented on, and went over with the greatest care the manuscripts of pagan authors, of the Fathers of the Church, and of Christian philosophers, all of which had been collected into the libraries of the monasteries. It is difficult to know whether such men as Lanfranc or St. Anselm could read Greek authors, but it is certain that they knew the translations of and commentaries on Aristotle that were attributed to Boethius. The opinions of Plato had also come down to them. The works of St. Anselm, always stamped with the purity and humility of heart so natural to him, nevertheless also exude the spirit of the learned dialectician and metaphysician that he was. Dialectic and logic had come from the East to the West. The methods of the philosophers of Byzantium had followed the great intellectual movement on which Charlemagne had put his stamp. From the eleventh century on, Western theologians made use in their writings and discussions of all possible resources of reason and logic in order to arrive at demonstrations and proofs of all the mysterious truths of religion.[22] No one is ignorant of the immense popularity that Abelard acquired in the twelfth century through his work as a teacher. His was an elevated and subtle spirit. Although he was a believer, Abelard did lean toward rationalism; he formed the youth of Paris with a kind of scholastic argumentation and rigorous method of reasoning that led those intelligences not enlightened by a living faith almost infallibly to a state of doubt. We find this same rigorous analytic spirit in all the works of art of the Middle Ages; this was especially true in architecture, which is as dependent upon the positive sciences as it is upon artistic inspiration. St. Bernard grasped the danger; he understood that putting into the hands of youth in times still so close to barbarism the weapon of such a method of reasoning would inevitably result in a blow struck against the Catholic faith. Thus, St. Bernard did not hesitate to compare Abelard to Arius, Pelagius, and Nestorius. In 1122, at the Council of Soissons, Abelard was forced to burn with his own hands, and without the opportunity of being heard, his *Introduction to Theology,* in which he had proposed to defend the truth of a unity of God in a Trinity, and this against the arguments of the philosophers. He proposed to do this by subjecting the dogma to all the resources of a rigorous dialectic. In 1140, following the censures of the Council of Sens, he was obliged to retire to the Abbey of Cluny, where the last years of his life were devoted to penitence. In spite of his condemnation, the art of dialectic nevertheless became more and more familiar to writers who remained completely orthodox; and from the resulting school of scholasticism came men such as Roger Bacon, St. Albert the Great, and St. Thomas Aquinas. St. Bernard and Abelard stood each at the head of one of the two great principles that coexisted in the clergy in the course of the twelfth century. St. Bernard represented pure faith, the necessity of remaining on the right path; he firmly believed in theocracy as the only way to escape from barbarism. He was perfectly sincere in introducing reforms among those whom he also wished to make masters of the world; the spirit of St. Paul resided in him. Abelard, for his part, represented all the resources of scholasticism, the subtleties of logic, and an analytic spirit—with all these things pushed to the extreme limit. His position, it is necessary to add, was more in conformity with the tendencies of his era than was that of St. Bernard. Thus it was that the clergy did not so much seek to destroy the rational weapon of Abelard as it tried to make use of it. So it adopted the methods of the learned doctor while preserving the orthodoxy of the saint. We must insist upon this point because it clearly characterizes in our view both the movement that dominated the arts and sciences and the conduct of the higher clergy in the face of that movement. The higher clergy understood the importance of the movement; so it took it over and directed it to the great profit and benefit of the arts and, indeed, of civilization. Everything that arose in that era was an irresistible force: the Crusades, the thirst for knowledge, the quest for freedom—all these things were mighty torrents that needed to be channeled. The West, which for so long had been sunk in its torpor, was suddenly revived and full of life and health; it was caught up at one and the same time in both expansion and self-absorption. Never had the desire to learn produced such marvels. Abelard, condemned by a council and turned into a fugitive despairing of human justice, no longer able to find a corner of the earth where he might teach freely, except on the banks of the Ardisson with the consent of the bishop of Troyes, soon found his solitude broken by a swarm of disciples. But let Monsieur Guizot tell the story:

> No sooner had his disciples learned the place of his withdrawal than they came from all directions, building around him along the river small huts to live in. There, sleeping on straw and subsisting on coarse bread and wild vegetables, they were only too happy to have found their master again. They were avid to hear his words; they nourished themselves on them, meanwhile cultivating his fields for him and seeing to his needs. Priests were there among these followers of his, along with members of the laity. These priests, Héloïse said, "who lived from ecclesiastical benefices and who were thus accustomed to receive offerings rather than to proffer them—whose hands were habituated to take, rather than to give—were prodigious, and almost importunate, in the gifts they brought." It proved necessary to enlarge the oratory; it was too small for the number trying to gather there. Buildings of wood and stone replaced the huts made out of reeds, all constructed by the labor or at the expense of his philosophical colony. Abelard, in the middle of such studious and affectionate youth, had no other thought than to instruct, to impart knowledge and doctrine. Eventually he saw built there the religious edifice that, in memory of the consolations he found there amid his own bad fortune, he dedicated to the Paraclete, or Comforter.[23]

The combination of faith, the simple need to travel, and the desire to atone for crimes committed had never before resulted in such an impetus as the one generated by the Crusades. Nor were there ever any more courageous or persistent efforts of a single nation to get an administration organized for itself, or, in order to transform itself into a true nationality, to take into its own hands responsibility for its own fundamental liberties, than was exhibited within the veritable explosion of all the new *communes.* The higher clergy may have condemned the teaching of Abelard, but it also operated at its own proper level when, at one and the same time, it both upheld orthodoxy and inspired the great movement that was the Crusades—all the time benefiting from both. At first the higher clergy did not understand the *communes,* and so it anathematized them. However, it shortly discovered, among the same bourgeois corporations of these very same *communes,* the active, capable, and bold artisans who could build and adorn its own temples, monasteries, hospitals, and palaces. It was an admirable epoch for the arts, one full of youth and vigor!

At the end of the twelfth century, architecture, as carried on by lay artists, still retained something of its theocratic origins. Yet, even though it was still contained within Roman traditions, it had a fluidity about it which gave some hint of what it would be like 50 years later; it sometimes exhibited a startling boldness; sometimes innovative exceptions appeared that soon became the rule. Each province was erecting its own large constructions, which would become rules. Among all these rapidly developing but partial building activities, those in the royal domain maintained the first rank. In the histories of peoples Providence always raises up men to fit the circumstances. King Philip Augustus reigned at this point in time. As a result of both his competence as a politician and his personal character, which was both bold and prudent, he brought the monarchy to a degree of power unknown since Charlemagne. He was one of the first rulers who knew how to enlist his nobles in enterprises that were truly national. Under him feudalism shed the last vestiges of its old habits of local conquest and became an integral part of the nation. A large number of towns and even simple villages were willingly granted charters. The higher clergy began to play a smaller part in secular affairs as it underwent reforms of its own. The country was becoming a real country, and the *de facto* royalty, in Guizot's expression, was raised up to the level of a *de jure* royalty. True governmental unity made its appearance, and, under its influence, architecture too began to shed its allegiance to the old forms, forms borrowed from all over. Architecture began to be practiced in accordance with rules that would soon transform it into a national art form.

To the existing royal domains Philip Augustus added Normandy, Artois, Vermandois, Maine, Touraine, Anjou, and Poitou; that is to say, he added the richest provinces of France and those that contained the most active and industrious populations. Little by little, the preponderance of the monarchy had taken hold in the provinces, particularly in the Île-de-France; it replaced secular feudalism and the influence of the great religious establishments. The towns, too, grew in the shadow of the rising royal power; they were better protected in their liberties, and better able to organize their municipal administrations with greater strength and security. Some of them, such as Paris, did not even need to establish themselves as *communes* in order to develop their industry, since they already lived under the immediate protection of the royal power and that was sufficient for them. It seems to us that too little account has ever been taken of the influence of the monarchical power on the development of the arts in France. It sometimes appears that Francis I was the first king thought to have influenced the arts significantly. In point of fact, however, from the twelfth century on, we can attest to the incredible vigor displayed by architecture and the arts allied with it precisely in the royal domains, especially in the Île-de-France—that is to say, in that portion of the royal domains that, as a result of the feudal dismemberment that took place at the end of the tenth century, had become the direct appanage of the kings of France. From Philip Augustus to Louis XIV, the overall spirit of the French monarchy evidenced some most striking characteristics: it was impartial as well as great; it maintained both logic and solid content in its direction of affairs, distinguishing itself in these respects from all the other monarchies in the history of the peoples of western Europe. The French monarchy, at the end of the twelfth century, was perhaps the only monarchy that was truly national and identified itself with the spirit of the people; this was the source of its always growing strength and power, even in the face of its errors and setbacks. In its relationships with the court of Rome, with its own great vassals, and with the nation as a whole, the monarchy exhibited (we are speaking, of course, of its conduct in general) the firm moderation and an enlightened spirit that were supposed to characterize the man of good taste (to employ a modern expression). The monarchy's way of seeing things and conducting its affairs was reflected in the arts all the way up to the time of Louis XIV. In the royal domains from the thirteenth century on, architecture, the living expression of the spirit of a people, exhibited a grandeur that yet avoided any character of exaggeration; it remained always contained, even in its flights; and, in periods of decadence, it continued to remain within the limits of good taste, sober yet rich at one and the same time, always clear and logical. This architecture adapted itself to all legitimate demands without, however, ever abandoning its *style.* It was an art that belonged to a people who were now formed, who knew how to say and to do only what was necessary in order to be understood. Let us never forget that, during the twelfth and thirteenth centuries, the schools in Paris that made up the university attracted everybody, not only in France but in Europe, who wished to acquire true knowledge. The teaching of the arts there had to be on the same level as the teaching of letters, the teaching of what was then called "physics" (that is, of the sciences), and the teaching of theology. Germany, Italy, and Provence in particular all sent their doctors to Paris to complete their studies. We have already seen how the great religious establishments, from the eleventh century on, sent out their monks to build monasteries in England, in Italy, and even in the depths of Germany. At the end of the twelfth century, lay corporations from the royal domains began to assume in the same fashion the direction of the arts throughout all the provinces of France.

Before moving any further, however, let us rapidly examine the various elements that, in each region, gave to the local architecture a distinct character. From Marseilles to Châlon, the valleys of the Rhône and the Saône had preserved a large number of ancient buildings that remained more or less intact; there more than anywhere else, Roman traditions left their traces up to the twelfth century. Construction along the banks of the Rhône during the eleventh and twelfth centuries recalled the architecture of the late empire. The churches of Thor, Vénasques, Pernes, the porch of Notre-Dame-des-Dons at Avignon, as well as those of Saint-Trophime of Arles and of Saint-Gilles, all exhibited in their details, if not in the sum total of their various modifications made in response to new needs, examples of Roman style still present on the soil of Provence. The frequent relationships of the littoral towns with the East resulted in Byzantine influence to be found in them, both in their ornamentation and in their general construction. Such features as the following indicate Eastern origin: apses with canted sides, polygonal cupolas supported by successive corbeled arches, blind arcades adorning the walls, moldings projecting out only slightly and composed of numerous elements, flowing ornaments depicting imaginary plants as well as pointed and jagged foliages, all tinged with their Eastern origins. These foreign elements become rarer as we move up the Rhône; or, at any rate, they take on a different character when combined with the Eastern influence coming from across the Rhine. The latter represents another and different influence, and the reason it does is that the peoples on the shores of the Mediterranean had direct and continuous relationships with the East. In the twelfth century, they were influenced by what was the contemporary Eastern art of the day; it was not an archaeological influence exerted by oriental art of an earlier day. It was from this factor that came the elegance and delicacy that is to be seen in the edifices in Provence that date from this period. However, the Byzantine influence that had left its traces on the banks of the Rhine dated back to the time of Charlemagne; since then the relationships of those regions with the East had ceased to be direct. Two different styles of architecture, then, one of which had once borrowed oriental features, and the other of which continued to borrow them, met in the upper Saône region, on the soil of Champagne and Burgundy; and it is from this that resulted the mixed style coming out of an indigenous Roman style, influenced by both contemporary Eastern models and the older Eastern models found in the Rhenish tradition. Examples of this mixed style include the churches of Tournus and the abbeys of Vézelay, Cluny, and Charlieu. Nevertheless, this mixed style resulted in a harmonious whole. These buildings were constructed by local men, men who were affected by influences whose origin they did not even know, and who were directed, as was the case at Cluny, by foreigners who did not go enough into the details of construction to prevent the local tradition from leaving its mark, both on the manner of building and on that of decorating. Moreover, Eastern influences did not appear on Gallo-Roman territory only as a result of the two ways described. In 984, foundations for a huge church were laid down in Périgueux. This church exactly reproduced, both in its plan and in its dispositions, a rather well-known model: St. Mark's in Venice, begun only a few years earlier. The abbey church of Saint-Front of Périgueux thus had domes on pendentives and was certainly erected by Gallo-Roman laborers under the direction of a Frenchman who either had studied St. Mark's or was working from the plans of a Venetian architect; for if the architecture of the structure is Venetian or quasi-oriental, both its construction and the details of its ornamentation belong to the era of Roman decadence. In no way do they recall either the sculptures or the building methods employed for St. Mark's in Venice. This building, despite the strangeness of its having been built when it was and its complete dissimilarity to anything that had preceded it in that part of Gaul, nevertheless exerted enormous influence on the things that were built north of the Garonne during the eleventh and twelfth centuries; it brings out the importance that the monastic schools of architecture represented up to the end of the twelfth century. One of our most distinguished archaeologists explains this migration of oriental architecture to the far ends of the Occident by the presence of Venetian colonies then present in Limoges and along the Atlantic coast.[24] In those days, a passage through the Strait of Gibraltar ran great risks owing to the many Arab pirates who held the coasts of Spain and North Africa. Thus, commerce between the Levant and the north of France as well as Britain (England) passed through Marseilles or Narbonne and followed a land route through Limoges in order to rejoin the sea again at La Rochelle or Nantes. The abbey church of Saint-Front de Périgueux was distinguished not only by the way it was laid out—which had no analogue in France—but also by its domes on pendentives.[25] It was most certainly a foreign importation, and one that exerted its influence far from Périgueux. Nevertheless, even if this church did indeed influence the religious architecture of the Atlantic coast region, it does not follow that it has to be considered the mother church of all the churches with domes built in France since the twelfth century. We must admit that the Levant transit trade brought foreign artistic principles into central and western France wherever there was any trade activity, or, more probably, wherever actual warehouses were established by the incredible energy of the Venetians. The contemporary written documents on this subject say little or are otherwise insufficient. It does not seem possible to establish an entire theory on such incomplete information as they provide; but if we examine the facts and draw the most natural conclusions from them, we may perhaps be able to clarify that most interesting question, the question of the introduction of the dome on pendentives into the French architecture of the eleventh and twelfth centuries. At the end of the tenth century, France was divided up as shown in figure 1. In the center of geographic France there was the great province of Aquitaine, of which Limoges was the central point; it was bordered to the north by the royal domain and by Anjou on a line that roughly followed the course of the Loire, and to the southwest by the ocean and a line that followed the course of the Garonne; to the south by the County of Toulouse; to the east by Lyonnais and by Burgundy. Now it was in this vast province, and only in this vast province, that French architecture adopted in the course of the eleventh and twelfth centuries the dome on pendentives carried on the principal arches of a vault. The manuscript collec-

Figure 1

tion of the antiquities of Limoges cited by Verneilh fixes the arrival of the Venetians in Limoges around 988 or 989.[26] It contains the following passage, speaking about commerce:

> The old accounts of the country recount that, formerly, Venetians trading in the goods of the East, being unable to move their ships and galleys coming from the East on the Mediterranean out into the ocean through the Strait of Gibraltar because of rocks blocking the strait, came instead to Limoges, where they established the Venetian Market. They brought spices and other Eastern goods there, landing them at Aigues-Mortes and transporting them to Limoges with mules and carts; from there they moved to La Rochelle, Brittany, England, Scotland, and Ireland. These Venetians remained in Limoges for a long time, residing near the Abbey of St. Martin, which they rebuilt on the ruins of the old one destroyed by the Danes [Normans]. . . .

If the Venetians had come to Aquitaine only to establish a depot to hold goods destined for the trade with "England, Scotland, and Ireland," it is not likely that they would have selected Limoges as the place for their depot. Rather, they would have selected a coastal town. Establishing a depot at Limoges, in the center of Aquitaine, indicates, it seems to us, a manifest effort to supply spices, rich materials, and Levantine commodities to the provinces of France as well as to the countries beyond the seas. During an epoch when the art of architecture was still trying to find the route that it would follow, when an active effort was going on in religious construction to replace structures likely to suffer destruction with stone vaults,[27] and when builders were yet familiar only with the barrel vault, which was applicable only to smaller buildings, it is not at all surprising under the circumstances that rich foreign merchants would hold up for imitation the architecture of their native land. Nor is it surprising that these foreign merchants would offer either to bring architects from Venice or to send monk-architects from Aquitaine to visit and study the churches of Venice and those on the shores of the Adriatic. The dome could thus have been introduced into France in any one of a hundred different ways. Each architect brought in by the Venetians, or returned from visiting the churches of the Adriatic, would have attempted to reproduce, to the best of his ability, and using workers unskilled at the particular task, those foreign models considered worth imitating. We therefore think it very probably an exaggeration to consider Saint-Front of Périgueux as the model and mother church of all the church buildings in France that happen to utilize domes. If Saint-Front is indeed copied from the plan and dispositions of St. Mark's in Venice, it does not follow that this particular abbey church is itself the unique source from which all other domed churches in Aquitaine and the Midi of France derived during the course of the eleventh and twelfth centuries. Saint-Front was perhaps the original of all the churches possessing domes on pendentives in Périgord and the Angoumois; but we believe that the domed churches in Auvergne and Lyonnais, like those of the cathedral of Le Puy, for example, were influenced by the East, or, rather, by the Adriatic, in a direct fashion, through Venetian commerce.[28]

However that may be, taking the fact itself as evidenced from the actual construction that went on in Aquitaine during the eleventh and twelfth centuries, it must be conceded to be a fact that has considerable importance in the history of French architecture; its consequences made themselves felt up through the thirteenth century, both in that province and beyond it.[29] The cathedrals of Poitiers, Angers, and even Le Mans, in the fashion in which the vaults of their great naves were constructed, preserve traces of the dome.

We know nothing about the buildings that existed in the northwestern part of France prior to the Norman invasion; the incursions of the Danes left nothing standing behind them. Once they were firmly established on the ground, however, the erstwhile barbarians who were the Normans became active and intrepid builders. In the course of a century and a half, they covered the territory that they had taken over with civil, religious, and monastic construction of a richness and extent uncommon for that day. It is hard to imagine that the Normans brought any elements of art with them from Norway; but they possessed a temperament that included both persistence and thoroughness; even their brute strength did not lack grandeur. As conquerors, they built castles in order to ensure their dominance. They also quickly recognized the moral influence of the clergy, and they endowed them heavily in consequence. Once they had set for themselves a goal, they pressed on to achieve it; they did not leave unfinished jobs that they had started, and, in this, they differed markedly from the people of southern Gaul. They were tenacious; among the barbarians who established themselves in France, they were perhaps the only ones who had a clear idea of order; they alone knew how to preserve their conquests and organize a state. They surely found the remains of Carolingian art in the territories where they established themselves; but they added to it their own national genius—a genius that was positive, expansive, even a bit rude, yet fluent and easy for all of that.

Since the Normans had frequent contacts with Maine, Anjou, Poitou, and the entire Atlantic coast of France, Norman architecture too was influenced by Byzantine taste. However, this influence was to be found in decoration rather than in construction itself, as in Périgord and Angoumois. We must not forget the trading centers for Levantine commodities and goods that existed in central France. The Venetians brought to France not just pepper and cinnamon, but also rich fabrics made out of silk or woven with gold and embellished with ornaments, scroll patterns, or bizarre animals; such materials were then manufactured in Syria, Baghdad, Egypt, or the coasts of Asia Minor, at Constantinople, in Sicily, and in Spain. These materials of Eastern origin are found in almost all the tombs of the twelfth century, just as they are depicted in the paintings of the time; they were very much in vogue in that age. The higher clergy in particular used them for sacerdotal vestments, as well as for curtains, altar cloths,[30] or to cover the shrines of saints. "Saracen" rugs, as they were called, had originally been manufactured in Persia; they were also used in churches and in the palaces of rich feudal lords. The early Crusades, as well as the conquests of the Normans in Sicily and in the East, only served to diffuse even more widely in France, and especially in Normandy, the taste for these admirable fabrics, which were as brilliant and harmonious in their colors as they were pure and gracious in their designs. The architecture of Saintonge, Poitou, Anjou, Maine, and especially Normandy adopted both their designs and their coloring. Everywhere in western France that Roman buildings of any richness of ornamentation remained, the influence of these oriental fabrics is little to be noted. Thus, at Périgueux, for example, in the ancient Vésone filled with Roman ruins, even though the form of religious construction was borrowed from the East, its decoration remained Roman, as we have already noted. In regions such as Normandy, however, where no Roman ruins remained, the decoration of buildings in the eleventh and twelfth centuries recalls the rich lace and braid and the ably fashioned scrolls characteristic of these fabrics from the Levant,[31] even when the architecture of these buildings holds to the Gallo-Roman traditions. Byzantine influence, then, as it is conventionally termed, exerted its influence very differently in the less accessible French provinces of that day. Statuary art, as found in connection with architecture, developed as it did at the end of the eleventh century for the same reasons. Everywhere that substantial Roman construction remained, statuary schools came into being: Provence, the valleys of the Rhône and Saône, Burgundy, Champagne, the County of Toulouse, the mouth of the Gironde, Angoumois, Saintonge, and Poitou. The architecture of the north, in Normandy and on the Rhine, however, was poor in statuary at the same time as it was rich in ornamental combinations of Eastern origin.

During the twelfth century, the royal domain, although reduced to a very small territory in extent, remained almost completely free of all these various influences, or, at any rate, underwent them only to a modest degree. More than in any other region of France, it preserved the pure Gallo-Roman tradition. And as the royal domain became extended in the reign of Philip Augustus at the end of the eleventh and the beginning of the twelfth centuries, it rejected what could be considered excessive in all these foreign influences; it made a selection among them of what was most closely in accord with its own habits and tastes. Thus, it fashioned a national art, just as it fashioned a national government.

Romanesque architecture[32] lacked a center, a unity in its influence that might have enabled it to become the art of a nation. As we have indicated, it was practiced and taught by the religious establishments and thus it came under their rules. These particular rules had no common link between them except the unique authority that they all recognized, that of the papacy; but that authority could not exert any material influence on forms of art. Romanesque architecture was thus reduced to remaining in a stationary state, or reduced simply to appropriating any new elements necessary for its progress from here and there, depending upon the impulses and tastes of the abbots. When the unity created by the monarchical power began to impose itself, however, the lay artists belonging to the recognized corporations powerfully reinforced that unity, and this in the natural course of events. In this way, a natural center of art was formed, which would see its influence radiated outward in every direction, just as political influence was being radiated outward from the same center. The results of all this began to be apparent by the beginning of the thirteenth century. Little by little Romanesque architecture began to fade, to become atrophied, in the face of the new architecture being initiated by the lay artists. Romanesque architecture retreated before the progress of the latter, being only doubtfully preserved by the monastic establishments, or else in those provinces where the action of the royal power had not yet made itself felt—but this was the case only until some new conquest of the monarchy in such areas abruptly destroyed its last vestiges there. Then, without any transition, new constructions of the royal domain type would suddenly be erected—as if a battle standard had been planted in the midst of a conquered city. From the thirteenth century on, the progress of architecture followed that of the royal power—indeed, accompanied it, and seemed to share equally in its prerogatives. Where the royal power was strong and uncontested, the new architecture developed with great energy. Where the royal power was weak and challenged, we find an architecture of mixed and uncertain forms.

It was during the final years of the twelfth century and at the beginning of the thirteenth that all the great cathedrals of the royal domain both were begun and were nearly completed, utilizing new plans. All of the following cathedrals were begun in the reign of Philip Augustus, and almost all of them were completed by the end of the thirteenth century: Notre-Dame de Paris, Notre-Dame de Chartres, the cathedrals of Bourges, Laon, Soissons, Meaux, Noyon, Amiens, Rouen, Cambrai, Arras, Tours, Séez, Coutances, and Bayeux. Champagne, so closely allied with the royal domain in the reign of St. Louis, similarly raised up the great cathedrals of Reims, Châlons, and Troyes. Burgundy and Bourbonnais also followed the new directions in architecture and saw constructed the cathedrals of Auxerre, Nevers, and Lyons. Soon the Viscounty of Carcassonne became part of the royal domain and, alone among its surrounding territories, where debased Roman traditions were to hang on until the fifteenth century, benefited from the advantage of the direct influence of an *official* architecture. As for Guyenne, which remained an appanage of the crown of England up until the time of Charles V, and as for Provence, which became French only under Louis XI, the architecture of the royal domain failed to penetrate into those regions; or, at any rate, nothing but sad imitations of it, which all seemed out of place, was ever produced in these regions. In Brittany, the architecture of the royal domain developed late and exhibited a character that bespoke English influence as much as it did the influence of Normandy and Maine. We show here in figure 2 the divisions of France at the death of Philip Augustus in 1223. The new architectural movement was followed everywhere in the construction that took place in the cities, towns, and simple villages. Soon even the monastic establishments were diverted into the channel that had been dug by the new art. Around the important buildings such as cathedrals, castles, and episcopal and lay palaces, thousands of other buildings were erected for which these grand and sumptuous buildings served as types—like so many children of the same family. The "mother" monuments often contained particular features dictated by an exceptional configuration of the ground at its site, by local needs, or even by the personal taste of the artist who erected it. Such features would then also appear in the secondary buildings, even though they were in no way required. An accident during construction, *second thoughts,* or an insufficiency of resources could all result in modifications of the model building. Yet its imitations could include even defects, impoverishments, and mistakes in construction resulting from various factors.

Figure 2

What was most striking about the new system of architecture practiced from the twelfth century on was its complete freedom from Roman traditions. We should not imagine that this liberation was a result of disorder or caprice. On the contrary, everything about it was ordered, logical, and harmonious. Once its principles had been laid down, the consequences followed with a rigor that did not admit of any exception. Even the defects of this architecture arose out of its principles, imperiously pursued. In the French architecture that emerged in the thirteenth century, everything—its dispositions, its methods of construction, its statics, and its ornamentation, even its *scale*—differed from these same features and aspects of ancient architecture. In studying these two art forms, we must assume two different and opposite points of view.

If we attempt to judge one of these two forms in terms of the principles that motivated the other, we will end up finding both types to be absurd. This is what explains the strange prejudices, errors, and contradictions that abound in the writings belonging to the two opposed camps of defenders of ancient and of Gothic architecture, respectively. These two architectures do not need to be defended from each other. They both arose out of two different civilizations, which themselves were based on different principles. It is, of course, possible to prefer Roman civilization to the civilization created by the French monarchy, but it is not possible to ignore or set at naught either one of them. It is even unprofitable to compare them; it is better all around to be conversant with both of them.

Roman monuments always represented a kind of casting or molding carried out according to established forms that required the expeditious use of an enormous mass of materials. Thus, a large number of workers, as well as extensive works and means of transport on a large scale, were always required. The Romans had at their disposition armies that were accustomed to constructing public works; they could assign a whole army of slaves to a given project, or otherwise requisition what they needed for it. The procedures they followed thus accorded with the social system they happened to have. To erect one of their great buildings, they did not need workers who had any particular experience. Specialists to direct the construction they certainly required; they also needed some painters and some skilled workers to stucco the enormous masses of masonry that they raised up. Some Greek artists were also needed in order to sculpt any of the marble employed. Aside from these few specialists, however, they simply needed strong arms to break rocks, carry bricks, mix mortar, and work concrete. Thus it was that, no matter how far it was from the capital that they happened to be building a circus, baths, aqueducts, basilicas, or palaces, the same procedures and methods of construction were always followed, and the same form of architecture was always utilized. Roman construction is always and everywhere Roman construction. This was true without regard to the lay of the land, the climate, or even the materials used or the prevailing local customs. Moreover, a Roman building was always a monument of the city of Rome; it was never the work of an individual artist. From the moment that Rome moved in anywhere, Rome immediately became dominant there, suppressing everything foreign to the Roman spirit. These practices constituted Rome's principal strength; and the arts followed the lead thus provided by politics. When Rome took over a territory, she abolished neither the customs nor the gods of the conquered people. Nevertheless, she habitually raised up her own temples and her immense public buildings at the same time as she established her own political administration. Before long the importance of these establishments, as well as of Roman administrative organization, absorbed the remaining vestiges of the civilizations over which she had cast her great shadow. There is surely to be found in all this many fit subjects for diverse studies and observations. In the middle of this unheard-of power human beings simply disappeared, becoming insignificant cogs in the operation of the whole vast political machine. Even Greece, so outstanding in the arts as in everything tending to the greater development of the human spirit—even Greece saw her light extinguished by the massive blast of the Roman wind. Alone Christianity was up to taking on the giant on his own terms. Christianity did this by giving isolated individuals the sense of their own personalities. However, centuries were required before the remains of pagan Roman civilization disappeared. Here we are able to consider only one of the many aspects of the immense human labor of the Middle Ages. By the end of the twelfth century, all of the basic principles that would assure the triumph of the ideas engendered by Christianity had been laid down (to speak only of the subject with which we are here occupied). The principle of personal responsibility had made its appearance; the individual person now counted for something in society, regardless of class. The arts, having completely thrown off the ancient traditions, now became the individual expression of the artist. The artist contributed to the common effort, accepting its rules, but at the same time giving to it the benefit of his particular inspiration. There was variety in unity. The guilds ensured this result, for they were founded on the basis of fixed rules. However, unlike modern academies, they did not impose unchanging forms. Unity constituted the great need and tendency of that era, but the unity that came about had not yet become tyrannical. Although painters and sculptors had to accept certain principles of construction, they were accorded ample liberty in the execution of their work. The architect might dictate the height of a capital or a frieze, but the sculptor could fashion his own work out of this capital or section of a frieze; he worked in an atmosphere where he had to take responsibility for his own work. Even architecture in the twelfth and thirteenth centuries, although committed to a uniform mode as well as to some absolute principles, preserved the greatest possible liberty in the application of these principles. Numerous examples abound in the *Dictionary* demonstrating the truth of what we are asserting here. With an invasion of the laity moving into the domain of the arts, there ensued an era of such rapid progress that we can barely trace it in all its aspects. No sooner did a new building go up than it turned out to be the basis for the next development. No sooner was a new mode of construction or decoration tried than it was pushed to its farthest limits with an incredible logical rigor.

In the history of the arts there are two principal elements that we must distinguish: necessity and taste. By the end of the twelfth century, nearly all Roman-style construction, whether religious or civil, could no longer satisfy the new needs that had arisen; this was particularly true in the royal domain. Narrow Romanesque churches with massive pillars, and lacking space, could no longer accommodate the numerous congregations of the faithful in towns and cities, where both the population and its wealth were rapidly increasing. These churches were sad and somber, crude in appearance; they were no longer in harmony with the new customs and with a civilization that had moved on beyond them. Old houses and castles presented the same problems in an even more marked way, since daily life could no longer make do with these old buildings; none of society's new needs could be satisfied by them. As regards military architecture, improvements in offensive methods also required new methods for defense that took the new advances into account.[33]

What was needed was the construction of new churches in which the bases or points of support of the structure took up as little space as possible. These new churches required more light and air; they needed to be more accessible and less closed in upon themselves, more healthful, and more capable of accommodating all the crowds. Moreover, in nearly all of the provinces of the north, the Romanesque churches had been constructed in such a way that they were not going to last.[34] Everywhere they were already falling down, or threatening to do so; they had to be rebuilt. It was also necessary to build palaces and castles for more people; for feudalism was everywhere taking on the characteristics stamped upon it by the monarchy. The king was assuming a greater share of authority over his great vassals, while they, in turn, were taking over smaller fiefs and centralizing power in their own hands in the same way the king was centralizing it in his. And for the newly enfranchised bourgeois as well as for the rising corporations, new construction of all kinds was required: meeting places, town halls, exchanges (or *parloirs,* as they were called then), quarters (or *chambres*) for administrators, structures for the better supervision of public morality, and, indeed, structures of all kinds. The enfranchised towns and cities also required external walls, for it was perfectly well understood that any conquest, if it was to be permanent, had to maintain a position that could be defended. Thus, there existed a need to rebuild practically everything to be in harmony with the new era in society. Furthermore, we must not forget that the ground was everywhere strewn with ruins arising out of all the feudal battles, the Norman invasions, and the establishment of the *communes,* none of which took place without upheavals and popular excesses. Moreover, earlier and ignorant builders had erected structures that could not last and could only be left to crumble. Along with imperative necessity, then, which the history of the times sufficiently explains, there were quite simply new tastes among these Gallo-Roman peoples, who were once again assuming their rightful rank among other nations. We have attempted to indicate some of the diverse sources from which these new tastes had sought inspiration. Above all, however, they arose out of the natural genius of the peoples who inhabited the basins of the Seine, the Loire, and the Somme. These peoples, endowed as they were with supple and innovative natures, were also quick to seize upon the practical side of things. They were active and energetic, given to reasoning things out; and they were driven by good sense as much as they were by imagination. They seemed destined by Providence to break the remaining shackles of barbarism in Gaul, not by material force or other abrupt means, but by means of an intellectual effort that had been fermenting since the eleventh century. Protected by the royal power, they in turn surrounded it with an aureole that did not cease to glow with a living light until well after the era of the Renaissance. No other people, perhaps, unless it was the Athenians, ever discarded so easily the old traditions that were in place. This entailed both an advantage and a disadvantage. Since these people never stopped trying to improve—at the same time that they never looked back—they sometimes ended up with the bad as well as with the good. They could become passionately attached to an idea. However, once they had pursued it as far as it would take them, once they had analyzed it down to its essence, or once the same idea began to take root among neighboring peoples, they could then throw it off with disdain, as if it were worn out and used up, a cadaver from which no more life could be expected, in order to pursue some other idea with exactly the same passion. This character trait has remained with us up to the present day. In our day, it has produced admirable as well as miserable fruits; it amounts to nothing else but what we have for about the last 300 years styled *fashion.* And fashion, of course, can apply to the futilities of life every bit as much as it can apply to the most serious of social questions and principles. Fashion can be ridiculous and terrible, just as it can be gracious and filled with grandeur.

However that may be, we must take into account the particular character of an important part of France if we are ever going to understand the great movement in the arts that burst out around the end of the twelfth century. We can only make reference to it generally here, since we will deal with it in connection with our analysis of each specific topic and of the forms adopted by each type of architecture. It is necessary to point out, though, that this great movement in the arts remained confined within specific limits so long as architecture, in both theory and practice, remained in the hands of the religious establishments. In that situation, everything contributed to keeping it within bounds: compulsory traditions that had to be followed; the rigor of life in the cloister; the reforms attempted and carried out among the clergy during the eleventh and part of the twelfth centuries. Once architecture had passed out of the hands of the clergy into the hands of the laity, however, the national genius was not slow in quickly making itself dominant. Eager to free itself from the Romanesque envelope in which it found so little comfort, the national genius ended up stretching the boundaries of that envelope until they burst. One of the earliest efforts in that direction involved the construction of vaults. What was needed was to try to take advantage of the rather confused results that had been obtained up to that point; this goal had to be pursued with the same rigorous logic that characterized all intellectual efforts in that era. The basic principle, which we have already developed in the entry "Flying Buttress," was that vaults exert oblique thrusts; thus it was necessary, in order to maintain them in place, to construct a counter oblique resistance.[35] By the middle of the twelfth century, builders had already recognized that the round, or semicircular, arch had too great a thrust to allow it to be raised to great heights on thin walls or separate pillars, especially over large open spaces, without enormous piers or abutments. So they replaced the round arch with the pointed arch.[36] They continued to use the round arch only for windows or narrow spans. They abandoned the barrel vault entirely, since its thrust could be supported only by a continuous abutment. Reducing the points of resistance of their structures to the piers, they ingeniously arranged it so that all the weight and thrust of their vaults were conducted to these piers, which they then supported by independent flying buttresses, which transferred to the outside all the weight of these large edifices. To provide a firmer foundation for their piers or separate buttresses, they charged them with supplementary weight, out of which they then fashioned some of their richest decorative motifs.[37] As they thus progressively reduced the mass of their structures, they recognized the tremendous resistance strength that the pointed arch possessed while, at the same time, it had only a slight separating action. Accordingly, they began to use the pointed arch everywhere, totally abandoning the round arch, even in civil architecture.

From the beginning of the thirteenth century on, then, architecture developed in accordance with a wholly new method—a method in which all the related parts could be rigorously deduced, one from the other. Now, it is by means of such changes of method as this that revolutions in the sciences and in the arts begin. Construction dictates form: piers destined to carry several arches will have as many separate columns as there are arches; these columns will have a greater or a lesser diameter depending upon the weight they must carry, and they will be raised up to the vaults that they are designed to support; their capitals, too, will assume an importance proportionate to the load they carry. Arches will be wide or slender, or will rest upon one or several rows of springers, depending upon their function.[38] Walls, having become superfluous, will disappear completely in the most magnificent constructions, to be replaced by gratings decorated with stained glass. Everything that is necessary to the construction will become just another motif for decoration: roofs, waterspouts, the introduction of daylight, the means of access and circulation on different stories of the building, even its ironwork, supporting structures, sealing, leading, heating, and ventilation. All these things will not be concealed, as has been a regular construction practice since the sixteenth century; they will, moreover, be kept right out in the open, and, through various ingenious methods, they will contribute to the total richness of the architecture—always taking for granted, of course, the level of good taste that will invariably govern how they are decorated. There will, in short, never be any mere ornament that could really have been dispensed with in one of these exquisite structures of the beginning of the thirteenth century. Each and every ornament will also represent the fulfillment of some specific need. If we move outside France and look at some of the imitations of these French buildings, though, we will encounter some rather strange things; for these imitations are often found to have copied the mere forms without any inner understanding of why an architectural member has taken the form that it has. Consideration of this fact may serve to explain how it is that, in accordance with our national habit of always trying to seek our good at a distance somewhere (as if distance somehow enhanced value), the loftiest criticisms of the type of architecture commonly styled "Gothic" almost always have in view the cathedrals of Milan, Siena, Florence, or certain German churches. It never seems to occur to such critics of the "Gothic" to take a trip of a few short miles, where they could seriously study the actual structure and features of the cathedrals of Amiens, Chartres, or Reims. French architecture of the Middle Ages should surely not be studied in those places where it was nothing but an import; it should be studied on the soil that gave it birth, and among the various moral and material elements that nourished it. Furthermore, this architecture is so intimately tied to our national history, to the achievements of the French mind, as well as to our national character (whose major traits, tendencies, and directions are vividly reflected in this same architecture) that it is only barely understandable why all this is not better known and appreciated, or why the study of it is not required in our schools every bit as much as is the teaching of our national history.

It was precisely at the moment when research on ancient literature, science, philosophy, and legislation came to be pursued with real seriousness that architecture, too, abandoned the last remaining features of the tradition of antiquity in order to establish a brand-new art whose principles were in manifest contradiction with those of ancient art. Must we therefore conclude that the men of the twelfth century were not consistent with themselves? The contrary is the case: what distinguishes the *Renaissance* of the twelfth century from the *Renaissance* of the sixteenth century is that the earlier of these awakenings actually succeeded in penetrating the inner spirit of antiquity, whereas the later Renaissance allowed itself to be seduced by forms alone. The dialecticians of the twelfth century studied the ancient pagan authors, the Fathers of the Church, and the Scriptures; but they saw all these things with the eyes of men of their own times; they saw them as Aristotle himself would have seen them, had he lived in the twelfth century. The form that was given to those things that pertained to art was thus derived from the needs and ideas of their own period. Let us take a striking example of this, fundamental in architecture, namely, *scale.* Everybody knows that the *orders* of the architecture of the Greeks and the Romans could be considered as typical *unities* always employed in construction, even while the *dimensions* could be greater or lesser. Meanwhile, proper *proportions* were always maintained in accordance with whether the edifice was smaller or larger in scale. Thus, the Parthenon and the Temple of Theseus in Athens are very different in their respective dimensions; yet the Doric order is applied to these two monuments in an almost identical, though proportionate, fashion. To make this point clearer, we may say that the Doric order of the Parthenon is the same as that of the Doric order of the Temple of Theseus viewed in a magnifying glass. Thus, nothing in the ancient architectural orders, Roman or Greek, brings to mind any unique *scale.* Nevertheless, there is such a scale, and that an invariable and imperative one, namely, *man* himself. The human dimension does not change, regardless of whether the building happens to be large or small. Thus, if you make a geometric design of an ancient temple without including any dimensions or indicating the scale, it will prove impossible to say whether the columns of your particular temple are four, five, or ten meters high. For the type of architecture styled "Gothic," however, the same situation does not obtain. The human scale is to be encountered everywhere in Gothic architecture; it is encountered independently of the actual dimensions of any given structure. Go into the Reims cathedral or into a village church of the same era, and you will find that things are generally of the same height; they also have the same architectural profiles. Columns may be longer or shorter, but they will have the same diameter. Moldings may be more widely employed in a larger building, but they will be of the same dimensions as the moldings in a smaller building. All the other details and features that enter into the order of construction will similarly always be on the same scale, namely the human scale: balustrades, supports, socles, platforms, galleries, friezes, bas-reliefs, and the like. The human being enters into everything; the edifice is erected by him and for him; it becomes practically an article of his clothing. However grand and rich a building may be, it is nevertheless always constructed according to the measure of man. Thus it is that the monuments of the Middle Ages seem larger than they really are. This is the case because, even in the absence of people, we are continually being reminded of the human scale. Our eyes are continually obliged to compare the dimensions of the whole with a human standard of measurement. However, exactly the contrary impression is produced by ancient monuments; we do not realize their actual dimensions until we have taken some thought about them. When someone is placed near one of them as a point of comparison, it is the person who appears small rather than the monument appearing large. Whether or not all of this amounts to a virtue or a defect is not the issue we are discussing here. Rather, we are only pointing to the fact of it, a fact of the greatest importance. For it points to the abyss that separates the methods of the arts of antiquity from those of the Middle Ages.

We do not assert, though, that the art brought to birth on a portion of French soil at the end of the twelfth century is the quintessential *Christian art.* St. Peter's in Rome, Santa Sophia in Constantinople, St. Paul's Outside the Walls in Rome, St. Mark's in Venice, our own Romanesque churches of Auvergne and Poitou—all of these churches are certainly examples of Christian art, since they were constructed by Christians for religious purposes. Christianity is sublime in the catacombs, in the deserts, in St. Peter's in Rome—or in the Cathedral of Chartres. But we may well ask: would the unique constructions of northern France ever have been created if it had not been for Christianity? Evidently not. Thus, the great principle of *scale* with which we have just been regaling the reader—does it not appear to be a particularly striking symbol of the Christian spirit? To indicate man's relationship to God by continually emphasizing his littleness with respect to the grandeur of a vast and magnificent structure erected for religious worship—is this not a truly Christian notion, one that occurs immediately to people? Is it not, indeed, a rigorous application of a principle of construction that precisely inspires the indefinable sentiment we experience in the presence of the great Gothic churches? Whether or not the architects of the twelfth and thirteenth centuries applied this principle consciously or instinctively, it remains the principle that presided over their work of construction, civil and military as well as religious, up to the time of the Renaissance. The Renaissance, of course, was frankly inspired by ancient models. However, the architects of what we may style the age of ogival architecture—the architecture of the pointed arch—were every bit as consistent in their use of their forms as Greek architects were in the application of their system based on the *proportion of the orders,* a system that the Greek architects applied independently of a building's dimensions. For the Greeks architecture was an abstract art. Greek art was a unity. It dictated; it did not obey. It dictated both the materials and the men; it was the ancient *fatum.* By contrast, the architects of the Middle Ages were subject to the law of Christianity, which, even while it recognized the sovereign power of God, also recognized human free will, human responsibility for human efforts, and the value, however infinitesimal overall, of an individual creature made in the image of the Creator.

If we follow the logical consequences of these principles, which arose out of Christianity, we will see architectural forms becoming subject to the materials employed in each locality, as provided there by nature. If the materials were small in scale, the architectural members consequently assumed a lesser importance.[39] If materials were larger, the outlines, the ornamentation, and the details of the architecture became more ample. If these materials were more refined, or were easy to work, the architecture took advantage of this, too, by ordering its decoration accordingly, so that everything became more fluid. If the materials were hard and crude, on the other hand, the architecture simplified everything. In ogival architecture everything assumes its proper place and preserves its proper value. Every man counts for what he is, just as every object counts for what it is—just as in creation itself everything assumes its proper place in the divine plan. Since it seemed that this ogival art could not help being methodical even in its refinements, we see it from its very beginnings simply abandoning all the ornamentation once utilized by the Romano-Byzantine tradition in favor of its own designs for its friezes, cornices, grooves, capitals, and moldings, utilizing instead the leaves and flowers familiar from the fields and forests of northern France. It was a marvelous thing: the architectural imitation of vegetation seemed to follow an order similar to the order of nature. We have examples at hand that demonstrate this. *Buds* represent the first signs of life in a plant; buds in turn produce *shoots,* or young branches, with leaves and flowers on them. When, at the end of the twelfth century, French architecture decided to make use of plants as motifs of decoration, it began with imitations of *cotyledons, buds,* and *shoots,* only to move on later to the representation of stems and fully developed leaves.[40] It goes without saying that this same synthetic method was *a fortiori* followed in statics and in all the methods employed by architecture to create resistance to natural destructive agents. Thus, the pyramidal form was adopted as being the most stable one. Horizontal planes were excluded since they would permit rainwater to accumulate; steeply inclined planes were preferred, without exception. Along with these general overall considerations we will also be struck, if we examine things in detail, at how the interior of these buildings was organized. Just as the human body is supported and is able to move around on two slender, simple supports, occupying the least possible amount of ground space (while the body itself is much more complicated and highly developed higher up, where the most important organs are to be found), so *Gothic* construction also makes use of the simplest possible kind of supports, utilizing a kind of basic structure whose stability is maintained only by the development and combination of its upper parts. The *Gothic* building remains standing only on condition of its being complete. It is impossible to withdraw a single one of its "organs" without killing the entire organism. Its stability comes only from the laws of equilibrium. Indeed, this is one of the reproaches most willingly leveled against this type of architecture, and it sometimes appears to be a reasonable one. But would we similarly reproach the human organism for the perfection of its various elements, considering it inferior to that of a reptile, for example, because it is more fragile and more susceptible to outside agents? In Gothic architecture, matter is subordinated to the idea. This architecture arose out of a modern spirit, which itself arose out of Christianity.

However, the principle governing this architecture could never be absorbed by mere form, and that for the very reason that its principle was based on human reason. Once architecture had become so completely identified with the ideas of a particular era and of a given people, it was surely inevitable that it would have to undergo its own changes once those basic ideas were changed. During the reign of Philip Augustus, it was perceived that the architectural art was striking out on new paths under the influence of a group of men united by a community of principles, even while each one of them retained his own personality and originality. Some of the more timid were still attached to the Romanesque tradition; they adopted the synthetic method only with reservations. The bold adopted it resolutely. It is for this reason that we find in some of the buildings constructed around the same time, at the end of the twelfth and beginning of the thirteenth centuries, some rather notable differences both in methods of construction and in those of decoration. Some of these efforts served as points of departure for the new rules of architecture; others were abandoned as soon as they were tried. Artists who were all going in the same general direction, even while they preserved the individuality of their own particular genius, formed themselves into various provincial schools. These schools, though, also tended to move closer together and did not differ among themselves, except in the case of details of little importance.

From 1220 on these provincial schools could be classified: the schools of the Île-de-France, Champagne, Picardy, Burgundy, Anjou and Maine, and Normandy. The divisions were never so clear-cut that we could not find intermediate types of construction appearing in one or the other of them at the same time; their development, however, followed the order we have given here. In the Île-de-France and Champagne, for example, *completely Gothic* structures were already being built at a time when Anjou and Normandy had barely thrown off the old Romanesque traditions, and had not yet adopted the new methods of construction and decoration entailing all the rigorous consequences that adoption of them would bring in its train.[41] It was only at the end of the thirteenth century that all the distinctions disappeared, and provincial genius was swallowed up by the royal domain. Everything then became blended into a single type of architecture, which was successively extended until it covered the entire territory of France. The fact is, though, that Auvergne (with the exception of the construction of the cathedral at Clermont-Ferrand), like Provence, never adopted Gothic architecture; the latter province, which became French only at the end of the fifteenth century, moved from a debased Romanesque directly into the architecture of the Renaissance; the influence of northern construction there was both late and incomplete. The focus of French architecture in the thirteenth century was thus concentrated within the royal domain; it was there that were created the immense cathedrals that we still admire today, as well as all the sumptuous palaces, the great public buildings, the castles and enclosures, and the rich monasteries. However, as architecture lost its provincial or personal originality, as it passed into the exclusive hands of the corporations of the laity, it was no longer executed with the same minute care in its details, nor with the same discrimination in its choice of materials, that strikes us in the buildings that were constructed at the end of the twelfth century, when lay architects were still imbued with the monastic traditions. If we put to one side certain rare examples of construction such as the Sainte-Chapelle in Paris, or as the Cathedral of Reims, or even certain features of the Cathedral of Paris, we can make an apt observation that the buildings constructed in the course of the thirteenth century were often victims of neglect in their execution, and this in about the same degree as they were the beneficiaries of a highly skilled and scientific system of construction. What emerged in the building of these edifices was the spirit of *enterprise.* It was necessary to put up a great deal in a short time and with very little money. The haste to enjoy the end product came to the fore, while the foundations were relatively neglected. Buildings went up rapidly; and the builders made use of all kinds of materials, good and bad, without taking the time to be discriminating. Stones were literally snatched out of the hands of the workers before the latter even had time to dress them properly. Joints were uneven; rubble was piled up in haste. Construction was sometimes abruptly stopped, and sometimes just as abruptly resumed, often with major modifications of the original projects. Lacking was that wise slowness that had characterized the old *masters* of the religious orders who did not even begin construction until after they had carefully chosen and laid in all the necessary materials; until they had accumulated the necessary finances; and until they had allowed their plans to ripen properly through careful study. It appears that the lay architects essentially did not occupy themselves with the details of execution; they were primarily concerned with finishing their work. It was almost as if they were already under the sway of the veritable fever of activity that currently dominates modern civilization. Yet even in the projects that went up so rapidly, we still see art undergoing modifications as construction proceeded. These modifications had reference to an increasingly absolute application of the principles on which Gothic architecture was based; this was a regular occurrence. *Symmetry,* that basic need of the human spirit, was sacrificed to an incessant search for a true absolute, for the outer limits to which one's material could be extended. Rather than continuing to follow the original plan of a work that had come to seem to him imperfect, the architect of the thirteenth century, not at all tied down by considerations of symmetry, did not hesitate simply to change his original plan and to proceed to the immediate application of new ideas—ideas that were nevertheless developed under the inspiration of the basic principle that drove him on. Thus it was that many of the great constructions of that day were begun with some hesitation, continued under a direction that was still unsure of itself, and yet ended up being carried through quite expeditiously, developing progressively in accordance with the ideas of a builder who was in the process of learning and perfecting his art at each step as he went along—who never, indeed, ceased striving anew for the best up to the very moment when the work was finally complete. Nor was it only in the overall work that this forward-moving approach was to be observed; all the artisans were moved by similar sentiments. Almost from one day to the next, statuary shed its preoccupation with the old hieratic forms of the eleventh and twelfth centuries; it did so in order to imitate nature more faithfully and to achieve an improved expression, as well as to render more understandable the gestures being depicted. The ornamentalist, who had at first striven to give his work a more monumental character by seeking his models in plant shoots or sprouts, quickly moved on to making exact copies of actual leaves and flowers; he re-created in stone both the freedom and the true aspect of actual plants. Painting advanced more slowly along the route being followed by the other arts. Painting was more attached to its traditions; it retained conventional types longer than did its sister, sculpture. Called to play a greater role in the decoration of the new architecture, however, painting too became caught up in the same general spirit, and allied itself more freely with architecture in order to assist the latter in the effects it was trying to achieve.[42] It is worth remarking here that the two arts, painting and sculpture, became entirely subordinate to architecture at the moment when the latter reached its apogee. It was only when architecture fell into decadence later that these two arts recovered a certain independence (which, however, did not benefit them greatly, considering that architecture had declined to such a low ebb by then).

From the fact that many of the great constructions of the Middle Ages were begun at the end of the twelfth century, and not finally completed until the fourteenth or fifteenth, many have concluded that two or three centuries were always required in order to build them. However, that was not the case. The truth is that, until our own day, perhaps, buildings were never constructed as rapidly as were the monumental buildings that went up during the thirteenth and fourteenth centuries. The thing was, however, that these buildings were erected using the resources of particular bishops, monasteries, chapters, or feudal lords. Construction could therefore be interrupted by political events or by a lack of money. When the resources were there, however, architects carried out their work with prodigious speed. Examples are not lacking to justify this assertion. The new cathedral of Paris was begun in 1160; by 1196 the choir was complete; and by 1220 the entire building was finished. The later chapels of the nave, the two gables at the intersection, and the chapels of the choir were all modifications of the original building plan, and could have been dispensed with. Thus, what we have here is a vast edifice, which could not have cost less than sixty or seventy million of our francs, and which was erected in the course of sixty years. Nearly all of our great cathedrals were built in an equally limited number of years—except for later additions made to them. The Sainte-Chapelle in Paris was begun and completely finished in less than eight years.[43] When we think of the innumerable statues, sculptures, surfaces covered with stained glass, and ornaments of all kinds that were involved in the construction of one of these churches, we can only marvel at the amount of activity and at the number of artists, artisans, and workers who must have been involved, especially when we know that all of the sculptures, whether ornaments or figures, like all the stained-glass panels, were finished and installed as the work went along.

Now if these vast religious edifices, abounding as they did in rich decorations, could have been completed as rapidly as they were, then it stands to reason that monasteries and castles based on a rather simpler architecture, and required to fill immediate material needs, must have gone up in a relatively short time. Even when the dates of the foundations are lacking, there always remains the construction itself, which often shows signs, for anyone familiar with the art of construction, of how rapidly these projects were brought to completion. Great military establishments such as Coucy and Château-Thierry, among others, and, later, Vincennes and Pierrefonds, were raised up out of nothing, and, within a very few years, were delivered into the hands of their garrisons.[44]

There is, in the histories of peoples who live in centuries that turn out to be fecund, indications of how great efforts of the human intelligence can be fruitful under particularly favorable kinds of circumstances. Such creative periods that are tied to particular eras are encountered everywhere. What particularly distinguishes the age with which we are concerned here, however, is the unity that marked all its productions at the same time as the high quality that characterized them. The thirteenth century saw the appearance in the intellectual order of such men as Albert the Great, St. Thomas Aquinas, Roger Bacon, and other philosophers, encyclopedists, scientists, and theologians, all of whom worked to perfect the methods employed in the intellectual disciplines of their time. They brought together what was available to them from the philosophy and science of antiquity in order to subject it to intense Christian scrutiny; their aim was to promote the spiritual welfare of their contemporaries. The study and practice of the arts also became better coordinated; and from that time on the arts witnessed regular progress as they all moved in the same direction. There is no better way to compare the development of the arts in that era than to speak of a crystallization. This crystallization consisted of a synthesis in which all the parts came together in response to a fixed law that was both logical and harmonious as well as forming a homogeneous whole from which no part could be removed without destroying the whole.

In the architecture of the thirteenth century, science and art boiled down to pretty much the same thing. Form was the consequence of mathematical laws, just as, in the moral order, faith and the beliefs attached to it had to be established and validated on the basis of human reason, on proofs taken from the Scriptures, and on observations of natural phenomena. It is remarkable with what boldness and breadth of view questions of faith and belief were openly treated in public discourse. Happily for the great century that the thirteenth century turned out to be, the intellectual elite of the time was orthodox. Albert the Great and his pupil St. Thomas Aquinas brought together and synthesized the knowledge that they themselves had been able to acquire; this knowledge, in combination with their acute intellectual penetration, they applied to the dominant subject of interest of the day, namely, theology. The same kind of process was at work in the arts of the thirteenth century; it explains the perfect unity they achieved.

We should not imagine, however, that religious architecture was the only kind of architecture there was, and that it simply imposed its forms on civil architecture. Far from it! We should not forget that French architecture developed among a people who had been conquered, and who had had to come to terms with their conquerors; the inspiration for it arose out of this indigenous, conquered portion of the nation, which was the most numerous portion. This architecture then moved predominantly into the hands of the laity shortly after their first attempts at emancipation. French architecture was thus neither theocratic nor feudal. It was an independent art, and a national one at that. It fulfilled national needs, whether it was engaged in building a castle, a house, or a church; and it made use of the forms and procedures appropriate to each of these types of structure. If there was nevertheless a harmony among all these different branches of the architectural art—if, indeed, each branch grew from the same trunk—it was also true that each branch developed under such different conditions that it is impossible not to be able to distinguish between them. Not only did the French architecture of the thirteenth century adopt diverse forms with respect to the needs that it had to satisfy; it also underwent modifications as a result of the materials it employed. Whether the building was to be of brick, of stone, or of wood, it was given a different appearance depending upon which of these materials was being used. Wrought iron, cast or embossed lead, wood, marble, terra-cotta, hard or friable stone—the proper use of all these materials was dictated by the different dimensions of a building. This was true to such a fixed and absolute extent that it was possible to conclude merely from the appearance of a design or molding: "This ornament, this molding, or this architectural member applies in this or that fashion." Such a quality of essentiality belongs to the original art of all great epochs. It is unnecessary to add how it confers value and charm on the slightest of its productions. It is this judicious use of various materials, indeed, that distinguishes the construction of the thirteenth century from the centuries that preceded and followed it. It appeals to people of taste as it does to the least sophisticated of people. Nothing less than a poor education is responsible for failing to have such a natural and true reaction.

However, there is no human work that does not contain within itself the seeds of its own possible dissolution. The very qualities of thirteenth-century architecture, carried to exaggerated lengths, became its defects. The progress of this aspect of development in Gothic architecture was rapid. This architecture was filled with youth and strength in the early years of the reign of St. Louis; but abuses began to appear by the year 1260. Barely 40 years lie between the construction of the west facade and the south portal of the Cathedral of Paris; the great west facade still shows some remaining traces of Romanesque traditions, while the south portal already belongs to an architecture that has begun to show signs of decadence.[45] By the end of the thirteenth century, especially in religious architecture, we no longer find that individual mark or stamp that characterized the buildings of the beginning of the century. Both the major arrangements and dispositions made, as well as the methods of construction and ornamentation employed, have taken on a monotonous aspect, which makes the architecture easier to study, but which in fact favored mediocrity at the expense of genius. We perceive that commonplace rules have been established, bringing the architectural art within the range of the most vulgar of talents. Everything has become completely predictable. One form or feature inevitably begets another; reason has replaced imagination; logic has killed poetry. However, the execution of everything has become more uniform and more scientific, just as the choice of materials has become more judicious. It begins to appear that the genius of the builders no longer had anything to discover, and henceforth, builders satisfied their need for new discoveries by focusing on details—by seeking the quintessence of art. All the various architectural members became less substantial. Sculpture came to delight in the execution of the minutely small. Any feeling for the whole, along with any sense of true grandeur, became lost. Henceforth, builders sought surprises through an increasing boldness or audacity, through the creation of an appearance of lightness, and through mere ingenuity or finesse. Science superseded art and indeed took it over. It was during the fourteenth century that greater knowledge of the thrust of vaults was developed, that is to say, a greater knowledge of the projection and distribution of force. This period witnessed the construction of buildings where the extension of walls or surfaces was reduced as much as possible in order to allow light to penetrate into the interior by every practicable avenue; where denticulated spires were projected up into the air from points of support that seemed incapable of supporting them; where moldings were divided up into an infinite number of separated parts; where piers were composed of multiple little columns as numerous as the moldings of the arches they had to support. Sculpture lost some of its importance, impoverished by the geometric combinations of the new architecture; it came to seem out of place, and its aims confused, by the effort to achieve delicacy. This was true in spite of the incessant search for new combinations—and in spite of the *rationalism* that now ruled over all aspects of architecture. We are left cold by so many efforts arising out of calculation rather than out of inspiration.

It is necessary to add, though, that the thirteenth century left little for the fourteenth century to do in the field of religious architecture. Our great churches had mostly been completed by the end of the thirteenth century. Little remained for the architects of that era to do except to complete the great cathedrals and their dependencies.

But it was during the fourteenth century that civil life underwent greater development. The nation, based on the royal power, began to play a more important role, pushing feudalism to the margins of political life. Towns and cities built town halls, markets, and ramparts. Prosperous bourgeois built larger and more comfortable houses; luxurious living appeared. Feudal lords constructed manor houses that were considerably less severe in appearance; no longer was it merely a question of defending themselves against powerful neighbors, or erecting fortresses designed either to protect them against another's resort to force or to guard the products of their own plunder and rapine. With the sovereignty of the royal power better established, and with respective rights better regulated, nobles could consider living on their domains no longer as conquerors but rather as possessors desirous of governing their holdings and functioning as the protectors of the vassals grouped around their castles. Thus, their habitations, which had once been so enclosed and somber, began to be decorated; large windows appeared destined to let light and air into the living spaces; porticoes and ballrooms, where large numbers of people could congregate, were constructed. Lodgings for visitors went up outside the interior enclosures. Promenades, churches, or hospitals for the inhabitants of the towns or villages were even sometimes constructed around the central manorial habitations.

The misfortunes that afflicted France at the end of the fourteenth and at the beginning of the fifteenth centuries significantly slowed down the impetus of both civil and religious construction. Architecture continued to follow the impulse established during the thirteenth and fourteenth centuries, while gradually forgetting where it had started from; a profusion of details came to smother the dispositions made for the whole. *Rationalism* was carried so far, both in plans sketched out and in actual construction, that whatever architectural members were laid down at the foundation of the building were relentlessly extended against all possible obstacles, mounting vertically up to the summit without any interruption. Piers and moldings with prismatic, curvilinear, or concave shapes (these last with projecting arrises) appeared and reappeared everywhere, tiring the eyes, and preoccupying rather than charming the viewer, forcing him to exert a perpetual effort without ever being able to arrive at that sense of peaceful admiration that ought to be the effect of any work of art. Surfaces became so divided up with an innumerable quantity of projecting features, or denticulated little compartments or divisions, that any sense of the whole surfaces of the building became lost, along with any sense of its total layout and structural dispositions. Horizontal lines were eliminated—to such an extent that the eye, obliged to follow long vertical lines, could no longer find a stopping place, and could only imagine that the thing went on up indefinitely, losing itself in the clouds. Sculpture assumed a greater importance by following the basic method that had been in use since the thirteenth century: imitations of plants. However, these imitations were carried to extreme lengths, producing exaggerations of the natural models. Flowers and foliage were no longer organic to the construction. The result was a jumble of vegetation that could evoke surprise at what must have been the difficulty of its execution, but which was also distracting, causing the viewer to lose sight of the total construction. What had been admirable in the ornamentation of the architecture of the thirteenth century was its perfect harmony with architectural lines; the thirteenth-century ornamentation helped rather than hindered understanding of why a given form had been adopted; it was impossible to displace it; it literally went with the stone. In the fifteenth century, by contrast, ornamentation became nothing more than an added appendix, which could have been eliminated without doing great harm—as easily, indeed, as one might remove flowers and plants placed around a monument for a celebration. The continued rather puerile pursuit of the exact imitation of natural objects could scarcely be in harmony with the increasingly rigid forms of the architecture, especially since, by the sixteenth century, these forms were taking on a sharpness and rigor, and were reproducing geometric patterns, that ill accorded with the exaggerated suppleness of the sculpture. The systematic application in every detail of vertical lines, in spite of the horizontality of the stone constructions, is rather shocking to common sense, even after the reasons for this kind of pattern have all been explained.[46]

The architects of the thirteenth century, in reducing the extension of their walls and surfaces, eliminating walls, and replacing them with openwork, had certainly been obliged to decorate the empty spaces thus produced with stone tracery.[47] It is necessary to add, though, that the compartments of cutout stone that formed the framework and the enclosures of their bays had been put together following rules dictated by statics. In other words, stone continued to fulfill its accustomed role. By the fourteenth century, however, this tracery became too delicate and could be maintained only with iron reinforcements, even though their original dispositions were preserved. By the fifteenth century, the tracery was as intricate as lace and presented combinations of curves and countercurves that were in no way motivated or inspired by the construction they were part of; they included in their sections sharp prismatic forms, which could no longer be solidly maintained except by the artificial arrangements of the stones or else by the use of ironwork, which became one of the principal causes of the destruction of the stone. Not content merely to embellish their bays with stone tracery traced out according to complicated drawings, the architects of the fifteenth century covered the bare parts of their walls with blind mullions; this amounted to nothing more than filling spaces where the eye, no longer knowing where to come to rest, really required a plain surface. Already by the fourteenth century, this practice of covering bare spaces with false mullions had come to be favored; but at least in that earlier period this type of decoration was employed in judicious fashion.[48] It was employed between supporting structures and in spaces that by their position needed to appear light and airy. By the fifteenth century, however, such decorations for false bays covered buttresses and indeed even those parts of the architecture that were supposed to present aspects of strength and resistance. It seemed that these later architects had a horror of the void, and could not bring themselves to allow their supporting structures to appear plainly as what they were. Instead, they exerted all their efforts to disguise them, while, in the meantime, some walls that carried no load and served no purpose except to fill space themselves remained bare instead of being decorated with blind arcades or false bays. Nothing is more jarring than these cold, smooth walls located between buttresses covered with infinite details, small in scale, which only served to diminish the very parts of the edifice that were supposed to project the idea of strength.

The further removed from the territory of the royal domain, the more these defects appeared in the architecture of the fifteenth century. Builders departed from the principles laid down in the thirteenth and fourteenth centuries; they adopted extravagant combinations, and thought they were performing great feats of skill in stone. Their architecture adopted forms alien to the nature of the materials employed; these forms were usually fashioned by some artificial means and required prodigious resort to ironwork and sealing techniques. Buildings were burdened with an ornamentation that was no longer on the same *scale* as the buildings themselves. It was the architecture of this period that inspired the use of the term *Gothic*—but that was comparable to judging Roman architecture by the monuments of Baalbek or Pola [Pula], without taking into account the masterpieces of the age of Augustus.

Here we must make an observation of major importance: although English political domination became quite firm in the north and west of France during parts of the fourteenth and fifteenth centuries, we do not know of a single building in those areas that resembles those that were being constructed in England at the same time. The architecture of these regions remained French. This does not mean that those who attribute certain edifices in Normandy and the western provinces to the English are mistaken; we can concede without difficulty that the English indeed had things built; but they only made use of French artists, as it happened. This fact is easy to show for anyone who has seen the respective architectures of the two countries. The dissimilarities are striking, in fact, whether we are looking at the principles of construction, the decorations employed, or the methods of execution of the work. During the thirteenth century, French and English architecture differed only in certain details or dispositions in their general plans. From the fourteenth century on, however, the architectures of the two countries began to follow different paths; these paths moved farther and farther apart. Up until the Renaissance no foreign element interrupted the steady march of architecture in France. French architecture was nourished from its own sources, even when it made ill use of its own principles or pushed logic to a point where it distorted its own methods by trying to follow them out to an extreme limit and to work out all the possible consequences of them. All the examples we give in this *Dictionary* illustrate how the twelfth century moved fatally down a gradual slope to arrive at the fifteenth. Each effort, each initiative, and each success proceeded rapidly to its apogee, and, as quickly, declined into its decadence. At no point was anyone ever apparently able to say: “We must stop here!” The whole process was an uninterrupted chain of inferences; it was not possible to break a single link in the chain; for each and every subsequent link had been forged by virtue of the same principle by which the first link had been forged. And we may say that it would perhaps be easier to study Gothic architecture in its decadence, moving from its effects back to their causes, and from its consequences back to their principles, than it would be to trace its natural developments as they occurred. This, indeed, is the way most of us who have studied the origins of this kind of art have approached the subject. We took Gothic architecture in its decline as our starting point and then moved back upstream to its source.

In point of fact, by the end of the fifteenth century, Gothic architecture had spoken its final word. It was not possible to go any further: all the materials had been mastered; architectural science no longer paid any attention to them. The utmost manual skill of the artisans could no longer be materially improved. Human reason and the human spirit had fashioned what could be fashioned out of stone, wood, iron, and lead—indeed, had gone beyond the limits of good sense in their utilization of these materials. The materials themselves finally rebelled, and any further developments could really exist only as drawings in plans or in the minds of the builders.

In the fourteenth century, Italy, which had never clearly abandoned the traditions of antiquity and had been only partially influenced by the traditions of the North and the East, revived the arts of ancient Rome. Filippo Brunelleschi was born in 1375 [1377] in Florence. He studied the ancient monuments of Rome, not only in order to be familiar with their exterior forms but, even more, in order to be able to understand the procedures employed by the Roman builders. Returning to Florence at the beginning of the fifteenth century, he succeeded, in the face of many difficulties stirred up by both routine and envy, in constructing the great dome of the church of Santa Maria del Fiore. Italy, which preserves everything, has handed down to us even the minor details of the life of this great architect. Nor was his work limited to constructing this great dome. He built citadels, abbeys, and palaces in addition to the churches of San Lorenzo and Santo Spirito, among others. Brunelleschi was a man of genius. He can perhaps be considered the father of the architecture of the Renaissance in Italy, for he both was aware of and knew how to apply the models that antiquity offered to him. Nevertheless, his works exhibited a character of originality rarely exceeded by those of his successors. Perhaps he was equaled by Bramante, who distinguished himself among so many of the illustrious artists who were his contemporaries by a pure and refined taste, a simplicity of manner, and a great sobriety in his methods of execution.

At the end of the fifteenth century, the marvels that by then dotted the landscape of Italy began to be talked about in France. When Charles VIII returned from his foolish campaigns, he brought back with him a court that had been dazzled by ultramontane splendors—riches both ancient and modern in the cities that the temporary conquerors had passed through. From that time on everybody dreamed of palaces and gardens embellished with statues, marble fountains, porticoes, and columns. Italian art became the passion of the moment. Gothic architecture, meanwhile, was worn out; it was at the end of its rope as far as producing any new and surprising effects was concerned. Hence, it quickly made use of the new elements from Italy too. Its decoration soon included features reminiscent of Italian art. However, no art can just be changed, any more than a language can just be changed, from one day to the next. The Florentine and Milanese artists whom Charles VIII had been able to bring with him were very much out of their element in a France that was still entirely *Gothic*. Their influence could not have any direct effect upon the existing corporations or upon those in the building trades accustomed to reproducing the by then traditional forms of their own country. The organizations of artists and artisans had become very powerful; they dominated all branches of the arts, and they were not disposed to allow themselves to be dictated to by foreigners; the latter may have enjoyed favor at court, but they did not enjoy the same prestige among the middle classes. The majority of these imported artists soon grew tired of the struggle; they were forced to try to contend with workers who either did not understand them or did not want to understand them. Besides, as was bound to be the case, the artists who had decided to leave Italy in order to follow Charles VIII were hardly the cream of contemporary Italian artists anyway. Rather, they were likely to be mediocrities unable to make it in their own country and hence prepared to seek their fortunes elsewhere. Attracted to the promises made to them by the great, they found themselves instead forced to deal with established builders who were competent and conscious of their own knowledge, as well as being clever and given to mockery; they were also habituated to following an established system, one encumbered moreover with great inefficiency. They thus opposed the new Italian fashion in art with a strength of inertia that was dismaying. They responded to orders with a Gallic shake of the head, which actually portended many difficulties in store when everything should have been clear sailing. Enamored as it was by the new Italian fashion, the court could nevertheless not have been aware of all the practical difficulties to be encountered in attempting actual construction. People at court did not have the least idea about all the specialized knowledge possessed by the French builders. There was no way a few unhappy Italian artists who happened to be skilled in the new forms developed in Italy (but who were probably very poor tracers or stone dressers) could be effectively set down in the midst of working French carpenters and stonecutters accustomed on their own and on a daily basis to overcoming all kinds of difficulties through the use of geometric patterns, and, moreover, totally knowledgeable about the execution of the most complicated kinds of building plans. In spite of its good intentions, then, and indeed of its power, the court in these circumstances still could not prevent its foreign protégés from coming to be considered either ignorant or impertinent. Thus, the efforts to introduce Italian styles into France at the end of the fifteenth century had only modest results. The indigenous architecture might allow itself to borrow a few details from the Italian Renaissance, adopting an arabesque here, a capital there, a finial here, a keystone mask there—all imitated from ancient models in place of the usual sculptured Gothic foliages, baskets of flowers, cabbage leaves, and spikes. But the local architecture continued to maintain its own methods of construction and of tracing or drawing, as well as its own accustomed dispositions, both in details and as a whole.

The arts that developed at the end of the twelfth century arose from the very soul of the Gallo-Roman nation. These arts reflected the spirit of this nation, both its general tendencies and its particular genius. We have seen how these arts were born outside of the circle of the privileged classes at the same time as the first free political institutions were being won by the urban populations. The arts of the Renaissance, however, arose from a completely different source; the upper classes were the patrons of these new arts. For a considerable period of time the regular clergy as well as the middle classes were in fact ranged against them. We shall see, in fact, how the arts of the Renaissance came to ally themselves with the Reformation in order to establish themselves better on the old Gallo-Roman territory.

It was around the year 1483 when Martin Luther was born in a small village in the county of Mansfeld. However, let us first glance for an instant at the situation of the higher clergy at the end of the fifteenth century. Only a few years later Pope Leo X was to say: "Let us live in peace; the ax no longer strikes the root, but is merely pruning the branches." The papacy, resting after so many long and glorious conflicts, enjoyed a renown that it seemed could not be tarnished; it ruled over the Christian world as much through the moral predominance that it had so laboriously acquired as it did through the leadership in the arts and literature that it had also been able to give. Rome was the center of all light and all progress. The papal court, composed as it was of learned men, scientists, poets, and an extraordinary group of artists, attracted the admiration of the whole of Europe.

In both France and Germany, the bishops possessed more or less extensive feudal powers, just as did the secular feudal lords.

The great religious establishments, of course, had for a long time rendered immense services to civilization; they had put uncultivated land under cultivation, established workshops and factories, drained swamps, and preserved and propagated the study of both Christian literature and the literature of antiquity. They had fought against the spirit of disorder present in secular feudalism, and had long provided a refuge against all the physical and moral evils afflicting humanity. But they had now fallen into a state of quiescence for which they were going to pay dearly. In the Germanic lands, sovereign power was divided up among a large number of electors, including both ecclesiastics and the laity; there were marquises, dukes, and counts who answered directly only to the emperor. The secular portion of this nobility remitted only with repugnance the aid due to the Holy See. The latter was constantly obliged to operate beyond its means. In 1517 Leo X published a list of indulgences that could be preached in Germany, and preachers were thereby enabled to amass abundant contributions destined to help complete the great church of St. Peter's in Rome. Secular princes, meanwhile, encountered closed doors when they sent out collectors to try to gather taxes in the very same areas. It was at this point that a poor monk stood up behind a pulpit in Wittenberg to denounce indulgences. A battle with the Holy See ensued; it was an ardent, passionate battle on the part of the Saxon monk. He eventually came to be supported by the German nobility as well as by peoples who wanted to liberate themselves from the Roman yoke. The monk, of course, was Martin Luther, and he soon set Germany on fire. He triumphed there, in fact. The secularization of the monasteries and convents became an enticement for secular princes, who could suddenly lay their hands on the property of the abbeys and take from them all manner of gold and silver work and vessels made of these same precious metals. So the secularization of the monasteries was in fact carried out. Meanwhile, Luther thundered from the pulpit as well as in his writings against the papacy, the bishops, and the monks. Luther also knew how to manage and handle with care the secular princes who could have suppressed his message with a single word of their own. The people at large quickly got into the act as well, as was inevitable, once religious questions became partisan political matters. Within only three years after Luther had begun his war against the power of the court of Rome, his followers were everywhere, and they were already dividing the

Reformation up into innumerable sects: Bucerians, Carlstadtians, Zwinglians, Anabaptists, Oecolampadians, Melanchthonians, and Ilyrians. Thomas Münzer, an Anabaptist pastor of Allstedt, stirred up the peasantry of Swabia and Thuringia, only to perish, along with his followers, at Franckenhausen, under the blows of the same nobility that was protecting the Reformation. Luther, who at the very least could have foreseen such disasters, reacted without the slightest feeling of pity with these cruel words: "For donkeys, pricks, a pack saddle, and a whip! It was the sage who said it: peasants deserve nothing but oat-straw. If they refuse to knuckle under, the cudgel and the musket for them! Let us pray that they will obey. Otherwise, no pity. If they don't hear the whistle of the arquebus, they will prove to be a hundred times more wicked."[49]

Luther, however, wanted to preserve images in the churches. Nevertheless, one of his disciples, Carlstadt, broke up all the statues and stained-glass windows in All Saints' Church in Wittenberg almost in front of his very eyes. Germany, in fact, was soon covered with ruins; the hammers of the new iconoclasts were employed against the images of the saints even in private houses and oratories; richly painted illuminated manuscripts were burned.

This, then, was how the sixteenth century began in Germany. As things turned out, the people merely served as an instrument, and the secular nobility alone profited from the secularization, or, rather, the destruction, of the great religious establishments. Melancthon, a faithful disciple of Luther, remarked that "the electors kept all the treasures of the churches and convents but *did not even care to contribute to the maintenance of the schools.*"

However, during the reign of Francis I, France too began to experience the repercussions of the revolution taking place in Germany. The Holy Roman Emperor Charles V, preoccupied with his own vast projects, offered little more than a rather indecisive resistance. Perhaps the weakening of the power of the Holy See by the Reformation would even benefit some of his projects; perhaps he thought he could steer the whole thing in the direction of his own policies and then put a stop to it in good time. Luther, though, could never really have exercised the same influence in France that he exercised in Germany; his coarse and brutal speech, like his preaching strewn with abusive language picked up in taverns, would never have impressed the enlightened classes of our country. His doctrines, however, even though they were condemned by the Sorbonne, did attract some followers; novelty has always been attractive in France. By the time Calvin appeared, the diatribes of Luther against the pope and the princes of the Church had already proved convincing to certain doctors, educated nobles, theological scholars, and some of the artists jealous of the protection given to the Italians; they all no doubt hoped to gain by throwing off the yoke of Rome. Reformation was the fashion. We of all peoples should not be in the least surprised to see entire peoples carried away in this manner; for we, too, witnessed a total revolution happen from one day to the next, a revolution carried out to the accompaniment of cries of "reform"! John Calvin was born in 1509 in Noyon. Luther, the Saxon monk, was the man of rash speech, flushed face, and terrible voice and gestures. Calvin was rather the man of austere bearing, cadaverous visage, and sickly appearance. He kept careful watch over the form of his discourses as he did over that of his writings; by nature headstrong, he was yet prudent; he did not fall from one day to the next into the strangest kinds of contradictions, as did his predecessor in Wittenberg. Like a kind of theological diplomat, Calvin moved ahead one step at a time; he also never moved backward. Luther had no idea how to raise up dikes against the torrent he had unleashed; so he egged on the German nobility to massacre thousands of peasants who had been whipped up into a frenzy by a man who was insane. Calvin proceeded against Servetus, lodged denunciations against him, and had him burned at the stake alive because he had wounded his, Calvin's, vanity as a reformer. These were the two men who were to bring about change in a great part of Catholic Europe. . . . Yet did not these reformers represent expressions of some of the ideas of their times? Jan Hus was burned a century before Luther only because he lived earlier. The Reformation of the sixteenth century was in the air; people thought along these same lines; they merely became personified in Luther and Calvin. Only Rome was surprised. Thus, the majority of educated men in Germany, France, and England quickly adopted the views of the reformers. First, the nobility: they found honor and profit in it; they saw the rival influence of the clergy diminished; and they liberated themselves from the yoke of Rome. Educated men, scholars, and artists thought they would find in the bosom of the new church the intellectual freedom they had been seeking for some time; they failed to see—at least the artists among them failed to see—that this new church, by its very nature riveted to the temporal power, would remove from their crown some of its brightest jewels by insisting that everywhere reality—or the *governmental* idea—must henceforth rule in place of poetry.

The printing press gave a sudden—and immense—impetus to all these battles; without the printing press, they might not have progressed too far beyond the walls of Wittenberg. Thanks to this new method of spreading new ideas from one end of Europe to the other, as well as among all classes of society, each individual person could henceforth become a doctor, discuss the Scriptures, and interpret in his own fashion the mysteries of religion; each individual person, indeed, could found his own church. However, all this led first to anarchy, and then to temporal and spiritual confusion under a uniform despotism. Henry VIII, the king-theologian, was the first to understand the political importance of the Reformation. Henry had refuted Luther's doctrines; but then he had failed to obtain from the pope the annulment of his marriage with Catherine of Aragon. So he suddenly himself adopted the principles of the reformers, married Anne Boleyn, arrogated to himself the spiritual power in England, suppressed the abbeys and the monasteries, and confiscated their revenues and treasures. Such an example as this had to be tempting to the Catholic nobility: to get out from under the spiritual domination of the clergy at the same time that one enriched oneself with the temporal goods of the Church had to be attractive to secular feudal lords; in point of fact, it induced them to move toward the Reformation. In France, once again, fashion too entered in. Without enthusiastically enlisting under the banner of either Luther or Calvin, Frenchmen saw their curiosity excited. The battles against the papal power, which was still very strong, attracted their attention. There was a disposition in France as always, especially among the educated classes, to provide protection to new ideas without considering the long-term possible consequences of such a course of action. Marguerite de Navarre, in her little court at Nérac, granted asylum to both Calvin and Le Fèvre d'Etaples when they both happened to be in trouble with the Sorbonne. Great ladies scoffed at the Catholic Mass, and had their own masses "*à sept points*" composed; they also came out strongly against confession. There were rumbles at the Sorbonne about all this but everybody ignored them. The duchess d'Etampes thought of getting Francis I to listen to the reformers. There were debates. Every day saw a new preacher attempt to gain renown by coming out for some new and curious extravagance. Sensible people (and they are always in the minority) got discouraged; it was easy to see how the tempests that occurred would inevitably be stirred up by such salon discussions. But it is necessary to underline that this kind of agitation had also infected society at large. Traditional theological studies such as the serious and solemn meditations of the doctors of the twelfth and thirteenth centuries had all had their day; people wanted something else. The study of the law set itself against the feudal system. Francis I founded chairs of Roman law in France in imitation of those in Bologna; he also endowed a trilingual college of which Erasmus would have been the director if Charles V had not succeeded in preventing him. People became exclusively taken up with the literature of antiquity. It was an irresistible movement, not unlike the movement of the twelfth century that had lifted society up out of barbarism. In the sixteenth century, however, there was lacking a figure such as that of St. Bernard who could have channeled, regulated, and taken proper advantage of all the agitation that was going on. Instead, the whole thing was soon to dissolve in blood and ruins.

But the age was not without its strange contradictions, moving in several directions at once. . . . We have already made mention of the lack of success of the efforts of Charles VIII to make dominant in France the art of the Italian Renaissance. His efforts, we saw, could not break into the traditional way of doing things of the guilds of artists and artisans. We saw, too, how by the end of the fifteenth century the power of these guilds had assumed overall control of construction; the individual architect had little by little disappeared under the separate influence of each governmental entity acting directly.[50] Italy, especially Florence and Rome, had taught our artists, if only through the presence of the men brought in by Charles VIII (who were supposed to have assumed control of construction work) that the marvels that had come to be admired beyond the Alps had not been created by organized professional bodies acting separately one from the other. Rather, these marvels were the creations of individual artists—architects, and sometimes painters and sculptors at one and the same time. It was they who imposed a unity on the art of the Italian Renaissance. During the reign of Francis I there arose also in France men who, imitating their Italian masters—and operating, of course, with the favor of the court and the great lords—did succeed in assuming the direction of various projects over certain bodies of artisans, admitting the participation of the latter only as workers. Among these artists, who had learned in Italy how to upgrade their own profession as architects, and who were working under the inspiration of the classical Italian models that had now been so skillfully renewed, were those who also embraced the very party of the Reformation that Rome itself was trying to ban throughout Europe—and which Leo X, that enlightened patron of artists and man of elevated taste himself, had styled the Antichrist!

We must, however, take note of the fact that in France, unlike in Germany, the Reformation did not at first present itself as an enemy of the plastic arts; it neither broke up statues nor burned paintings and illuminated manuscripts. Quite the contrary: for the Reformation gained adherents almost exclusively from among the nobility and the upper middle class; it gained proselytes from the lower classes chiefly in certain western provinces, or in those regions where the Albigensians had already espoused a persistent heresy against the Catholic church in the twelfth century. The aristocracy was now better educated than it had ever been; it passionately embraced the literary study of antiquity, just as it seized upon the movement on which the king, Francis I, had placed his personal stamp; it gave itself over to a style of luxury previously unknown in the construction of its new châteaus and town houses. Old feudal manor houses were dismantled, giving way to habitations that were open, pleasing to the eye, and decorated with porticoes, sculptures, and marble statues. The monarchy set the example when it destroyed the old Louvre of Philip Augustus and Charles V. The large old tower of the Louvre, to which all the fiefs of France ultimately went back, was itself not even spared; it was torn down in order to make way for the elegant constructions of Pierre Lescot. Francis I sold his St. Paul town mansion, which was "vacant and in ruins . . . where we were not accustomed to reside, possessing several other fine lodgings and sumptuous palaces, while the mansion in question has very little value among our domains. . . ."[51] Civil architecture took over from feudal architecture, which, up to that time, had sacrificed everything else to considerations of defense. Francis I thus succeeded by means of art—by persuading his nobles to follow the new ways—in completing the great political revolution that Louis XI had begun. Feudal lords acting under the impetus of the empire of *fashion* themselves demolished their old fortresses; they poured their treasure into transforming their old closed-in and somber dwellings into habitations that could be enjoyed. In adopting the novelties being preached by the reformers, however, they did not notice that the people who so much applauded their taste in art were not following them in their ideas of religious reform. Meanwhile, the monarchy just let them go on. The time would come, though, when they would rue the day that they had been so imprudently carried away. Between the king and the people the last vestiges of their power would be taken away from them.

The study of the arts and literature, which up to that time had been engaged in exclusively by the clergy and by the third estate, penetrated into the aristocratic class and created a new element of fusion between the various classes in the country. In spite of the administrative disorder and the other faults and misfortunes that signaled the beginning of the sixteenth century in France, the country was actually quite prosperous; commerce and industry, as well as the arts and sciences, had undergone an immense development. France seemed to possess hidden treasures, which served to fill all the gaps in her credit brought about by her recent cruel reverses and the scandalous drains on her resources. Everywhere cities were demolishing their walls in order to be able to expand. Town halls, markets, hospices, and the like were all being rebuilt on a new and grander scale. New bridges went up across the rivers; new roads were laid down. Agriculture, which up to then had been one of the most powerful means by which religious establishments had been able to exert their influence, began to be studied and practiced by large landholders belonging to the third estate; it became "the object of legislative dispositions of which some remain in effect."[52] The state established its authority over waters and forests and mineral exploitation through mining. This effort began to eclipse the prominence of the monasteries that dated from previous centuries. Abbeys were secularized and their moral influence declined; many of them actually fell into the hands of the laity. France was provided up to capacity with churches constructed over the previous three centuries; these churches sufficed, and then some, to fill religious needs. Also, the number of the faithful diminished because of the Reformation. From the beginning of the sixteenth century on, Rome, along with the Catholic clergy generally, failed to grasp the importance of the new doctrines being preached by the innovators. The Church, after so many glorious combats, believed that she had definitively established herself on a divine basis at the very moment when she was in fact being abandoned both by the kings and by the secular nobility. At the Council of Trent the Church would seek a remedy for her problems, but she was quite tardy in doing so; reform within the Church had become a necessity, as she had solemnly recognized at the Fifth Council of the Lateran. The Church was overwhelmed by the prodigious intellectual activity of the sixteenth century, as well as by the new political tendencies of the peoples of both Germany and France; she also found herself betrayed by her ancient enemy, feudalism, at the very time that feudalism, too, was being carried away by the same tempest that it had been responsible for stirring up against the Church. The original and individual native spirit of peoples was becoming exhausted in the terrible battles that, in France, were to produce such desolation in the second half of the sixteenth century. The monarchy alone emerged from the ruins of all this with its power intact. Louis XIV closed the book on the Renaissance. As was always the case, the arts were associated with all these great political movements. Up until Louis XIV, the arts represented a rapid, fecundating river, which varied in its course, sometimes flowing in a narrower one; but it was a river that did not fail to gather in water from all its tributaries as it proceeded to flow around its many bends. Under Louis XIV, however, this river became an immense dormant lake, barren, reflecting light uniformly, surprising in its grandeur but a body of water that no longer carried anybody anywhere—which, indeed, wore out one's gaze with its sheer monotony in all its aspects. Today, of course, the dikes have again been breached, and the waters of the lake are flowing out in all directions, in disorder, from many different holes in the dikes. Where are these waters flowing? Nobody knows.

With the Renaissance religious architecture ceased in its development. It dragged on through the sixteenth century in a most indecisive fashion, both trying to maintain its traditions and breaking with them at one and the same time; it possessed neither the courage to break with the old forms and the system of construction of the previous centuries nor the means to preserve and maintain them.[53] Monastic architecture, mortally wounded, stopped cold. Civil architecture, however, got a new lease on life during the sixteenth century and alone produced some truly original work.[54] As for military architecture, it is hardly necessary to add that it underwent profound changes; for the development of artillery had changed the entire system of attacking, as it did also that of trying to defend strong points.

CONSTRUCTION
an overview

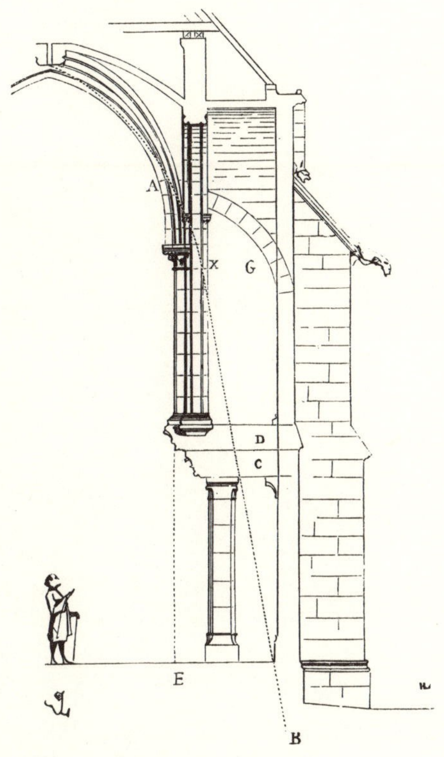

CONSTRUCTION, s.f.—*overview.* Construction is a science; it is also an art. What is meant by saying it is an art is that a builder must have not just knowledge and experience but also a "feel" for building. Builders are born and not made, in fact. The technical knowledge and science of construction can only be based upon elements already present in the brains of those who are going to fashion for practical use and give durable form to brute matter. Moreover, it is as true of peoples as it is of individuals that some are born builders from their cradles on, while others will never become builders under any circumstances. The progress of civilization adds very little to the native human faculty for building. Architecture and construction must be taught and practiced together: construction is the means; architecture the end result. Yet there are architectural works that cannot be considered construction, just as there are certain types of construction that can scarcely be numbered among the works of architecture. Even some animals construct: sometimes cells, sometimes nests, or sometimes mounds, tunnels, hutlike structures, or webs; all these things are certainly constructions, but in no way does this mean that they constitute architecture.*

*This excerpt covers the first main section of Viollet-le-Duc's entry "Construction" from vol. 4, 1–62. [Editor's note]

To build, for the architect, is to make use of materials in accordance with their qualities or their own nature—all this with the preconceived idea of satisfying a need by the simplest and solidest means; of giving to the thing built the appearance of duration, and of giving it appropriate proportions in accordance with the human senses, human reason, and human instinct. The methods of the builder must accordingly vary by reason of the nature of the materials he is working with, the means he disposes of to employ these materials, the human needs he must satisfy, and the particular civilization into which he is born.

The Greeks and the Romans were builders. In their construction, however, they departed from different and opposing principles; they did not make use of the same materials; they employed different means to make use of the materials they did use; and they sought to satisfy aims that were not the same in the two cases. For all these reasons the appearance of Greek construction essentially differs from that of Roman construction. The Greek employed nothing but the lintel, or post and lintel, in his construction; the Roman employed the true arch and, later, the vault. This fact alone shows how the opposing principles from which each departed resulted in very dissimilar construction; this was as true of the means employed as it was of the appearance of the finished construction. There is no need to discuss here either the origins of the opposing principles or their consequences. We will simply begin with Roman architecture at the point at which it had arrived in the last years of the Roman Empire; for this was the source that the Middle Ages would tap at the beginning of its own construction efforts.

The principle of Roman construction was the following: establish points of support that presented, by their seating or placing and their perfect cohesion, solid, homogeneous masses capable of supporting the weight and thrust of vaults. Weights and thrusts were divided up between fixed piles or piers whose inert resistance was sufficient to carry both the weight and the thrust. Thus, Roman construction was nothing but a skillfully devised concretion calculated to maintain itself by means of the law of gravity and the perfect adhesion of all its parts, themselves deprived of any elasticity, however. With the Greeks, stability was obtained by the judicious observance of the law of gravity; the Greeks did not aim at achieving the adherence of all the parts of a particular construction; for, in a word, they neither used nor knew about mortar.

Since with them weight exerted its pressures only vertically, or downward, they required only vertical means of resistance. Vaults were unknown to them. Hence they had no need to be able to deal with oblique pressures—what we call "thrusts." How did the Romans proceed in order to achieve their goals of providing sufficient passive resistance and perfect adherence between all the active and inert parts of a given structure, that is to say, between their vaults and the points of support of these vaults? They put together homogeneous masses of masonry constructed out of small component materials such as pebbles or masses of small or broken stones held together by an excellent mortar; they then enclosed the resulting rubble within an embankment of bricks, small building stones, or freestones. As for vaults, they built them with arches placed on centering structures and made them out of brick or stone in front and concrete within—all laid on beds of wood lagging. This method presented a number of advantages. It was quick. Also, it enabled buildings to be built everywhere and in all different countries according to the same plan; it made possible the use of the Roman armies to carry out construction work or to requisition workers into these armies for this same purpose. It was a durable and economic method as well. It required only competent direction in order to succeed; it also required only a small number of skilled and intelligent workers, under whom a large number of unskilled laborers could work. It further eliminated the need for the slow and onerous transport of bulky building materials, as well as the need for equipment to handle such materials. This Roman method of construction was, of course, the logical consequence of the social and political system that obtained in Roman society. It is true that the Romans also constructed buildings such as temples and basilicas in imitation of the Greeks; but these kinds of buildings were frankly importations and hence they need to be classified apart from Roman-type construction, properly speaking.

The barbarians who invaded the Roman provinces did not bring with them the arts and methods of construction, or, at any rate, whatever elements they might have introduced into the milieu of a dying Roman civilization could have had nothing but a very weak and tenuous influence. The barbarians found buildings already constructed in the places they invaded, and they simply made use of them. For a long time after the invasions of Gallo-Roman territory, many ancient edifices remained standing. This indicates that the Germanic hordes did not destroy everything in their paths; the barbarians even tried to repair the buildings they found and sometimes to imitate them.

After a long and unbroken string of disasters, however, the traditions of the Roman builders came to be lost, for the most part. Under the Merovingians, construction in Gaul was limited to barbarian copies of those ancient buildings that had been spared from the ravages of war or had otherwise been able to survive the long neglect and destitution of the times. The few buildings remaining to us that were constructed prior to the Carolingian period provide only a pale reflection indeed of Roman art; they were nothing but crude imitations of models whose numerous ruins could be seen. Only under the reign of Charlemagne do we see builders making some effort to go beyond the ignorance into which the previous centuries had been plunged. Charlemagne's relations with the East, as well as his contacts with the Lombards (among whom the last traditions of ancient Roman art appeared to have taken refuge), enabled him to attract competent builders into the countries he ruled. And he knew how to make use of such builders; he did so with a zeal and perseverance that were really quite remarkable. Certainly his goal was to revive ancient Roman art. However, the sources he was obliged to tap in order to attempt to achieve his goal had already profoundly modified their own principles of construction. Charlemagne could scarcely send architects to study the monuments of ancient Rome because there weren't any, in effect; he could import artists, geometers, and skilled workers only from Spain, Lombardy, or the East; these were the only places such people then existed. And these people brought with them methods that already diverged from those of antiquity. The Carolingian renaissance, therefore, probably produced very different results from the ones its author had hoped for. In spite of everything, however, the main goal was attained; the new elements introduced into western Europe soon gave rise to numerous creative efforts; for it was from this point on that the arts began to progress once again. It is the history of that progression, from the point of view solely of construction, that we shall attempt to trace here, otherwise referring our readers to the entry on "Architecture"[1] for everything pertaining to the art of architecture in general in the period from the tenth to the sixteenth centuries.

In the course of the Roman Empire, whether in Rome or

Byzantium, it is quite easy to verify that the dominant preoccupation of builders was the vault. From the barrel vault these builders quickly progressed to the groined vault; and from the dome or cupola carried on a circular wall or drum, they were able to go on to build the church of Santa Sophia with its great hemispheric vault carried on pendentives. This was an immense step forward; it established a line of demarcation between the Roman construction of antiquity and the construction of the Middle Ages. Neither Rome nor Italy nor Roman Gaul had ever witnessed the construction of even a single Roman edifice with a hemispheric vault carried on pendentives. The church of Santa Sophia was the first example of this type of construction, and, as everyone knows, it had the largest dome in existence. How was it that the Roman architects established in Byzantium came to conceive and execute a construction of this type? This is a question that we shall not attempt to sort out here. We accept the fact that, for the first time, the thing came about and was executed with an unchallenged freedom and grandeur. Covering a circular enclosure with a hemispheric vault was a perfectly natural and inevitable idea; the thing had actually been done for quite a long time—indeed, a time stretching back into remote antiquity. To extend the cylindrical constructions that we call barrel vaults into the circular drum was the first step. But then to raise up a hemispheric dome on a square plan, that is to say, upon four freestanding piers situated at each angle of a square, was not simply an inevitable logical deduction from a first principle. It was an innovation; indeed, it was one of the most daring of all architectural innovations.

However that may be, the builders whom Charlemagne imported into the West from Lombardy and the East did not bring this particular method of construction along with them. They contented themselves with constructing, as at Aix-la-Chapelle, vaults on an octagonal or circular base of support. It was only later that features derived from Byzantine-type construction had a direct influence in the West. As for Carolingian construction methods, they resembled Roman methods—that is to say, they consisted of fillings of rubble enclosed within facings of brick, small building stones, or larger building stones; or of small stones alternating with courses or layers of bricks—all held together with thick joints or seams of mortar, as can be seen in figure 1.

A indicates courses of triangular bricks with their long edges showing outward on the facing. *B* indicates courses of more or

Figure 1

less regular small building stones presenting their dressed surfaces on the facing; for the most part they are squared. *C* represents a brick whose thickness varies from four centimeters to five centimeters. *D* shows the type of small building stones used for the facings. This type of Roman construction represented a rather rough way of building things. The Romans normally employed this type of construction only when they intended to cover over their facings with marble or stucco. When they constructed facings with freestones, they normally joined them together dry, without mortar, along the grain of the stones as they had come out of the quarry. The Romans gave these stones a broad foundation so that such facings would be transformed into something that constituted a reinforcement capable of resisting pressures that the masses of masonry alone could not have carried.

From the early years of the Carolingian era builders wanted to erect structures faced with freestones in imitation of certain Roman models; but they could neither transport nor raise up to any height the large blocks of stone required. They therefore contented themselves with the appearance of having done this—that is, they made facings formed out of rather thin stone slabs or plating; as often as not, these stones were placed or fixed against the grain; in this type of construction the builders avoided grooves or hollows as much as possible and filled up the empty spaces with rubble drowned in mortar. Sometimes they even went so far as to try to imitate the structural disposition of Roman construction by employing stone slabs or plating joined together dry, without mortar. There is no need to dwell on how defective this kind of construction was, especially since the mortars the builders used were mediocre, their lime poorly burned or slaked, their sand earthy, and their rubble very irregular. Sometimes they adopted a middle way; that is to say, they built facings out of smaller freestones joined with thick beds of mortar.

These efforts and gropings in no way constituted art. What these architects revealed was evidence of the very low degree of their knowledge of the details of construction; they were very shaky in their imitations of the Romans; and it went without saying that their problems were only aggravated when it came to their buildings as a whole. They were constantly coming up against difficulties that they were quite incapable of resolving: they lacked the necessary knowledge of construction; they were the heirs of no living tradition within which they could work; they did not have skilled workers, any more than they had proper hoists or other equipment. They were obliged to exert—and they did exert—tremendous efforts in order to erect buildings of even modest dimensions; they had the problem of ensuring the solidity of these buildings and, especially, of providing them with vaulting. It was here that the insufficiency of these Carolingian builders was most readily to be seen; their difficulties and uncertainties—indeed, even their discouragement, for the latter was perhaps the inevitable result of their incapacity—were all too evident. Yet it was out of this very ignorance of ancient construction methods and procedures, combined with the constant efforts that the builders of the ninth to the eleventh centuries did keep on exerting anyway, that a new art of construction was to be born. It grew out of experiments that were unfortunate at first, but which, repeated with perseverance and steadily improved over time, eventually succeeded in opening up a new and uncharted path. It required no less than three centuries for these barbarians to become properly instructed in the art and science of construction; at the end of all their protracted efforts, though, these builders could pride themselves upon having made possible a new era for future builders, an era that owed very little to the arts of antiquity. The imperative needs with which the first medieval builders found themselves faced obliged them to look for their resources in their own observations rather than in the study of the monuments of antiquity. They knew the latter only very imperfectly; for in most of the provinces of Gaul such monuments no longer existed except in a state of ruin. The builders of the time were quite ready, of course, to take advantage of foreign products, but, in doing so, they necessarily subjected them to their own imperfect ways of doing things; this inevitably transformed them; it also pointed the builders toward a unique kind of art in which reason was to play a larger role than tradition. It was a hard school: builders were uncertain about basing themselves on the past; they were face-to-face with the new needs of a new civilization, where everything was up for grabs and everything had to be re-created anew. Builders possessed only the barest elements of the exact sciences; they literally had no other guide than the experimental method. Now the experimental method, even if it is not necessarily the quickest or most efficient of all methods, at least has this advantage: it tends to form practitioners who are alert and observant, ready to take advantage of every kind of improvement that might possibly help them.

Already in the edifices of the eleventh century, the art of construction made noticeable progress, a kind of progress that was often the result of defects more or less successfully remedied. Mistakes and their consequences are generally more instructive than is being able to do something perfectly the first time. The builders of the day could count on only the scarcest of resources; they lacked the various positive means that the Romans had enjoyed in the vast construction work they had carried out. The medieval builders lacked manpower, money, transport, networks, roads, tools, construction engines, and equipment; they were confined to their own provinces by the feudal system. Nevertheless, already by the eleventh century, they were expected to be able to erect huge monasteries, palaces, churches, and ramparts. With their own ingenuity and industry, they had to make up for everything that Roman organizational genius had provided. They simply had to improvise, as it were, in most of the very areas where modern civilization provides us in profusion with all the means we ever require. Yet these builders were still expected to achieve successful results at low cost (for the West was poor then); they also had to satisfy numerous and pressing needs that arose out of the fact that the entire territory had been continually ravaged by barbarism. Builders had to go find their own building materials; they had to occupy themselves with the means of transporting these materials; they constantly had to combat the ignorance of their own unskilled workers; they had to make their own observations and estimates about the qualities of their lime, of their sand, and of their stone; and they had to locate and provide lumber. The builders of that day similarly had to function as their own architects, quarriers, tracers, stoneworkers, drivers, carpenters, lime burners, and masons; and they had nothing to help them in all this except their own reason and intelligence, along with their own powers of observation. It is easy for us today, when the merest of merchants or notaries can have a house built without even having recourse to a professional architect, to look down on the earliest efforts of the medieval builders; but the all-around genius that was required of an architect in that day merely in order to build a simple room or church was surely much greater than anything we expect of an architect today. Today's architect is able to have his things built for him without himself having to possess the slightest knowledge of the most elementary principles of construction. In fact, this is the sort of thing we encounter all too often today. In times of ignorance and barbarism, the only ones capable of directing significant construction work had to be none but the most intelligent, those who had been able to rise above the level of simple workers by dint of their own genius. And when the direction of building projects was thus necessarily limited to a relatively restricted number of superior men, the resulting productions were by that fact alone likely to be works of great originality; in point of fact, these productions evidenced the degree of sheer reasoning and calculation that had gone into their execution; the forms in which they were clothed exhibited the kind of recognizable distinction that is always particularly characteristic of reasoned productions that respond to the actual needs and customs of a people. At the risk of being called barbarians ourselves, we must nevertheless recognize that the beauty of a work of construction does not reside in the steady improvements that a highly developed industry and civilization have provided us with over time; this beauty resides rather in the judicious use of the means and the materials that the builder has at his disposition. With all the different materials we have today—for instance, the metals produced by our modern factories—and with all the many skilled, practiced, and experienced workers to be found in our cities, we are nevertheless all too capable of turning out construction that is quite defective, even absurd, if not absolutely ridiculous—construction that has neither any reason nor any consideration of economy to commend it. At the same time it is quite possible to produce a fine, sensible, and beautiful piece of construction employing only wood and small building stones. So far as we can tell, the variety and quality of the materials employed have never in themselves established the artistic merit of those who were employing them. Materials of intrinsic excellence cannot escape from wretchedness if they are placed or made to function where they do not belong by an architect who has neither knowledge nor good sense. We are entitled to take pride only in the proper and judicious use of the materials we have, never merely in their quality or quantity. All this is said by way of parenthesis in order to persuade our readers not to look down upon or disdain builders who had at their disposition only poorly extracted stone or small building stones gathered up from here or there on the ground at random; only poorly burnt lime; and only defective tools and inadequate equipment. Yet it was with such crude means as these that the early medieval builders nevertheless earned the right to teach us some excellent principles of construction, principles that are applicable for all time. The proof that these builders are, indeed, able to teach us something resides in the fact that they were successful in forming a school that, from the point of view of both theory and practice, as well as from that of the judicious use of materials, reached a degree of perfection that has not been surpassed in modern times. It may perhaps be legitimate for those who teach architecture without ever having actually practiced the art of construction to judge the architectonic productions of ancient civilizations merely by appearances and by superficial forms that happen to attract them. Those of us who have been called to build, however, must seek to learn from the efforts and successes of a thoroughly ingenious school that, coming from nowhere, and having to do everything from scratch, succeeded in resolving the problems posed by the society of their times. To consider the builders of the Middle Ages as barbarians because they were constrained to abandon the building methods of the Romans is to fail to take into account the new society that had come into being; it is to fail to understand the changes that had been introduced by Christianity with the help of the genius of the peoples of western Europe; it is to eliminate several centuries of the slow but persistent work that was always going on within society, and which was tending toward the more activist and vital type of activity that characterizes modern civilization. Nobody admires the ancient world more than we do; nobody is more ready to recognize the superiority of the great ages of the

Greeks and the Romans over modern art. Nevertheless, we were born in the nineteenth century, and there is no way in the world that we can cancel out the fact that a great many things have happened between us and the time of antiquity. New ideas, new needs, and new ways and means of acting that are simply alien to those of ancient times stand squarely between us and them. We simply have to take account of the new elements and new tendencies that have characterized a new society. We may even mourn the passing of the social organization of ancient times; let us study it scrupulously and appeal to it when necessary. But let us not forget that we live neither under Pericles nor under Augustus; that we do not dispose of our own slaves; that three-quarters of Europe was not plunged into ignorance and barbarism merely in order that one-quarter of Europe might ultimately be the beneficiary; that society is no longer divided into two distinct but unequal parts, one of which is absolutely subservient to the other; that human needs have almost infinitely expanded since ancient times; that modern machines and structures have become immensely complicated; that today industry endlessly analyzes all the means available to us and modifies and transforms them as necessary; that old traditions and formulas have been replaced by reason; and that, finally, art, if it is to survive and flourish, must know and understand the milieu in which it is expected to live and work. Now, it was precisely the art of construction that, in the Middle Ages, took the first steps leading to all of these new things. We may well groan and lament that it all happened as it did, if that is truly the way we feel; but the fact remains that what has happened has indeed happened; we cannot, by wishing it, arrange things differently so that yesterday did not in fact lead to today; yesterday is gone and today is today. The best thing for us to be doing now is to find in the lessons of yesterday what is still useful for us today; to recognize in yesterday's task the work that still relates to the task to be done today. To do this is much more reasonable than simply to disdain it.

It has often been held that the Middle Ages constituted an exceptional era, an era related neither to what preceded it nor to what followed it, and foreign both to the particular genius of our own country and to modern civilization in general. Perhaps this particular thesis can be maintained as far as politics is concerned, although this would surely mean a very strange fact in the context of world history. In history everything is normally linked quite closely. Once party spirit comes into play, however, there is no paradox, however strange, that will not somehow find its ardent supporters. In architecture, and, especially, in construction, party spirit should not count for anything. We cannot for the life of us see how the principles on which modern civil liberties, and the equally modern laws of the regime under which we currently live, are based could ever be undermined merely because someone has succeeded in showing that the builders of the twelfth century really did learn how to build or that those of the thirteenth century were both liberal and generous in the way in which they made use of the means that they had at their disposal. Nor can today's modern regime be undermined by the demonstration that the builders of the Middle Ages attempted to carry out the programs confided to them in the simplest and least expensive possible ways or that they thought and reasoned in an exact and appropriate fashion and took the trouble to master the laws of statics and those of the equilibrium of forces. Certain customs of peoples may well be considered odious and oppressive; feudal lords and abbots were sometimes extravagant and wasteful, if you insist, and they exercised an intolerable despotism. Nevertheless, the castles and monasteries where they were domiciled could for all of that still have been constructed with economy and great good sense, as well as with considerable liberty in the use of the means of construction. A building can in no way whatsoever be "fanatical," "oppressive," or "tyrannical"; these are epithets that simply do not apply to a unitary assemblage of stones, lumber, and iron. A building is either a good building or a bad one, well thought out or devoid of any rational justification. Just because we no longer hold to feudal ways is not at all equivalent to imagining that the construction of that time has nothing at all to say to us. Some medieval court or other may well have condemned some unfortunate Jews or sorcerers to be burned alive; yet the room in which that court held its proceedings could easily have been of quite excellent construction—better built than the rooms in which our magistrates of today apply our own laws, so noted for their justice, in a spirit of modern enlightenment. A modern man of letters—indeed, a historian—had this to say about a feudal castle: "This den of brigandage, this dwelling of petty despots, tyrannizing over their vassals and constantly at war with their neighbors . . ." Faced with such a thing, is it not imperative upon us all to cry shame upon this castle and this castellan? Fine. But how can mute buildings really be the accomplices of those who inhabited them, especially if these same buildings were actually built by some of the very victims of the abuses of power perpetrated by their owners? Is it not the case, in fact, that the Greeks also exhibited on occasion the most odious kind of fanaticism? Are we thereby obliged not to admire the Parthenon or the Temple of Theseus?

We believe that the time has now come for us architects to cease being bedazzled by the opinions of those who know nothing of the actual practice of our art but who nevertheless pretend to be able to judge works of which they understand neither the structure nor the true and beneficial purpose. Moved by their passions and their personal tastes, as well as by their exclusivist-type studies and by their narrow party spirit, these critics pronounce their anathemas upon artists whose efforts, science, knowledge, and practical experience still remain useful to us today. It cannot be a matter of overriding concern to us architects if feudal lords were tyrants, or if the clergy of the Middle Ages were corrupt, ambitious, and even fanatical, if, at the same time, the builders responsible for the construction of the time were themselves ingenious and competent builders, lovers of their art, and careful and knowledgeable practitioners of it. It cannot be a concern of architects today if prisoners were immured in dungeons for years on end, provided that the stones of the dungeons in question were skillfully dressed, resulting in construction from which no escape was possible. Nor can architects today be concerned if a window grille happened to be installed in a torture chamber, provided the grille was skillfully designed and the iron bars properly forged. The confusion between social institutions and artistic productions cannot exist for us architects; it is our task to seek excellence wherever we can find it. Let us not be duped by exclusivist doctrines. If the manners and morals of a previous age do not meet with our approval, by all means let us condemn them; but let us not condemn and proscribe the arts of the same era before we have determined whether or not we can learn anything from them that might actually be to our own advantage. Let us leave to enlightened amateurs the task of establishing the preeminence of Greek architecture over Roman, and of the latter over the architecture of the Middle Ages; let these enlightened amateurs treat these insoluble questions. We can certainly listen to what they have to say (provided we have nothing better to do). Let them therefore carry on with their discourses on the art of architecture at the same time as they continue to be ignorant of even how to trace a panel or dress and lay down a single stone. It is not permitted to profess medicine or even pharmacy without actually being a physician or a pharmacist. In architecture, this does not seem to be the case.

In order to understand and appreciate the initial efforts of the builders of the Middle Ages, we need to know the elements they disposed of as well as the practical means that were in use at the time. The Romans were the masters of the world and had been able to establish a regular and uniform government among the many peoples, either allied or conquered, over whom they ruled; they accordingly disposed of resources that were absolutely lacking to the provinces of Gaul divided up, as a result of the establishment of the feudal system, into a number of small states and innumerable smaller entities. When the Romans wished to construct buildings of public utility in a particular region or country, they were not only in a position to concentrate there, at any given moment, literally an army of soldiers accustomed to carrying out construction work; they were also in a position to make requisitions upon the local population for construction work. The Roman system of requisitioning labor was in fact practiced on a vast scale. By the concurrence of this multitude of workers available to them, the Romans were able to achieve prodigious results in their construction. In order to build quickly and well, they had adopted methods that accorded with the kind of social system they had. Even if the builders of the Middle Ages had wished to employ these same methods, though, where would they have been able to find comparable armies of workers to carry them out? How, for example, in a region without stone, arrange to bring in the necessary materials, when the old Roman roads had long since been broken up, when there was no money available to purchase building materials or beasts of burden to haul them, when the neighboring provinces were in any case almost always at war with one another, and when each abbot, like each secular feudal lord, regarded himself as absolutely sovereign over his own particular territory, and was jealous of his power over everything that went on in it, and this almost in direct proportion to how scanty and exiguous that territory happened to be? How were the builders of the Middle Ages to organize the requisitioning of the necessary workers in jurisdictions where power was disputed among several claimants, or where the work force scarcely counted sufficient numbers to cultivate the soil, or where continual warfare was the norm? How could the enormous heaps of materials that were necessary for the Roman method of construction be accumulated? How could workers be assembled and fed and provisioned under these circumstances? The fact is that, at first, only the religious orders were in a position to undertake any kind of important construction. The reasons for this were as follows:

1) The religious orders were alone in being able to gather at any particular place a sufficient number of workers united by the same ideals, subject to the same orderly discipline, exempt from military service, and possessing the land on which they lived.

2) The religious orders alone had amassed sufficient resources through their practice of a regular administration, and they alone had secured regular relationships with neighboring establishments, cleared and improved uncultivated lands and laid out roads, had given to them or otherwise acquired the richest quarries for stones and the best forests for wood, and organized workshops or factories and therefore offered peasants relatively sure guarantees so that their lands had become populated with relative rapidity, to the detriment of the lands of the lay feudal lords.

3) Thanks to the privileges they enjoyed and the comparative stability of their institutions, they alone could form schools of artisans within the orbit of their monasteries; provide workers with a regular apprenticeship; clothe, nourish, and maintain them and put them to work under a single, unified direction; maintain the traditions of the arts and crafts practiced; and institutionalize any improvements made in the art of construction.

4) The religious orders alone were able to extend their influence abroad by founding daughter houses, which were at first dependent upon the mother abbey, and they alone were able to profit from all the various partial efforts that were being made in regions very different from one another with respect to climate, manners and morals, and ways of doing things.

It was owing to the activity of the religious orders, then, that the art of construction was finally able to emerge from barbarism in the eleventh century. The order of Cluny, being the most considerable, the most powerful, and the most enlightened of the religious orders, was the first to establish its own school of builders.[2] The new principles of construction developed in the Cluniac order were to produce, in the twelfth century, the first construction finally freed from the last vestiges of the Roman tradition. What were these new principles of construction? How did they develop? These are the questions that we must now proceed to examine.

Principles

In order for a new set of principles to develop, in any area of life, it is necessary that both new conditions and new needs be manifest. At the time when the Order of St. Benedict came to be reformed, in the eleventh century, the reformers aimed at nothing else but the entire renovation of a society that, although it had just been born, was already falling into disarray and decomposition in certain respects. These monastic reformers were able men, and they began their reforms by simply abandoning the worm-eaten traditions of ancient society. They started with nothing. They wanted no more of habitations that were both sumptuous and barbarous at one and the same time, and which had served as refuges up to that time for the corrupt monks of a previous era. They built for themselves wooden huts and lived in the midst of the fields; they lived as men thrown entirely upon their own industry in order to survive as in the middle of a desert. These initial steps of theirs were to have a persistent and continuing influence, however, even as the wealth of the monasteries increased and their growing importance in the society of the time led them to replace their former hovels with durable housing, quite elegantly constructed. The first law that was observed in all their construction prescribed the rigorous satisfaction of real needs, not only in the ensemble of the construction that went up but also in its details. The second law that was observed in construction was never to sacrifice the solidity of the construction to the vain appearance of richness. None of this meant that wood and stone were ever anything but wood and stone, of course; for even when these materials are employed in great quantities in any given construction, their functions have always remained the same among all peoples and in all different historical periods. As wealthy as the monks became, they could still never hope to build as the Romans had built. They therefore exerted their efforts to ensure that their construction was not just solid and durable (for they quite consciously intended to build for the future) but also economical. To employ the usual Roman method of amassing rubble enclosed within facings of brick or building stones would have required more manpower than they had at their disposition. To build by means of enormous blocks of stone, carefully dressed and laid down, would have required means of transport unavailable to them; it would have required usable roads, large numbers of skilled workers and beasts of burden, and construction equipment that was either too expensive or too difficult to assemble. Faced with all these problems, the monks adopted a middle way. They built their principal piers or vertical supporting structures using freestone facings as a revetment, or retaining wall; and then they filled in the inside between these retaining walls with rubble. For the facings of their walls to be filled in they used an arrangement of small spalled or scabbled building stones or square stones; in between, the inside was filled in with a rubble of pebbles and mortar.

Figure 2 provides an idea of this type of construction. In order to link together the diverse parts of a building and bind or tie together the walls along their lengths, the builders sank into the masses of masonry, at different heights, under the windowsills or below the cornices, longitudinal wooden beams, just as we have indicated with *A*.[3] In this type of construction the builders economized on stone as much as possible; no stone presented any

Figure 2

grooves or hollows; all the stones were laid down alternately lengthwise and widthwise. The entire revetment was executed with the greatest care; not only were the facings tooled with a bushhammer, but so were the joints and edges; the stones were laid down one directly on the other, without mortar, as in the typical Roman disposition or arrangement.

This type of construction is to be found in the great monastic buildings at Cluny, Vézelay, and Charité-sur-Loire (eleventh and twelfth centuries). The building materials employed by the monks consisted of what could be obtained in the vicinity or in quarries that they themselves owned. It is important to recognize that the monks employed these materials in a fashion that took into account their qualities and defects both. If the materials presented any flaws or blemishes, if a stone was split or cracked by frost, for example, then they would simply take care to place it in the least disadvantageous position, where it would do the least harm, since they could not procure other stone without considerable expense. In order to preserve their building materials from damage caused by humidity or the effects of frost, they tried to protect them from these atmospheric agents by covering them with projecting roofs and by separating them from the ground outside by placing them on strong foundations made of stones acquired from more distant quarries.

In the productions of those who when they act are able to count only on their own resources and their own strength to succeed, there can always be found a certain sum of intelligence and energy, which can be of great value to anyone willing and able to discern its presence. Sometimes the productions in question are rough and imperfect creations; their like would never be found among the productions of refined and civilized men, whose needs are served by myriads of modern industries, which furnish them with practically everything; they are not obliged to make any effort in order to be able to satisfy their every need. Yet those true pioneers who fashioned the earlier, rougher productions often became true masters of their crafts, and therefore their efforts can provide a true lesson for us, since it should be evident that it requires considerably more intelligence to produce something when all the resources are lacking than it does when they are within easy reach even of the most mediocre and unintelligent.

Roman construction, given the absolute stability of its supporting points or structures and the perfect concretion of all its upper parts (a result obtained, as we have already indicated, because of the considerable resources it had at its disposal), presented passive, immobile masses, as would structures fashioned out of a single block of tuff stone. Romanesque builders, however, who did not enjoy as many of the same effective means as had their Roman predecessors, soon had to recognize that their buildings did not constitute the same concrete wholes as had those of the Romans—namely, that they were agglomerations that were perfectly stable. Their piers were made up of outer stone facings or platings enclosing a rubble inside that was too often held together with inferior mortar. Their walls, disconnected or unbound along their entire height, could also undergo unequal settling or sinking; all this caused fissures or rents and could result in serious accidents. It became necessary to seek ways of eliminating such effects as these. Romanesque builders from the eleventh century on wanted to provide vaulting for the majority of their great edifices—for motives that we have discussed elsewhere.[4] They had inherited the tradition of Roman vaults; but they did not have any way of supporting these vaults that could compare with the effective means the Romans had employed. Thus, once again, they had to make up with their own intelligence for means they lacked that the Romans had enjoyed. The Roman vault could be maintained only if its vertical supporting points or structures were absolutely stable, for the Roman vault, whether it was a barrel vault, groined vault, or hemispheric vault, formed a homogeneous shell without any elasticity; it was liable to break in pieces if cracked in its concavity. The Romanesque builders nevertheless wanted to imitate these Roman vaults; but since they were unable to ensure that their vertical points or structures of support were absolutely stable, they had to find a new method to support them, one that would counter the instability of the vertical supporting points intended to hold up the vaults and buttress them. This was no easy task; the various efforts, trials, gropings, and experiments that were carried out were numerous. But it was as a result of these efforts that a new system of construction was eventually born, a new system based on the principle of elasticity. This latter principle was destined to replace the principle of absolute stability on which the Romans had relied. Roman vaults, with rare exceptions, had been made out of rubble; if they were reinforced with brick arches, these arches were generally embedded in the mass of the rubble to such an extent that they became virtually a part of it. Romanesque builders, on the other hand, instead of constructing their vaults out of rubble, built them either with small rough building stones embedded in mortar but laid down like voussoirs, or wedge-shaped arch stones, or with dressed stones, forming a kind of masonry in which all the stones had been precut to occupy a determined place. Even if there was a certain amount of movement in the supporting vertical points or structures, already these new kinds of Romanesque arches presented a certain amount of elasticity as a result of the way the arch stones were fit and joined. The resulting structures accordingly did not consist of homogeneous shells liable to break; they could move to some extent with the piers or pillars that supported them. Nevertheless, this first modification in the old methods of vaulting was not entirely reassuring to the Romanesque builders; they therefore established at different points under the vaults, and at right angles with the strongest vertical supports, transverse arches made out of bonded stones and centered under the extrados of the vault. These transverse arches served as sorts of permanent support that both strengthened the vault and provided more elasticity to it. As does any arch composed of a certain number of individual voussoirs joined together, these arches tended to follow the movements of the vertical supports, or piers; they also lent themselves to the settling or spreading of the latter, and maintained the concavities of the masonry above them just as wooden centering would have done.

The Romanesque builders also took from the Romans the groined vault constructed according to a square plan; this kind of vault was formed by the interpenetration of two half cylinders of equal diameter. When they wanted to construct vaults over supports placed at the angles of a parallelogram, however, the Roman groined vault could not be used; in these cases, they adopted the continuous barrel vault or half cylinder, without interpenetration, and at right angles with the piers, or vertical supports. They reinforced these barrel vaults with transverse arches made out of bonded stones; they counted on the latter to avoid the troublesome effects of any longitudinal ruptures in their barrel vaults caused by the movement of their vertical supports. Once again, and we must insist on this point, we are talking about a permanent kind of centering with arches, which they were trying to devise to help support their vaults. Nevertheless, difficulties and obstacles continued to present themselves, just at the point where the Romanesque builders believed they had found the solution to the problem. The effect of the thrusts of vaults, which had been very well known to the Romans, was not very well known at all to the Romanesque builders. The first Romanesque builder who had the idea of placing a barrel vault on two parallel walls certainly thought that he had eliminated forever the inconveniences of open timberwork ceilings; he seemed to have hit upon a type of construction that was at one and the same time solid, durable, and of a truly monumental aspect. His illusion surely did not last very long, however, for once the temporary wooden centering and lagging were removed, the two parallel walls were inclined to lean outward and the vaults to collapse between them. It became necessary to devise the means to prevent such calamities as these. First of all, the walls came to be reinforced by exterior buttresses and by interior projecting pillars. Then, at right angles with these buttresses and pillars, transverse arches were thrown across, beneath and supporting the barrel vault. By embedding longitudinal beams of wood in the thick mass of the walls between one pier and the other, at the springing of the vault, the Romanesque builders believed they could arrest the thrust exerted by the arch between the piers. However, this procedure proved to be a mere palliative. Some edifices vaulted in this manner proved to be resistant to the force of the thrust of the barrel vault; a large number of them, however, collapsed not too long after they had been put up.

But it is important for the reader to get an exact idea of the type of construction we are talking about. In figure 3, we provide a view of its essential details. *A* represents the interior pillars helping support the transverse arches, *E*. *B* represents the exterior buttress of the pier designed to resist the thrust of the arch, and *C* the wooden beams serving to retain the vault at the springing. In order to carry the thrust of the transverse arches as far down as possible, the builders added a strong projection to the capitals, *G*. If vaults designed in this fashion rested on piers constructed solidly enough and out of materials that were joined together with equal solidity or else were very heavy; if the walls were thick and more or less solid from top to bottom; if the buttresses had sufficient projection; and if the transverse arches and, consequently, the piers were not too far apart—if all these conditions obtained, then barrel vaults reinforced in this fashion with arches underneath could be maintained. If, however, as was the case with naves

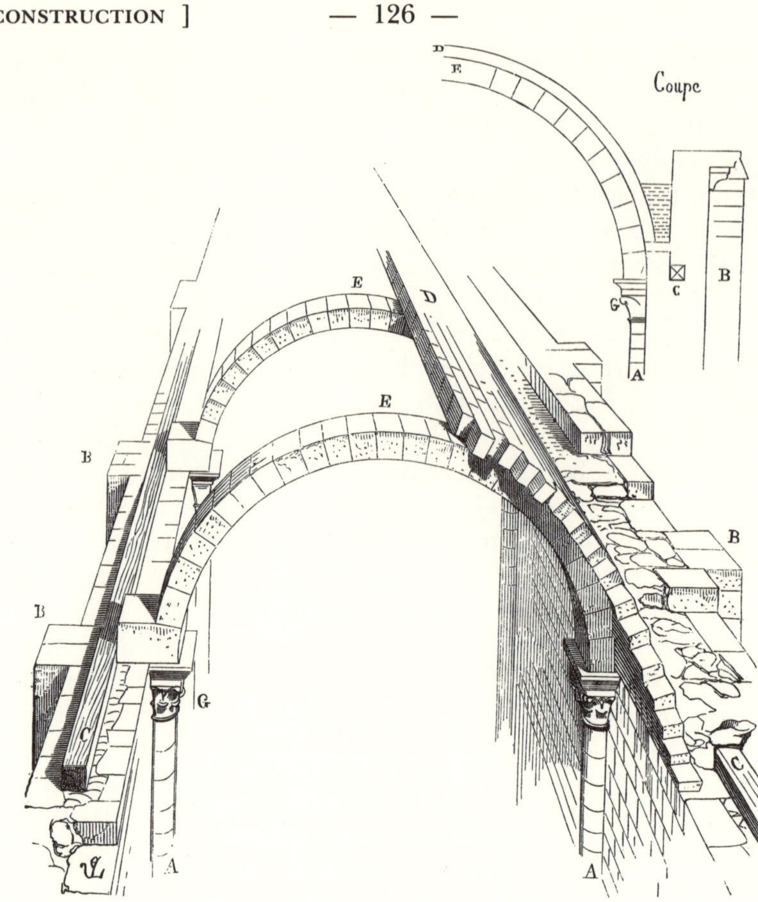

Figure 3

bordered with aisles, the walls were carried on archivolts and on isolated, freestanding pillars—and if these pillars were typically designed to be as thin as possible in order not to hinder traffic or vision—then they did not present a solid enough foundation to receive the exterior buttresses projecting over the vaults of the aisles. In that case, the higher barrel vault, in spite of the fact that it was reinforced with its transverse arches—or, indeed, along with these transverse arches—tended to push outward both the walls and the pillars. Hence, the whole structure would collapse. By the end of the eleventh century, many churches and rooms vaulted in the manner we have now described had already fallen into ruin and reconstruction of them had become necessary. Such accidents as these served as effective teaching moments for the builders; they gave them opportunities to observe certain phenomena concerning architectural statics about which they previously had apparently not had the faintest idea. Builders discovered that wooden beams, deeply embedded in the masonry and cut off from the air, promptly rotted, and the void this created within the structure merely hastened the collapse of the whole structure. They discovered that, as soon as walls began to lean, the thrust of their vaults actually increased as a direct result of this displacement. They discovered, finally, that if barrel vaults were placed upon naves with aisles, the disorders occasioned by the thrust of these vaults was such as to make impossible the maintenance on a vertical plane of their piers and walls.

However, the moment had not arrived when builders were able to find an exact resolution of the problem of the stability of these vaults placed on parallel walls. Builders first had to exert themselves to discover how to avoid the effects of thrust on lateral walls. Roman builders knew that groined vaults had the advantage of exerting pressure and thrust only on the four points of support receiving their imposts. Recognizing that barrel vaults exerted a continual thrust on the tops of walls, they wanted to get rid of them and replace them with groined vaults, even in the case of naves composed of bays having one side longer than the other, because they thought this would cause all the thrust and burden to be absorbed on the piers, which they hoped to be able to make stable. However, as we mentioned above, the Roman groined vault could be constructed only on a square plan. Thus, it was necessary to find some new combination involving the groined vault that would lend itself to construction on a parallelogram plan. Since, however, no drawing of a groined vault could actually be traced out, it could be only by groping and by trial and error that the new combination could be found.

Already during the eleventh century, builders had fashioned vaults that at one and the same time were inspired by both the cupola and the groined vault. These vaults, instead of being formed by two half cylinders brought together at a right angle to each other, were formed out of four semicircular arches joining the four supporting piers, and with two diagonal arches, themselves also semicircular arches, and therefore with a greater radius than the original four arches. Anyone acquainted with the methods used to construct a groined vault will easily understand the reasons for modifying the Roman groined vault. In order to construct a vault, it is necessary to construct wooden scaffolding on which to lay down lagging. To construct a Roman groined vault, it is necessary to cut four semicircular arches and two diagonal arches, with the curves of the latter being fixed by the meeting of the half cylinders; these curves of the diagonal arches will not be semicircular, however, but rather elliptical. This result is arrived at by means of ordinates, as indicated in figure 4. Let *AB*

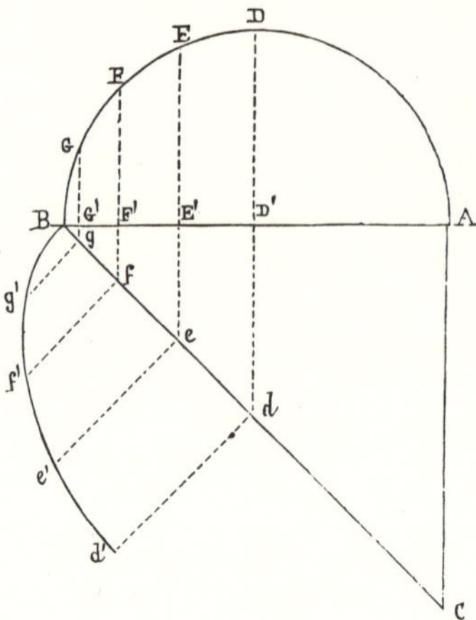

Figure 4

be the diameter of the cylinders and *BC* the horizontal line of the plane on which the two cylinders *AB* and *AC* meet. Working on a quarter point and dividing the rotated semicircle into an equal number of parts, *DE, EF, FG,* and *GB,* it is necessary to drop the perpendicular lines of the divisor points *DEFG* on the diameter *AB,* extending them until they meet the diagonal line *BC.* In this way the divisor points *defg* are obtained; from these points, raising the perpendicular lines on the diagonal line *BC* and adopting lengths where *dd'* is equal to *D'D,* and *ee'* equal to *E'E,* etc., one arrives at points *d'e'f'g',* through which must pass the curve of the meeting of the two half cylinders. This curve has a sine *dd'* equal to the radius *D'D,* and a diameter, *BC,* greater than the diameter *AB.* Hence, it cannot be a semicircle. This geometric outline is surely a simple enough thing; nevertheless, it appeared to be too complicated for the Roman builders. Having traced a semicircle, *AB,* in order to make it possible to cut out the framework of the four basic arches of the vault, they simply traced a second semicircle on the diameter *BC,* in order to fashion the two diagonal arches. As a result, the meeting point and keystone of these two diagonal arches, *d,* was higher than those of the four basic arches, *D;* and the vault, instead of being formed out of the meeting of two half cylinders, became a kind of composite of curved surfaces without any name but mostly resembling the cupola. It is necessary to provide this elementary demonstration because it is the key to the entire system of vaulting in the Middle Ages. This initial result, due to ignorance more than to any calculated proceeding, proved to be one of the most fruitful principles in the history of construction. Moreover, it involved something else besides crude ignorance; it indicated the presence of a certain conscious freedom in utilizing common methods of construction. This was of considerable importance. In effect, once emancipated from Roman traditions, the builders of the Middle Ages worked more consistently in accordance with their own principles; they soon came to understand the full extent of these principles, and they frankly embraced them. Let us, however, follow them step-by-step. The basic question was, then, once the principle of the Roman groined vault had been modified, to construct such vaults according to asymmetrical plans, where one side was longer than the other, for these builders certainly recognized the dangers of wide barrel vaults.

Thus, let *ABCD* in figure 5 be the parallelogram of a bay of a planned nave that must be covered with a groined vault. Let *AEB* represent the semicircular extrados of the rotated transverse arches, and *AFC* represent the semicircular extrados of the similarly rotated lateral arches. It is clear that the radius *HF* will be shorter than the radius *GE*. Consequently, the key *E* will be higher

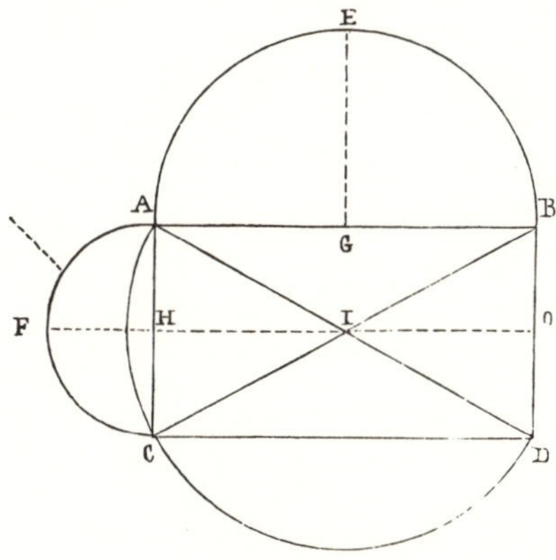

Figure 5

than the key *F*. If we trace a semicircle on the diagonal line *AD* to represent the curve through which the vaults formed by the semicircles *AEB* and *AFC* must meet, the result will be that the meeting points *AI, BI, DI,* and *CI,* instead of projecting outward, will on the contrary be hollowed inward for nearly two-thirds of their length and principally as they approach the key *I*.

Let figure 6 be the transversal section or plan of the vault following the line *HO*. Let *H'F'* be that of the lateral arch, *H'I'O'* the vertical projection of the diagonal arches *AD* or *BC*. A straight line drawn from the key *F'* to the key *I'* will leave a segment of the circle *KLI'* above this line; as a result, this portion of the vault must be convex at the intrados instead of being concave. Conse-

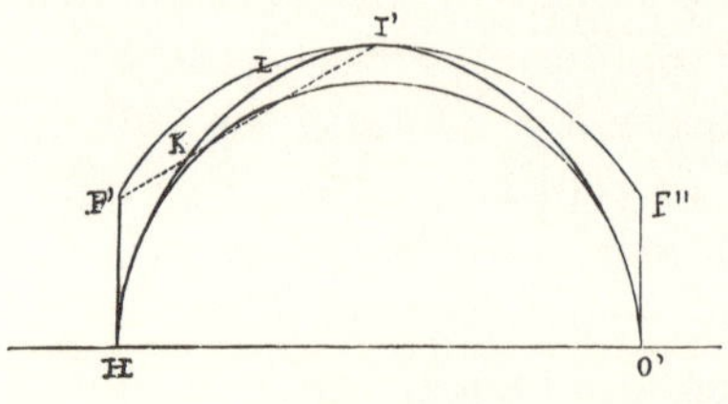

Figure 6

quently, such a vault would not be constructible. Placing, therefore, both the lateral arches and the transverse arches on the diagonal arches, as well as on wooden plank lagging in order to be able to close the triangles of the vaults with masonry, the builders filled this lagging with a thick mass of earth, following a curve given by the three points *F'I'F''*—that is, a curve given by the summits of the diagonal arches and the lateral arches. In this way, the arrises, or ridges, of the diagonal arches became salient, or projecting, again. On this mass of masonry the builders laid down rows of small building stones parallel with the section in order to close the vault.

The result of this process of groping or trial and error was that groined vaults were no longer interpenetrations of cylinders or cones but were ellipsoids. The initial difficulty had been overcome. And rapid improvements were not long in coming. First, however, we must consider how and by what mechanical means these vaults were actually constructed. The Roman groined vault, built over bays, did not have transverse arches; it was carried on piers or columns projecting from piers, as shown in figure 7. *A* is the horizontal projection of one of these vaults. The diagonal arches *BC* and *DE*, produced by the penetration of the two half cylinders of equal diameters, and forming salient arrises or ridges, carry down onto the projecting angles of the piers. The Romanesque architects, having first reinforced their great barrel vaults by means of transverse arches, as we saw in figure 3, and having then replaced them by groined vaults on asymmetrical plans (which meant, of course, that they then lacked symmetry), nevertheless kept the transverse arches as well. They could not have done otherwise, since the diagonal arches of these vaults were semicircles and their summit was above that of the arches, of which the diameter was already given by the spacing of the piers.

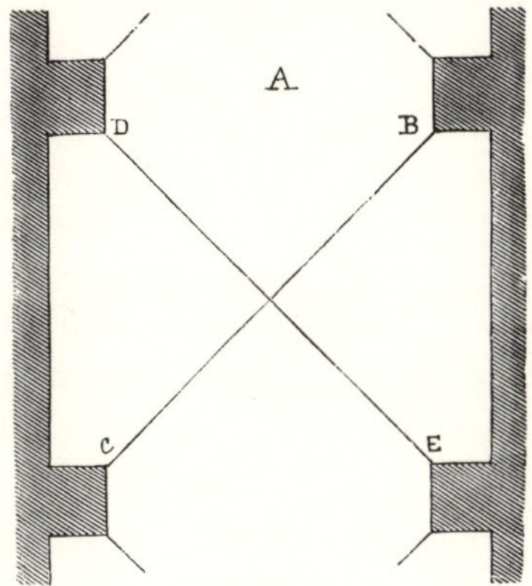

Figure 7

To help make ourselves better understood, let figure 8 be the longitudinal section of a groined vault composed of bays. The line *AB* is horizontal, and is the plan or section of the longitudinal half cylinder. Let figure 8-II be the longitudinal section of a groined vault of asymmetrical plan, where one side was longer than the

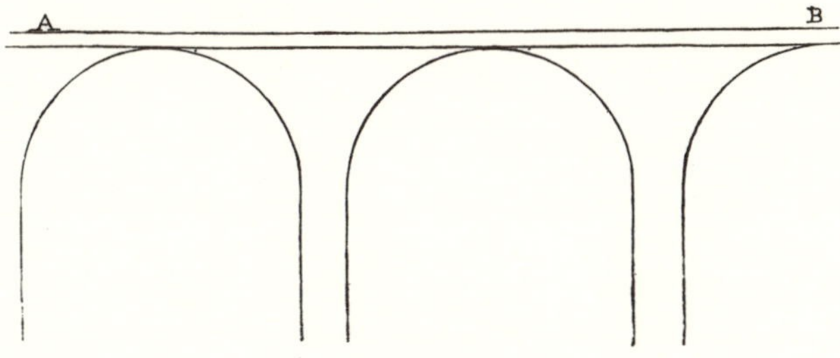

Figure 8

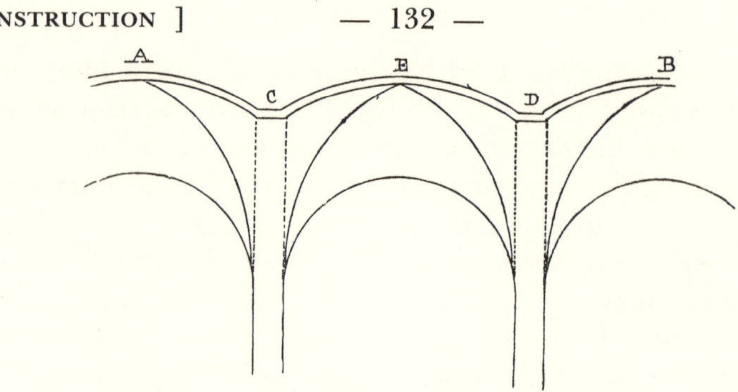

Figure 8-II

other. Line *AB* is a series of curves where, at the very least, broken lines unite the points *CD,* which are the summits of the transverse arches at the meeting points, *E,* of the diagonal semicircles. It was absolutely necessary to maintain salient transverse arches under points *CD;* these arches, as we have already mentioned above, amounted to a permanent centering of the vaults. Given this feature, the diagonal arrises had to take their point of departure from a recessed or setback point on the projections of the columns, since the latter were uniquely placed to carry the transverse arches. What this means, as we see from figure 9, is that these arrises or ridges had to take their point of departure from points *F* instead of points *G,* and that the imposts of the transverse arches had to rest on points *FHGI* as their foundation seats. When it was a

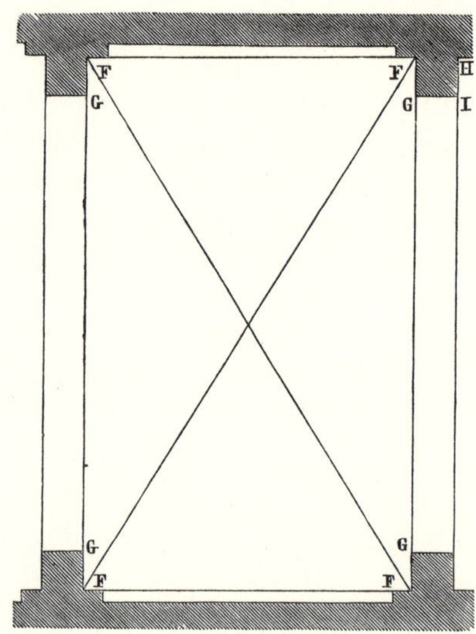

Figure 9

question of closing these vaults, the builders constructed lagging to carry earthen masses or forms on the extrados of these transverse arches and on two diagonal wooden centering supports, which they also built for temporary support while construction was going on.

In the kinds of construction carried out by peoples who are naturally builders, logical deductions generally follow one another with a fatal rigor. One forward step can never be the last step; it is always necessary to go on. Once a principle has been established as a result of a valid chain of reasoning, reason soon becomes the slave of that principle. Such do we find the spirit and outlook of the peoples of the modern West to be, in fact, and this same spirit and outlook had already emerged full blown from the moment that the society of the Middle Ages first began to be conscious of its powers and to organize its resources accordingly. Moreover, this spirit and outlook can find no stopping place, for no one who has ever established a principle based upon a valid chain of reasoning can then just turn around and say to reason: "You cannot take me any farther!" Even the builders of the eleventh century who were still working in the shadow of the cloister recognized this fundamental principle. A hundred years later, no one at all could any longer have prevented Romanesque architecture from becoming the new architecture that came to be called "Gothic." This new architecture was the inevitable consequence of the logical development of the old. Those who imagine they see in Gothic architecture anything else but the emancipation of artists and artisans who had quite simply learned how to use their own heads and to reason for themselves—who had indeed come to be able to reason better than their own masters, and who, therefore, with the weapon reason had thus placed in their hands, ineluctably carried everything before them to a place far beyond where they had originally intended to go—do not understand the unifying principle of the new architecture that had come into being. Gothic architecture was in its entirety a creation of lay people, and it stemmed from nothing else but a very rigorous analogical application of the system of construction inaugurated by the Romanesque architects. Those who imagine that Gothic architecture is some kind of oddity or eccentricity or exception in history fail, once again, to understand its elementary principle. We shall have no difficulty demonstrating this elementary principle, however. Let us therefore proceed.

Already by the end of the eleventh century, the principle on which the Roman groined vault was based had been laid aside.* Transverse arches had now been definitively accepted as a vital, free, and elastic feature, which provided a frame on which the vault, properly so called, could rest. If builders had now accepted that such a permanent type of crosswise centering, or support, was usable, then they logically had to admit that the same kind of support had to be acceptable lengthwise, or longitudinally, as well. Vaults were no longer seen as homogeneous concrete shells or crusts but rather as a series of *panels* with curved surfaces that were both free and resting on flexible arches. The rigidity of the Romanesque side walls still contrasted with the new system, however; it was necessary that the new system of joined panels should be flexible in every direction; otherwise rents and breaks could be even more dangerous, since the vaults were now being carried on flexible transverse arches in one direction but on rigid walls in the other direction. Thus, builders began to construct lateral arches between one pier and another, along the walls, in a longitudinal direction. These lateral arches were merely one-half of a rib embedded in part within the wall but not dependent upon the particular construction of the wall. By this means, vaults came to rest completely on piers or pillars. Walls became merely enclosures or partitions, in other words; if need be, they could be constructed after the basic structure of the building was completed; indeed, they could be eliminated entirely. Of course it was necessary to give these lateral arches a stable foundation, a specific point of support. For this reason the Romanesque builders added a new architectural member; the vault henceforth came to originate in a recessed angle formed by the impost of the transverse and of the lateral arches, as indicated in figure 10. *A* is the transverse arch; *B* the lateral arch; *C* the ridge of the vault; *D* shows the plan of the entire pier. If, however, the pier or pillar was isolated and freestanding, and the nave had side aisles, it took the form indicated in figure 10-II. *A* is the transverse arch of the grand vault, and *B* the archivolts carrying the wall. Above these archivolts, the wall is recessed, as shown by *F,* in such a way as to permit

*It was in the nave of the church of Vézelay that the abandoning of the Roman system can be seen. There, high groined vaults constructed according to an asymmetrical plan are already ellipsoids with projecting transverse arches and lateral arches. [Author's note]

the pilasters, *G,* to carry the upper lateral arches. *C* is the transverse arch of the aisle; *D* the ridges of the vaults of this aisle; and *H* the ridges of the grand vault of the nave. The vaults of the aisles are integrated into the transverse arches, *C;* the extrados of the archivolts, *B;* and a lateral arch that is in part embedded in the wall of the aisles, like the upper lateral arches shown in figure

Figure 10

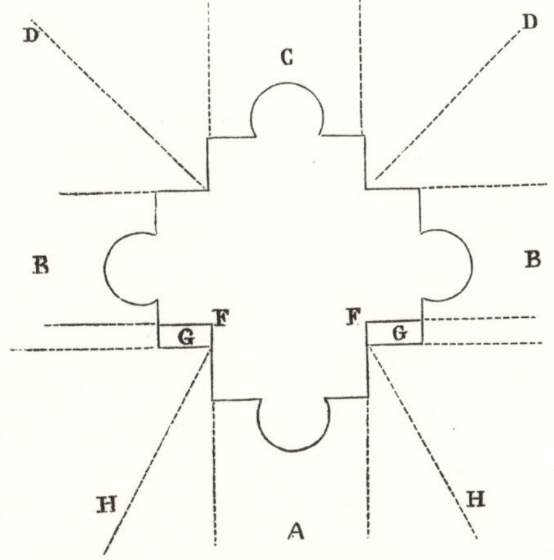

Figure 10-II

10. Thus, the particular architectural members of the vaults give to the horizontal section of the piers the form derived from these members. Even with all this, however, the vaults remained insufficiently buttressed; movements could be verified in the piers. Moreover, the transverse arches, which constituted the principal nerves of this vital new system, could become deformed. Since they still did not really know how to contain thrusts, the Romanesque builders at first tried to minimize their bad effects. They had observed that the more the stones of an arch presented a large section of the intrados and extrados, the more movement within such an arch caused damage. They were not the first to recognize such a law. The Romans before them, when they had a great arch to erect, had taken great care to construct several rows of concentric arch stones independent of each other, as indicated by *A* in figure 11. Arches constructed in this fashion functioned like so many hoops, acting separately from each other, and thus they retained much greater elasticity; they had much greater resistance than an arch constructed according to the method indicated in *B*.

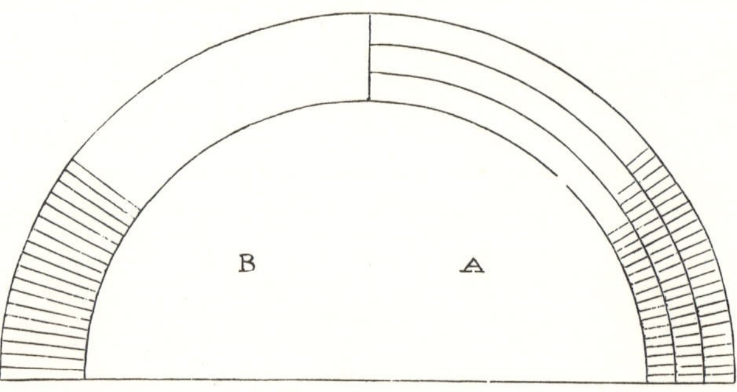

Figure 11

Following this principle, the Romanesque architects began to construct their transverse arches in two rows of concentric stones; one of them, the row belonging to the intrados, took a portion or section of the radius longer than the one belonging to the extrados. Since these transverse arches really amounted to permanent support, or centering, destined to receive the ends of the lagging on which the masonry of the vault was constructed, the builders added a second row of projecting stones on top of the first; they did this precisely in order to receive these ends of the lagging.

Figure 12 illustrates the method. *A* is the row of the arch stones of the intrados, and *B* the row of those of the extrados, with the projections, *C*, destined to receive the ends of the lagging, *D*, on which the masonry of the vaults was laid down. The lateral arches, having a smaller diameter, and not being subject to the same effects from thrusts, were composed of a single row of stones, as figure 12-II shows; but they also included the projection necessary to make it possible to lay down the lagging. It is clear from this

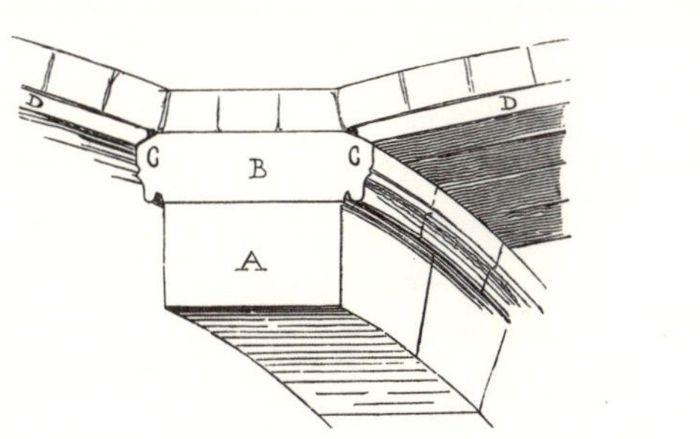

Figure 12

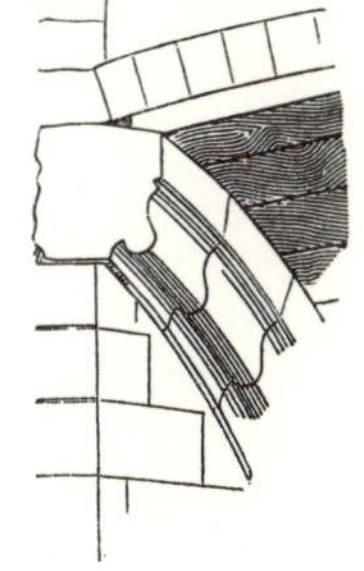

Figure 12-II

that the Romanesque architects were allowing the evidence of how they had carried out their construction work to remain as part of the finished structure. Far from seeking to dissimulate these means of construction, they fashioned their architecture around them in a very basic way. Do we need other proofs of this? The Romans crowned the summits of their columns with capitals; but the projection, or jutting out, of the abacus of these Roman capitals carried no member; it was simply an ornament. Thus, when the Romans placed a groined vault upon columns, as they frequently did—in their baths, for example—the impost of the vault was placed directly above the bare part of the column, as in figure 13. Then, as strange as it is inexplicable by reason, not only did the shaft of the column still carry its capital; it carried the complete entablature of the architectural order. Thus, the entire structure comprising *A* and *B* served no function whatever; and the strongly protruding ledges, *B*, also served no function except to hold the scaffolding that was necessary in order to close the vault. One must admit that all this constituted a great deal of ornate elaborateness expended on objects that were merely accessories. When the Romanesque builders placed an arch on a column, however, whether it was an isolated column or an engaged column, the

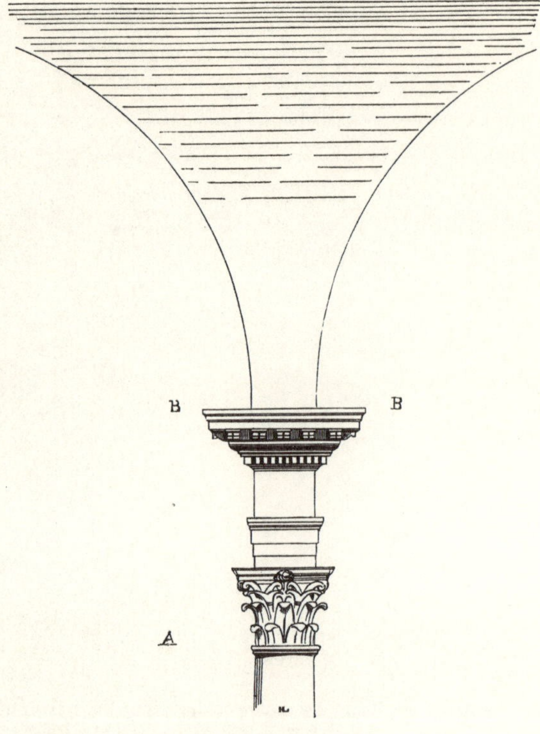

Figure 13

capital served as a corbeling destined to receive the impost of the arch; that is to say, the capital was a projection serving as a transition between the cylindrical shaft of the column and the square foundation for the impost. See figure 14. In this latter case, the capital is no longer merely an ornament but is one of the useful architectural members of the construction.[5]

If the Romanesque builders had a crowning cornice to place at the summit of an exterior wall, they did not go to the great expense and trouble of shaping or grooving all the various members of this cornice in a single stone; they were generally too parsimonious both of their time and of their materials for that; instead they fashioned projecting corbels out of the last row of building stones they used and placed on these corbels a stone tablet to serve as a drain for the roofing.[6] However, we do not need to insist further on these details; they will automatically find their rightful place in the course of this publication.

The construction of vaults was thus the great preoccupation of the architects of the Middle Ages. As we have been able to

Figure 14

show, these builders certainly succeeded in coming up with a number of very ingenious schemes and devices. However, they had not yet found the proper means to ensure the absolute stability of their vaults; they were still dependent upon various expedients. Thus, they made the masonry that they used to fill in their vaults out of light materials such as tuff stone in order to minimize the effects of the thrusts of their vaults; wherever possible they reduced thickness; they blocked up the space under the roofs of side aisles with masonry placed at right angles to the thrusts in the hope of preventing the tilting or tipping of the piers; they placed wooden ties or clamps across the bases of the buttresses that were concealed by the slope of the roofing in order to join to, and make their piers interdependent with, the exterior walls. All these various expedients proved to be sufficient in the construction of small buildings; in the larger buildings, however, they merely succeeded in weakening the effects of the thrusts of the vaults without eliminating these thrusts completely.

In order to understand the chain of reasonings and the process of trial and error through which the builders of the Middle Ages had to pass in order to move from ignorance to scientific knowledge, we must remind ourselves of the various effects they experienced as a result of what they did try. Let figure 15 be the cross section of a Romanesque church dating from the end of the

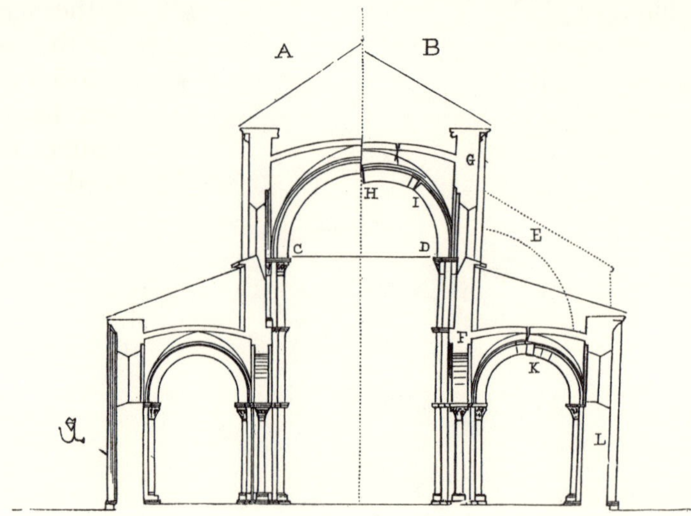

Figure 15

eleventh century; it was built, as was the church of Vézelay, with groined vaults over both the central nave and the side aisles. With *A* we see the construction as the architect conceived it; with *B* we see the deformation caused by its high vaults. Care was taken to put iron ties, *CD,* at the springing, or origination point, of the transverse arches. However, these iron ties broke; probably they had been badly forged. A century and a half after the construction of the nave, the effects produced by thrusts had already caused the collapse of several vaults. Exterior flying buttresses had also been constructed hastily, as shown by the dotted lines, *E,* on our design. The effects produced included (1) tilting or tipping of the piers and of the walls linking these piers between *F* and *G,* resulting in the sagging of the keystones of the transverse arches, *H,* and the crushing of the beds of the voussoirs of the intrados at the haunches of the arches, *I;* and (2) dislocation of the transverse arches of the aisles, *K,* as indicated in our figure 15, which in turn caused the tilting or tipping of the exterior walls of the aisles, *L.* These effects were produced everywhere in exactly the same fashion. In studying them, the builders came to believe, not without reason, since the same effects were consistently produced, that they were caused by the thrusts of semicircular arches and by the vaults that these arches were in part supporting. It appeared that the too-flat concavity of these vaults exerted an oblique action and a thrust that was simply too great; and that the thrust of a semicircular arch actually increased as a result of the action it exerted. The kind of deformation that occurred in the case of these arches indicated where the weak points were to be found, namely, at the keystones of the arches and in their haunches. Whenever a semicircular arch was not perfectly buttressed—so that the piers that supported it could not be displaced—a deformation would result, as indicated in figure 16.

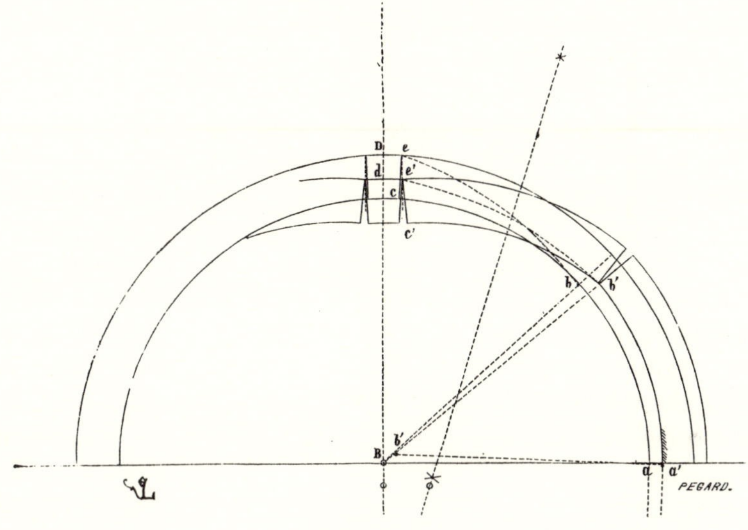

Figure 16

Let figure 16 represent a vault of which the diameter is 7 meters and the thickness of its arch stones 60 centimeters. At the point where the arch is sprung, the walls become displaced by 20 centimeters each. From that point the diameter of the semicircle of which the center is *B* reaches 7.4 meters. The springing points, *a,* of the transverse arch are removed to the point *a′*. The segment *ab,* which is a little less than one-quarter of the semicircle, is carried on *a′b′;* for if we suppose that the pier will break at a point 3 meters below the springing point, this point will sink below the level of point *a* and the center, *B,* will then rise to *b′*. The consequences of this first movement will be the lowering of the keystone, *D,* to *d,* and the sagging of the segment *bc* to *b′c′*. This effect will continue until the diagonal curve *be,* traced from the intrados to the extrados of the segment *bc,* becomes shorter than the distance between *b′* and *e′*. It is worth remarking in passing that these Romanesque vaults, commonly believed to have been constructed with these "basket-handle" (three-centered) arches, in fact acquired this particular configuration only with the displacing of the piers supporting them. Forty centimeters of displacement from the vertical between the piers yielded 40 centimeters of sagging at the summit of the arch; the difference between the half diameter of.the arch, in this case, and the rise of the arch's curve was thus 80 centimeters. The builders must have observed these effects and sought to devise methods to prevent them. The first attempt to do this appears to have been as follows: given a nave of which the transverse arches have a diameter of 7 meters at the intrados and a thickness of 60 centimeters, and once it had been noted (figure 16) that the segment *b′c′*, in sagging, pressed the lower segment *a′b′* down to *b′*, and the key to the extrados to *e′*, the builders concluded that the curvilinear triangle *b′e′c′* was useless and that only the diagonal *b′e′* offered any resistance. Departing from this principle, therefore, they traced the two semicircles shown in figure 17: the intrados *ABC* and the extrados *DEF*. Then, on the diameter *AC,* they tried to find the center, *O,*

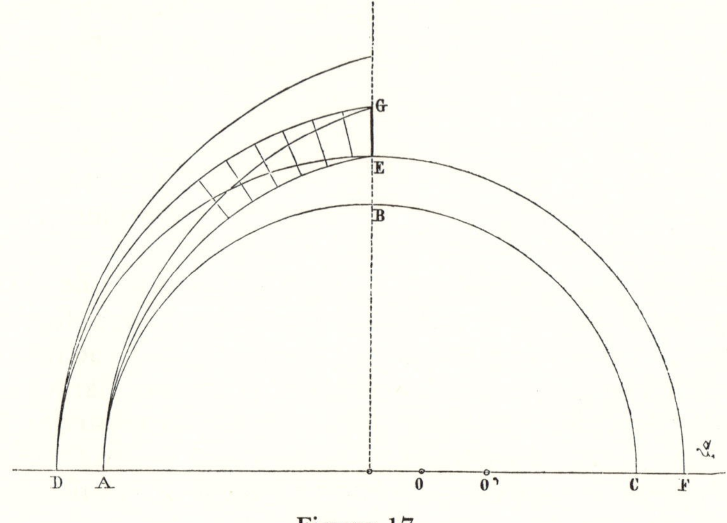

Figure 17

of a circular arch uniting point *A* of the intrados to point *E* of the extrados of the semicircular arch. Placing a joint at *EG* instead of a keystone, in order to avoid the effect of equilibrium that had been so evident in figure 16, they cut the stones of the new arch, *AE,* following the normal lines of the curve *AE*—that is to say, tending toward the center, *O.* If breakage still occurred in the transverse arches thus composed of two diagonal curves, *AE,* the builders proceeded with the arch, *AE,* as with the semicircular arch; that is to say, they moved the center, *O,* back to *O′* on the diameter, in a way that resulted in an arch uniting point *A* with point *G.*

It was in this way that, in the vaults of the twelfth century, we see transverse arches moving away from the semicircular model to become pointed equilateral arches (or "broken arches"). The best proof we could find in support of the hypothesis we have outlined here would be a precise summary of the large number of early broken arches that in fact can be shown to have a rise longer than a half diameter, and of the thickness of their imposts, one, two, and three times as large. However, this proof is evident only to those who have been in a position to take exact measurements on a large number of the transverse arches of the period. We must therefore make an observation of a more general kind, which could be made by anybody without having recourse to measurements that are difficult to carry out.

There are regions, such as, for example, the Île-de-France, where Romanesque semicircular transverse arches were composed of stones that were not very thick. In these regions, the first vaults built with broken arches had an acuity that is scarcely even perceptible. In the provinces where the Romanesque semicircular arches were constructed with thick stones, however, as was the case in Burgundy, the acuity of the arches of the first vaults where the semicircular arch was abandoned is considerably more marked.

The adoption of the broken arch was surely the result of observations made by the builders of the deformations they found in semicircular arches: for example, the raising of the haunch of an arch and the sagging of its keystone. There exist a large number of arches of the twelfth century traced out as indicated in figure 18—that is, arches with four centers: two centers, *A,* for the portions of the arch *BC* and *DE,* and two centers, *G,* for the portions of the arch, *CD,* that constitute the haunch; this was so that the portion of the arch between *C* and *D* might present greater resistance to the elevating effect that had been verified between these two points; for the closer the line *CD* approached to being a straight line, the less it was subject to breakage from inside to outside. By using this sketch, the builders avoided giving their transverse arches an acuity that, since they were accustomed to semicircular arches, could hardly have failed to be rather shocking.

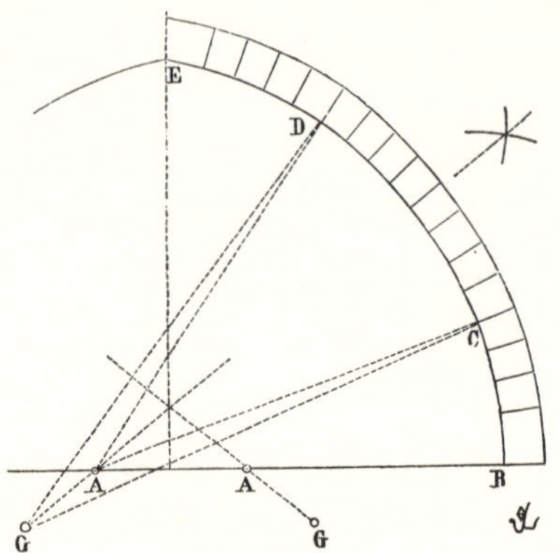

Figure 18

From the moment that an arch formed out of two circular arches came to replace the simple semicircular arch, a multitude of consequences necessarily followed that would lead builders far beyond the goal at which they had originally aimed. Used as a means of construction, the broken arch, or, to use its true name, the pointed equilateral arch, represented a true revolution in the art of building; this was particularly the case when we consider that its general structure was used in the vaulting of the vast open spaces eventually obtained as the fruit of the observation of the original effects of using the semicircular arch in vaulting. It has been said, of course, that "the builders of the Middle Ages invented nothing new when they adopted the pointed equilateral arch. The ancient monuments of Greece and Etruria used broken arches. The section of the Treasury of Atreus at Mycenae had a pointed equilateral arch, etc." This is all true. However, this particular viewpoint also omits some rather important considerations. They are these: those arches were placed on corbeling; their beds are not normal, that is, perpendicular, to the curve; and they are horizontal. For those who are concerned only with external forms, all these things amount to less than nothing. For those of us who are true practitioners of the art of construction, however, these details have considerable importance. Besides, even if the Greeks and Romans had built vaults derived from broken arches, how meaningful would that have been if they had not done so as a result of the combination of these curves and the observation of their oblique effects? It is evident that from the day when the compass had been invented and therefore the means to trace circles, the invention of the broken arch was also an inevitable result. What does it matter to us whether or not a complete system for the observation of its properties was not also established? There are those who have wanted to see in the use of the pointed equilateral arch for the construction of vaults some kind of mysical or symbolic idea; some have attempted to demonstrate that these arches possess greater religious significance than semicular arches. However, everyone was just as religious at the beginning of the twelfth century as at the end, if not more so. But the pointed equilateral arch appeared, rather, precisely at the moment when the analytic spirit and the study of natural philosophy and the exact sciences were beginning to germinate within a society that had been pretty much a theocracy up to that point. The introduction of the pointed equilateral arch into construction, and the far-reaching consequences that flowed from that introduction, came, once again, at the moment when architecture began to be practiced principally by the laity—at the moment when it emerged from the enclosures of the cloisters where it had been exclusively practiced up to then.

The last Romanesque builders, those who, after so much trial and error, finally threw out the semicircular arch entirely, were not dreamers. They did not occupy themselves with such things as the possible mystical significance of curves. They had no idea at all whether the pointed equilateral arch was in any way more *religious* than the semicircular arch. They were builders—something considerably more difficult than dreaming empty dreams. The problem that they faced was how to support wide and high vaults on freestanding piers. They no doubt trembled every time they had to remove the temporary wooden centering of every bay they ever vaulted. Every day they thought of some new palliative for the problems that they were continually facing. They watched with uneasiness and disquietude even the slightest displacement of any building; they noticed even the most minor effects of everything they tried. These observations, which these builders incessantly made, proved to be a fertile source of education for them. Their traditions were vague and incomplete; they worked while surrounded by obscurity. The only models they had were the buildings they themselves had raised up. The only experiments they were able to conduct were on these same actual buildings. They had no recourse to anyone but themselves; they had to go by their own observations.

When the buildings that went up around the beginning of the twelfth century are carefully studied and classified in their chronological order, and when the progress of the various schools engaged in building is followed in France, Burgundy, Normandy, and Champagne, it becomes clear that the builders of the day were seized with a veritable fever. The student of their work comes to share their anxieties and their haste to find the sure result. The student can chart the progress of their efforts literally from one building to another. Moreover, the student can only applaud their perseverance and the rightness of their reasoning, as well as admire the development of their knowledge, so limited at first, but later so profound. A study of this type can only be of surpassing usefulness for those of us who are builders in the nineteenth century; for today we are all too prone to mistake appearance for reality, and, too often, to exemplify vulgarity instead of good sense.

Already by the beginning of the twelfth century the pointed equilateral arch had been adopted for great barrel vaults in parts of Burgundy, in the Île-de-France, and in Champagne—that is, in the most advanced and most active provinces, if not the richest. The high naves of the churches of Beaune, Saulieu, and Charité-sur-Loire, and of the Cathedral of Autun, are all vaulted with barrel vaults formed out of two circular arches intersecting each other, even while the archivolts of the doors and windows of these very same buildings remain semicircular arches. It was a necessity of the construction that imposed broken arches on these structures; it was not just somebody's particular taste or whim. It is a remarkable fact that all the architectural details of these edifices were borrowed from ancient Gallo-Roman monuments remaining in these provinces. Because of the innovation of using the broken arch for the vaults, however, these churches have remained standing up to our own day (although not without having had to undergo some other additional interventions, in order to prevent their falling into ruin, which were undertaken a couple of centuries after they were built).

The structure in which the transition between the Romanesque system of construction and the system later to be styled "Gothic" can best be seen is the porch of the church of Vézelay. This porch is by itself an imposing monument composed of three bays with aisles and a vaulted gallery above. The plan of this particular porch, which was built around 1150,* is entirely Romanesque and does not differ from the plan of the nave, built 50 years earlier; the porch's section, however, reveals notable differences from that of the nave. Already toward the end of the eleventh century, the builders of the nave of the church of Vézelay had made an important step forward when they replaced the high vaults, which up to then had been barrel vaults, with groined vaults; these latter vaults, however, were built according to an asymmetrical plan using semicircular transverse and lateral arches, and they provide graphic illustration both of the inexperience of the builders and of their continuing uncertainty.[7] In the case of the porch, however, all the arches are pointed equilateral arches; the vaults are groined vaults without salient diagonal arches and were constructed out of plastered, rough, small building stones. The high vaults are very skillfully buttressed by the vaults of the galleries of the first story. The entire ensemble presents a case of perfect stability.

In figure 19 we show a cross section of the porch at Vézelay. The vaults of the galleries arise out of the lateral arches, *A,* of the great vaults, which are veritable archivolts, and out of the lateral arches, *B,* which originate much lower down; from the inclination, *AB,* of the keys of the side vaults a continuous abutment is formed that encloses the great vaults. Since the bays are asymmetrical and the lateral arches originate at the same level as the transverse arches, *C,* the keystones of these lateral arches, *A,* are at a lower level than those of the transverse arches. As a result of this par-

*It is necessary to note that Burgundian architecture was at least 25 years behind that of the Île-de-France. However, transition buildings are lacking in the Île-de-France. The church of Saint-Denis, built toward 1140, is already almost Gothic in the manner of its construction. Intermediate edifices between Saint-Denis and earlier buildings that were frankly Romanesque either no longer exist or else were almost entirely modified in the course of the thirteenth century. [Author's note]

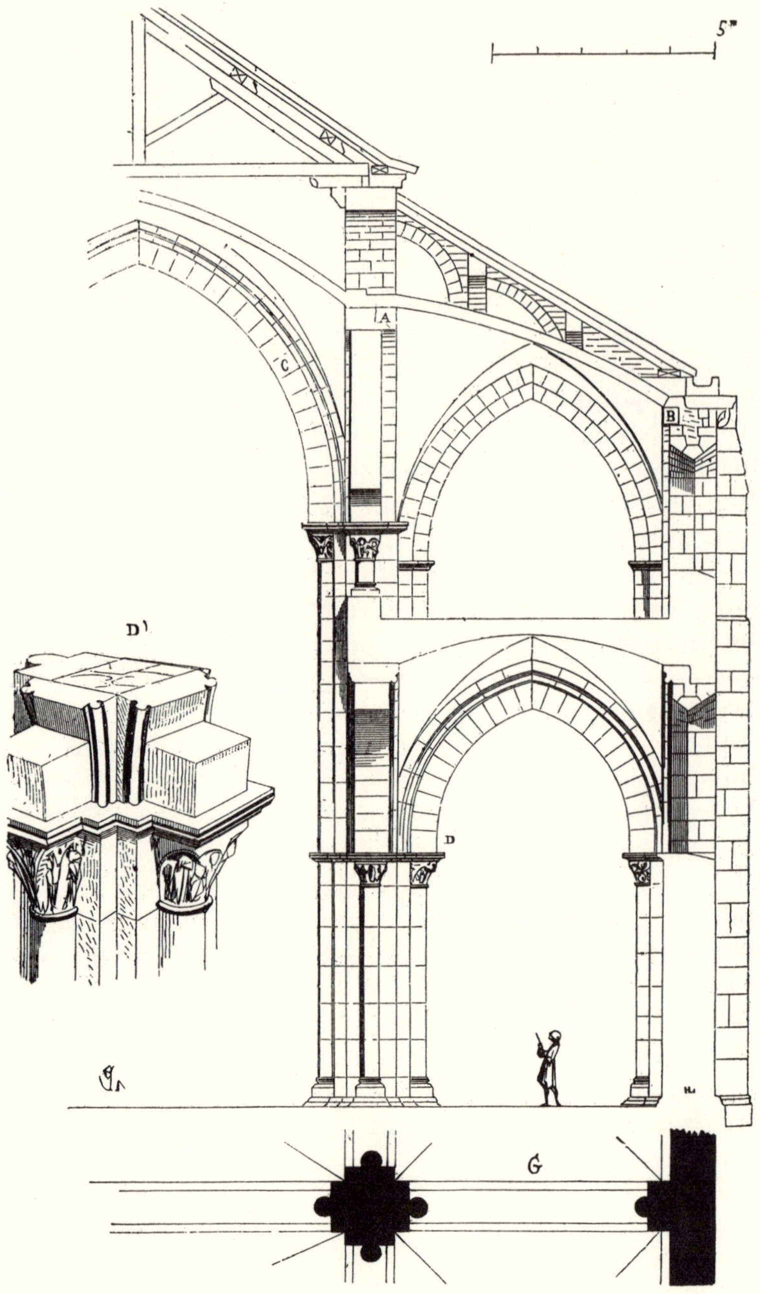

Figure 19

ticular disposition, the great vaults are well supported and their salient ridges scarcely noticed. With *D′* we show the details of the imposts of the arches at level *D* of the pier, and with *G* we show the plan for the origination of both the arches and the arrises or ridges of the vaults. This method of constructing vaults does not in any way resemble the Roman method of constructing them; already the principle of the independence of the various parts of the building has been accepted and is being rapidly developed.

However, all of the vaults of the porch of the church of Vézelay, except for two of them, have neither arris or hip ridges nor salient ogival arches. They are held together only by the adherence of the mortar used; each one of them forms a homogeneous concavity on its own, just as Roman vaults did. Moreover, the two vaults of this porch that do have arris ridges do not really count; for these ridges are merely decorations and do not consist of fillings enclosed within small building stones. However, the inclusion of this feature was an effort that would soon have important consequences. The builders had already obtained by means of their independent and resistant transverse and lateral arches for each vault a kind of elastic chassis or frame, which, if any sinking or settling took place, meant that each vault could move independently of all the others. In order to achieve this, the builders constructed their vaults out of two distinct elements: arches and fillings. The arches were now considered as permanent and elastic supporting structures; the fillings were used in neutral concave areas destined to close up the empty triangular spaces left between the arches. The builders thus began by avoiding an initial difficulty that had always given architects trouble; they returned to the vault constructed according to a square plan, but this time one consisting of two asymmetrical bays, if necessity required it. This amounts to saying that they traced out the plans of their vaults horizontally, as indicated in figure 20.

Let *ABCD* be a perfect, or almost perfect, square (for the approximation would suffice); this square comprehends two bays of a nave, *AE, BF* and *EC, FD.* The diagonals *AD* and *BC* give rise to this vault. Now these two diagonals are the diameters of two perfect half circles, rotated on the plan. Being of the same diameter, these two half circles necessarily meet at point *G,* which is the master keystone. Taking a length equal to the radius *GA* and carrying this radius to the perpendicular *GI,* we trace a broken arch in such a way that the point *I* falls on the point *G:* this is the transverse arch of which the horizontal projection goes to *EF*. Taking a length shorter than the radius *GA*, but longer than half of the width of the nave *AB*, and carrying this radius to the perpendicular *HK*, we trace the broken arch *AKB:* this is the trans-

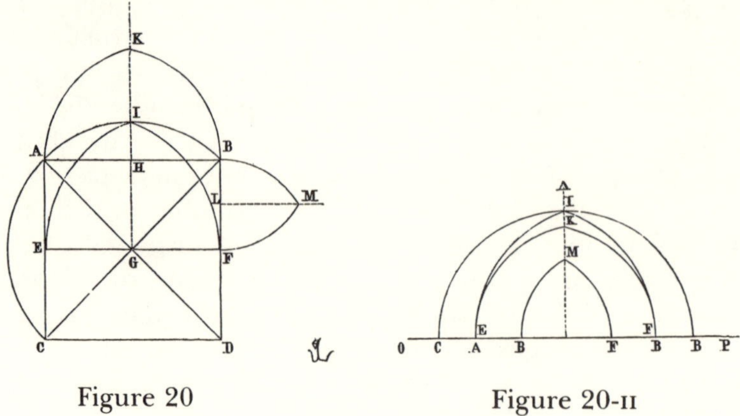

Figure 20

Figure 20-II

verse arch of which the horizontal projection goes to *AB* or *CD*. Finally, taking a length *LM* less than the line *HK* and greater than half of the line *BF*, we trace the arch *BMF:* this is the lateral arch of which the horizontal projection goes to *BF, FD,* etc. Cutting temporary wooden arches following these four curves rotated on the same line *OP* (figure 20-II) and then laying down the stones in a curved line on the curved surface formed by the temporary wooden arches, we obtain the framework of the vault as shown in figure 21.

These, then, are the original vaults that came to be called *ribbed vaults.* It will be noted that they arise out of a semicircle that gives rise first to the diagonal ribs; and it is this semicircle that dictates the height of the broken arches. These ogival arches, we may remark in passing—for thus are these diagonal rib arches commonly named—are semicircular. This is why the term *ogive* does not really describe the broken, or pointed, arch.[8] We offer this remark here only to point to one among the many common errors that are made concerning a type of art about which many people do not know very much. As we saw earlier, the broken arch was adopted by the last Romanesque architects in order to diminish the effects of thrusts. Then the role of this kind of arch became further expanded; it turned out to be the most practical means to close the very vaults generated (in the truest sense of the word) by the semicircular arch.

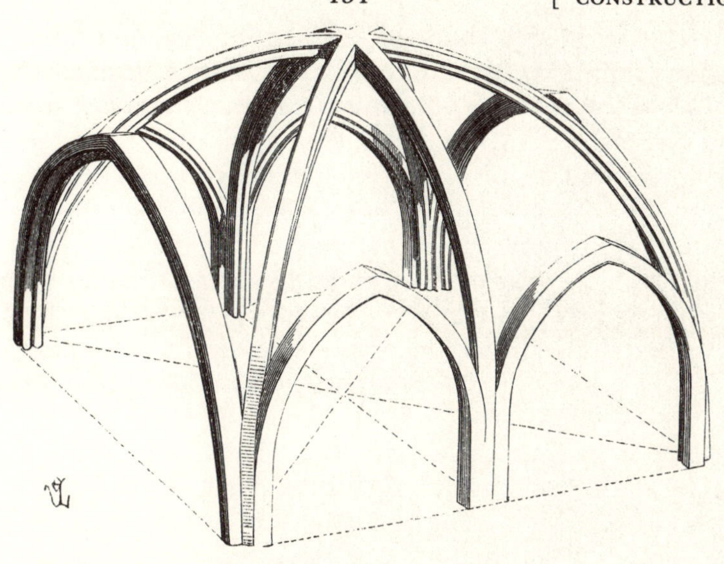

Figure 21

When, as in figure 22, a groined vault is formed by two half cylinders interpenetrating each other at right angles, the arches *AB* and *CD* and those *AC* and *BD* are semicircular arches and the penetrations *AD* and *BC* are less than semicircular; hence, the

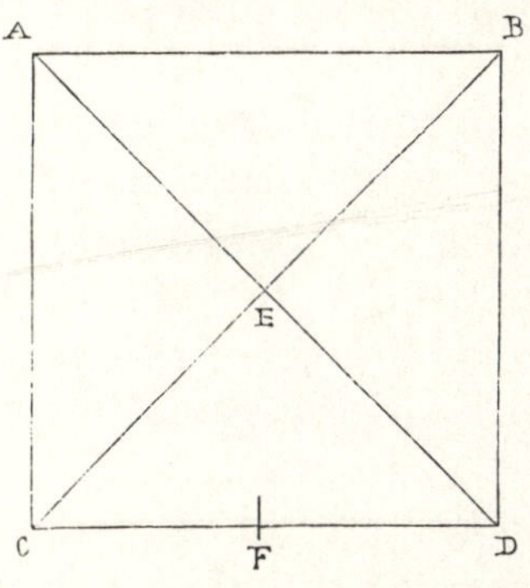

Figure 22

latter have to be flat or segmental arches, since the keystone *E* does not exceed the level of the keystone *F,* nor are the diameters *AD* and *BC* longer than the half circles *AB* and *CD.* There is no danger here if the vault *AB CD* is homogeneous and concrete—that is, if it forms a single crust or shell in the manner of the Roman vaults. However, if the builder wants to retain some elasticity in the triangles formed by his vaults; if he wants to strengthen the diagonal ridges *AD* and *BC* by turning them into true ribs; if he wants the triangles *ABE, CDE, ACE,* and *BDE* to rest on such ribs of a permanent supporting kind; and if, finally, his vault is to be one of great compass or extent—then it would surely be very imprudent on his part under the circumstances to trace the diagonal arches *AD* and *BC,* destined to fill such an important function, along any curve that was not at the very least a half circle. If such a tracing is not absolutely contrary to good construction, it presents certain difficulties, especially at the time of execution; these difficulties include finding the points through which the flat curves have to pass and deciding how to cut the arch stones. The semicircular arch eliminates such difficulties as these and is incomparably more solid. The first builders who were frankly Gothic builders did something that in appearance was very simple; instead of tracing the semicircle on the diameter *AB* as the Roman builders had done, they traced it on the diameter *AD.* This was, in reality, their only innovation; and, in adopting it, they did not suspect, we believe, the far-reaching consequences that would stem from something that appeared to be so natural and so simple. However, the builder's art is essentially a logical one; it is based on reasoning. The slightest deviation from accepted principles quickly leads to rigorously logical and necessary consequences far from the original point of departure. It is important to note that the first Gothic builders who, not without reason, had been so put off by the efforts of their Romanesque predecessors, since the initiatives of the latter had mostly led into dead ends, did not take fright at the consequences of their own initiatives as the latter began to open up before them. On the contrary, they immediately jumped in to take advantage, with rare sagacity, of the new opportunities and possibilities that their new methods had opened up for them.

The Gothic builders did not discover the broken arch. This same type of arch could be found in buildings that were frankly Romanesque in their construction, as we saw above. However, the Gothic architects did make use of the broken arch in order to develop a system of construction of which they were indeed the true and sole inventors. There were broken arches to be found throughout western Europe in the twelfth century. Gothic construction properly so called, however, could then be found only in France, and only on a small part of French territory at that (this is said with all due respect, of course, to those who will not accept that anything was ever invented here prior to the sixteenth century!).

What is true of all the inventions in this world that are present in latent form before their true application is finally found can also be said of the broken arch. Gunpowder was invented in the thirteenth century, but it was not utilized until the fifteenth century, when the proper moment arrived for the application of this particular agent of destruction. The same was true of printing; stamps for impressing marks had been fabricated throughout all history; but the idea of bringing together letters made out of wood or metal and using them to print books never came to fruition until there were more people around who knew how to read—that is, until knowledge and instruction had been disseminated among all classes of society and were no longer the monopoly of clerks closed up within their monasteries. Leonardo da Vinci, and perhaps others before him, clearly saw that steam could very easily provide the means of locomotion; yet nobody before our own time ever bothered to construct steam engines—that is, until the moment arrived when this powerful source of energy alone sufficed to fulfill the needs of our modern industry and activity. Thus, it is simply puerile to go on repeating that because the broken arch has been known all down through history, the builders of the twelfth century therefore have no claim on it as their own particular invention. Certainly they did not "invent" it; but they did recognize its qualities and potentialities for construction, and they put it to use in virtue of those qualities and potentialities. And we repeat: it was only in France—that is to say, only in the royal domain and some of the immediately surrounding provinces—that builders really understood how to apply the broken arch in the art of construction as a means to realize a principle, not just as another form chosen at random out of whim or caprice. We must now seek to draw out the consequences of this principle both as to their utility and as to their seriousness.

If, at the same time as they adopted the semicircular arch for the diagonal ribs of their vaults, the builders of the twelfth century had also tried to use it for their transverse and lateral arches, they would have taken a step backward. Their predecessors, too, had used broken arches, which they had adopted as a result of some of the unfortunate experiences they had had; they tried the broken arch since it appeared to have less thrust than the semicircular arch. But then they encountered great difficulties in trying to close their vaults. In effect, the keystones of transverse and lateral arches traced on a semicircular line would have been so far below the keystones of the ogival arches that it would have been difficult to provide filling in between with building stones; and even if the resulting vaults could have been closed, their aspect and appearance would have been very disagreeable. Their thrusts would also have been considerable, since they would have consisted of semicircular transverse arches with all the enormous weight of the stones filling in between. The advantages of using the pointed equilateral arch for the transverse arches where there were ribbed vaults, however, meant not only considerably less thrust; it meant considerably less weight in building stones for filling in (or, rather, it meant making this weight vertical). Let figure 23 be the plan of a ribbed vault. If the arches *AD* and *CB* are semicircular arches, and the transverse arches *AB* and *CD* are also semicircular arches, then the *rabattement*, or rotation, of the figure for these arches on a trace gives the semicircle *EFG* for the ogival arches, and the

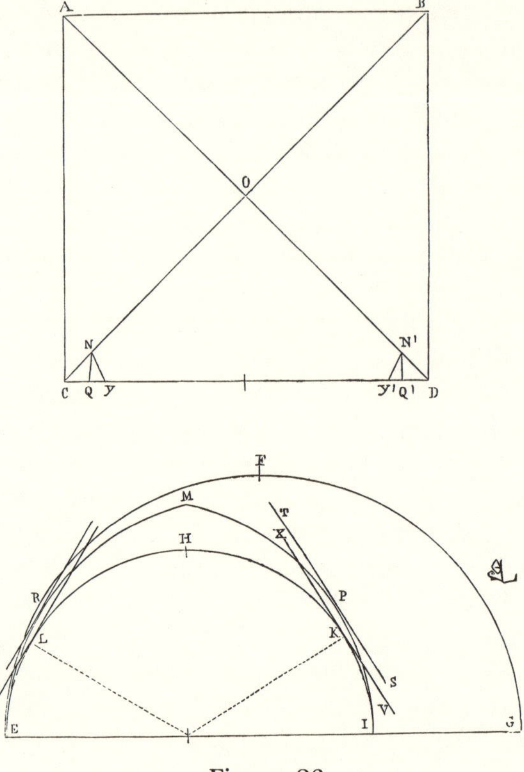

Figure 23

semicircle *EHI* for the transverse arches. In this case, the filling in with building stones of the triangle *COD* burdens the arch of the circle *KHL,* and this amounts to around three-fifths of the whole semicircle. But if the transverse arches are traced following the broken line *EMI,* then the filling in with building stones of the triangle *COD* burdens only the portion of that arch within the points *PMR,* the points *P* and *R* being given by a tangent *ST* parallel to the tangent *VX;* the portions to be filled in between *ER* and *IP* will act vertically. If the transverse arches are semicircles, the oblique weight or burden of each triangle filled in with building stones will be *ON′ QQ′ N′;* but if the transverse arches are traced as pointed equilateral arches, as indicated in our figure, then the burden will be only *ONY Y′ N′*.

The experimental method employed at the time actually yielded these results. The builders of the twelfth century had no other method but the experimental method that they could follow. It remains for us, however, to demonstrate the exactitude of this method that they followed with such results.

We have just said that the point *K* where the burden of the filling in begins gives an arch *IK,* which amounts to around one-fifth of the semicircle. In figure 24, let *AB* be a quarter circle and

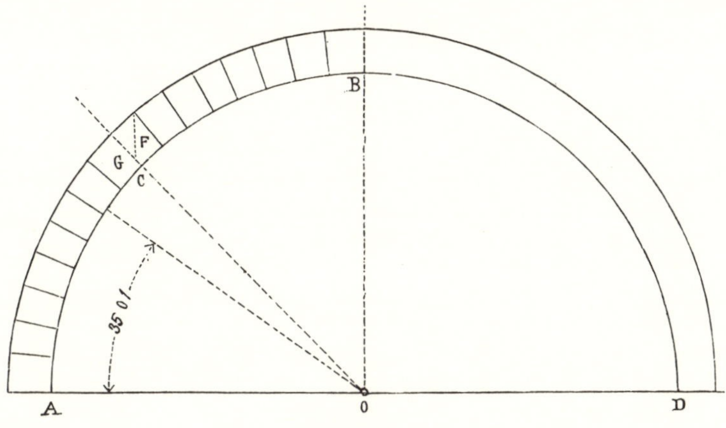

Figure 24

OC a line at 45 degrees dividing this quarter circle into two equal parts. The arch stones placed from *C* to *B,* unless they are maintained by the pressure of the arch stones placed from *B* to *D,* will tend to vacillate because of the laws of gravity and, as a consequence, they will push against those arch stones placed from *A* to

C. It is accordingly at *C* that the break in the arch should take place. However, friction at the surface of the beds of the arch stones, as well as the strength of the adherence of the mortar, also need to be taken into account. This friction and this adherence still suffice to maintain the arch stone *F* in its place and keep it bound to the arch stone below it, *G*. However, the arch stone *F* also shares in the burden of the stones from *F* to *B* and this forces the arch stone *G* and sometimes one or two of the stones below it to the point where the sections of these stones end up giving an angle of 35 degrees, which amounts to less than one-fifth of the semicircle. It is only above this point that a rupture takes place when one is going to take place (see figure 16) and only there, consequently, that the active burden begins.

Whether it was by theoretical or practical calculation, it is certain that the builders of the twelfth century counted on being able at some point to reduce the thrusts of vaults to the point where they could do away with abutments and maintain them on fairly thin pillars, provided they were weighted. They did not at first think it necessary to oppose thrusts with flying buttresses; they initially believed they had pretty much eliminated these thrusts, either by means of the obliquity of the ogival arches or by means of the broken curve of their transverse arches. Experience, however, quickly taught them that they had been mistaken about this. What resulted from the oblique thrusts of the semicircular ogival arches, added to the thrusts of the pointed equilateral transverse arches, was enough to overturn pillars raised up very high above the ground; the latter therefore turned out to be rather precarious structures without really solid foundations. Thus, builders had to turn to flying buttresses. At first they placed

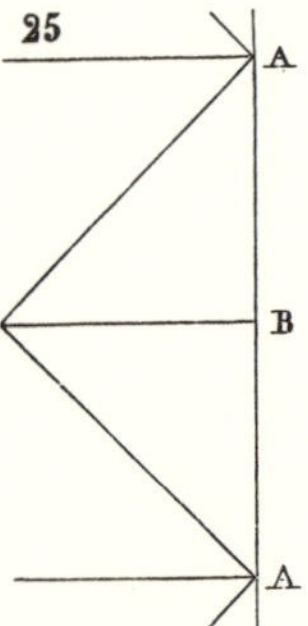

Figure 25

these only at right angles to the junction points of the three arches, as shown by *A* in figure 25. They did not place them against the points, *B*, receiving freestanding transverse arches. There was a question, though, of at what height or at what level the head of the flying buttress needed to be placed. This was a problem that was all the more difficult for the medieval builders when we consider that not even theoretical calculation can supply this point accurately; only long practical experience can indicate what it should be. Insofar as we can judge by the small number of primitive flying buttresses that have been preserved, figure 26 diagrams the method followed by the architects.

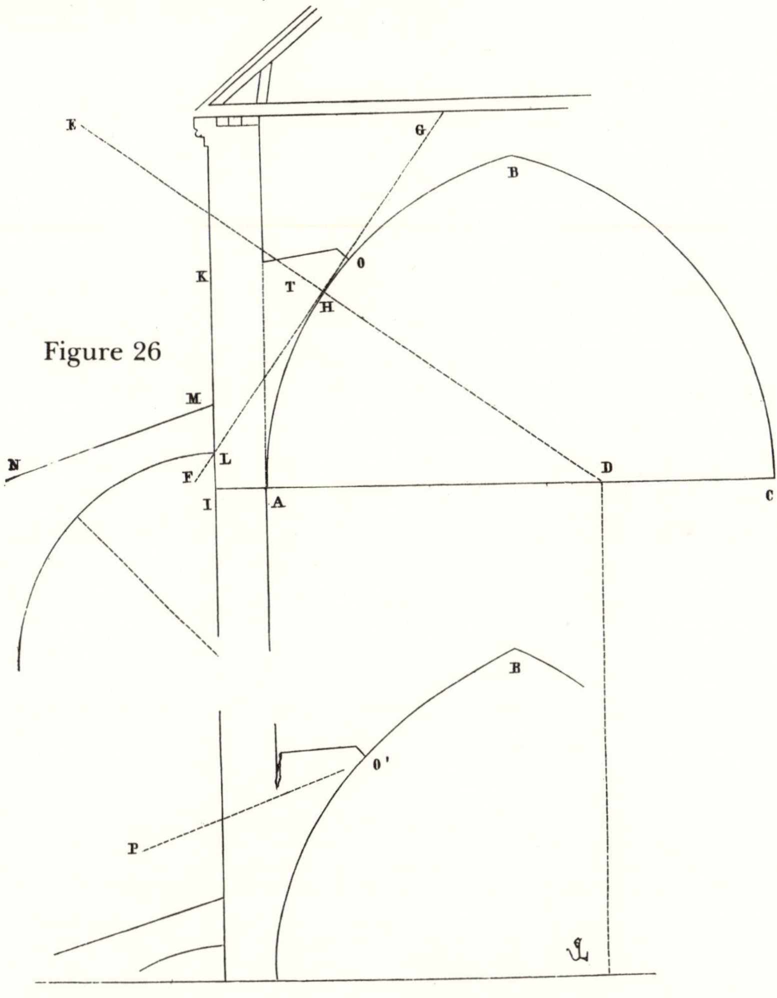

Figure 26

Figure 26-II

Let *ABC* in figure 26 be the transverse arch separating two great vaults. Let a line, *DE,* go out from point *D,* center of the arch *AB,* at 35 degrees above the horizon. Let *FG* be a tangent crossing point *H,* and *AI* be the thickness of the wall or pier. The tangent *FG* will meet the line *IK* outside the pier at point *L.* This was the point where the intrados of the headstone of the flying buttress was placed. Now this arch is a quarter circle or a little less, its center being placed on the extension of the line *IK* or a little inside of this line. The stress, *MN,* of the flying buttress is initially rather arbitrary, weak at the summit, *M,* powerful above the abutment at *N,* which results in a slight inclination along the line of the coping, or capstone, *NM.* Very soon certain effects manifested themselves in this type of construction. This was as a result of the thrusts of the vaults; and it occurred in spite of the flying buttresses. The reason for these effects is explainable: behind the haunches or sides of the arches and vaults at *T,* the builders were accustomed to fill up the space with crude, undifferentiated masses of masonry; this was done to strengthen the piers as much as it was to hold in place the haunches of the arches and their fillings. These masses in fact tended to prevent breakage of the arches at point *H;* but then the entire load of the fillings acted from *K* to *O,* and since this load could not be anything but considerable, it resulted in raising slightly the keystone *B* (for the arch had no load from *O* to *B*). The consequence of all this action was the deformation shown in figure 26-II. This deformation produced a break at point *O′* at a level above the masses of masonry; this brought about an extremely oblique thrust, *O′P,* which was exerted above the headstones of the flying buttresses, and thus tended to destroy the equilibrium of the entire structure. It actually became necessary to rebuild the flying buttresses of the original Gothic buildings within a few years after their construction. When that reconstruction took place, either the headstones of the flying buttresses were raised up, or else they were doubled with a second flying buttress.[9]

It should be obvious that we are not attempting to paper over the mistakes and false starts of the first Gothic builders. Like all who attempt to go down a new and uncharted path, they were able to succeed only after considerable groping and trial and error. It is easy today to criticize the efforts of the architects of the end of the twelfth century from the standpoint of later buildings constructed with such knowledge and care, such as, for example, the cathedrals of Amiens or Reims. But at the time they were building, these architects had no models to go by except the rather badly constructed Romanesque buildings. At that time construction was far from being based on the exact sciences; the exact sciences were scarcely known. The new task that the architects of the day imposed upon themselves bristled with all kinds of difficulties, which kept recurring; these difficulties could be overcome only by yet more careful and exact observations. It was these careful and exact observations that formed the basis of the great skill in construction that was exhibited in the thirteenth and fourteenth centuries. We must nevertheless observe, in high praise of the builders of the twelfth century, that having adopted a brand-new principle of construction, one for which they had no precedents, they pursued the development of this new principle with rare tenacity and perseverance; they did not look back, in spite of the obstacles and difficulties that arose at every step of the way. Their tenacity is all the more to be honored when we consider that, when they adopted the principle of the construction of Gothic vaults, they could not at that time have foreseen all the consequences that would follow in the nature of the case from this decision of theirs. Nevertheless, they acted as men who were motivated by strong conviction, and they therefore opened up for their successors a wide and safe road down which western Europe could travel for the next three centuries. Every human idea or conception is blemished and contains some admixture of error; the truly immutable, in any endeavor, must always be discovered. Even then, every discovery carries within itself the seeds of its own ruin. In the human world no sooner is a principle accepted than its imperfections and defects are also perceived; human effort must then be expended to combat and correct the imperfections and defects in an accepted principle.

Of all the conceptions of the human mind, those involved with the construction of buildings are among those that most regularly confront us with difficulties of a very serious kind—serious because they are sometimes in conflict with each other. Some of them are material, and some of them are moral. Builders must not only seek to give the materials they use the forms most appropriate to the nature of these materials; they must also put them together in a such a way that their constructions will be resistant to various forces and destructive agents. At the same time, builders are obliged to work within the limits of the resources they have at their disposition; they must satisfy the tastes and habits as well as the moral needs of those for whom they build. There are difficulties of conception in construction to which builders must apply their intelligence as artists. There are various methods of execution to which builders are necessarily subject. Throughout the entire Romanesque period architects exerted vain efforts in an attempt to reconcile principles that were apparently irreconcilable. These two principles were the thinness or lightness of the vertical supports desired, and the economy of the materials available for the construction of the modified Roman-type vaults. Some provinces even adopted a method of construction almost purely Byzantine as a result of Eastern influences alien to the Western mind.

Around the end of the tenth century, the church of Saint-Front was built at Périgueux. From this isolated example an entire school issued. Yet we must nevertheless recognize that this type of construction was alien to the new spirit that was stirring among the peoples of western Europe. The builders of Saint-Front in Périgueux constructed this church as if they were mere molders reproducing forms whose function and context they did not really understand. Thus, the pendentives that support the flattened domes of Saint-Front are bonded by means of foundations placed upon corbeling with beds that are not normal, or perpendicular, to the curve, but are horizontal. If these pendentives have not long since caved in, it is mainly because they held together by strong mortar and continue to adhere to the masonry, which gives them their concavity. Buildings such as this exhibit nothing but rote efforts to reproduce forms, the geometric reason for which is in no way understood; they exhibit both a complete ignorance of the art of construction and a pitiful recourse to mere expedients indifferently applied whenever difficulties were encountered. Certainly they exhibit neither foresight nor prudently taken thought.

There are a large number of Romanesque buildings, in fact, that betray a similar complete lack of foresight on the part of the architects. Such and such a building was begun with the vague idea that it would be brought to completion in some fashion; but then it was left half-finished, since the builder had not the slightest idea how to resolve the problems he encountered. Other buildings were completed but by means evidently alien to their original conception. It plainly appears that Romanesque architects built from one day to the next; they relied on inspiration, chance, or circumstances; perhaps they even relied on miracles to help them see their projections through to completion. Even if some of the edifices were not still around to bear witness to the distress and embarrassment of their creators, we would still have all the legends about the construction of some of these buildings; these legends abound with dreams about angels or saints taking the trouble to show the architects how they should be shoring up their vaults with masonry or providing reinforcement for their pillars. None of this, of course, prevented the collapse of some of these very same structures shortly after they were built. Faith alone does not suffice to make a builder.

The architects of the end of the twelfth century, however, without perhaps being any less believers, even though most of them belonged to the laity, nevertheless did not believe it prudent to await the intervention of an angel or a saint in order to put up a building properly. It is a curious fact of history that deserves to be noted that the monastery chronicles, which recorded the histories and legends of the monks, were effusive in their praises of the buildings constructed during the Romanesque period; they tended to go on at obliging length on the subject of the grandeur of these Romanesque buildings and the beauty of their decoration. This was true of buildings that, in reality, were little more than ugly collections of building stones, poorly conceived and poorly executed. At the end of the twelfth century, however, when the practice of architecture moved out of the cloister and passed into the hands of the laity, these monkish chronicles suddenly, and quite abruptly, ceased to hold forth on the subject of buildings, except for perhaps a chance word here or a dry, laconic phrase there. On the subject of the new master builders, these chronicles had nothing at all to say.

Is it even believable, for example, that in the voluminous cartulary, or register, pertaining to the cathedral of Notre-Dame de Paris, which includes documentation dating back to the twelfth century, there should not be even one single word about the construction of the cathedral itself? We are compelled to address ourselves in the following laudatory terms to the ones responsible for such creations as this cathedral: you were diligent and intelligent artists; you came from the people; you were the first to learn how to free yourselves from traditions that were worn-out and used up; you launched yourselves frankly and knowingly into the intelligent utilization of your very real practical knowledge; you organized and taught a veritable army of skilled workers who were soon to be found spread all over western Europe. You opened up the way to progress and bold and hardy innovations in construction; you already belonged, in short, and on many counts, to modern civilization; you were among the first to adopt, along with a desire for knowledge, a spirit of the impartial research that sought such knowledge. If your contemporaries nevertheless allowed your names to be forgotten; if they failed to recognize the importance of your efforts (from which they nevertheless profited); if, indeed, those who maintain the pretension of being in charge of the arts in our day similarly try to denigrate your work—if this is the lot that is reserved for you, then, amid so many past and present injustices, may our voice at least be raised here in your favor to demand for you the place that rightly belongs to you and which only your own modesty caused to be lost. If you had been less concerned about the excellence of your work, and if, like your confreres in Italy, you had spent more time talking up your science and knowledge and promoting your own genius, perhaps we would not be forced today to rummage around in your work in order to bring to light the profound results of your experience, all the practical means you so judiciously calculated and devised; we would perhaps not have to be defending you against those who are apparently incapable of understanding that genius can indeed develop anonymously and that it may even be part of its essence to have sought the silence and obscurity that your genius did seek. The fact is, though, that we have had to defend you; we have had to defend you against those who, instead of looking at the facts, accept on faith judgments already long since rendered by passion or by interest.

We must nevertheless go on to state: today it can no longer be permitted to deal with questions of history, whether these questions touch upon politics, literature, or the arts, by means of simple affirmations or negations. Those who think they can judge these questions merely by falling back on their passions or their old habits are the ones who are retrograde. No sensible artist today would dare to maintain that we ought to build our houses today the way they were built in the twelfth or thirteenth centuries; but any fair-minded person ought to be able to understand that the experience acquired by the master builders of the times can be useful to us, and all the more so because these particular master builders were such innovators. Actually, the most difficult obstacle we have to overcome here—the real obstacle, the obstacle that will not go away—is really nothing else but our own slothful spirits. We should frankly admit this. Everybody wants to be in the know, to be knowledgeable without ever having taken the trouble to learn. Everybody wants to be able to judge without ever going to the trouble of even looking at the facts. As a result of this attitude, the truest facts, the best writings, and the most useful things are all too often only classified as outmoded; some man of wit somewhere has treated them with derision. Meanwhile the crowd is only too happy to applaud, since this spares it the trouble of trying to find out anything for itself. It is a melancholy kind of glory, after all, merely to have helped prolong the obscurity into which Gothic art had fallen. Nobody should be able to profit from such a "glory" as this in an era that prides itself on being able to throw light on everything whatsoever—an era that, unable to find sufficient nourishment in the present for its intellectual needs, insists on parading the entire past before itself as well.

If it is true that the French architecture of the Renaissance was actually superior to the Italian architecture of the fifteenth and sixteenth centuries, as some of those who have studied the matter with an enlightened critical eye maintain, does this not really appear to be the result of the fact that our schools of Gothic architecture, in spite of the abuses of the latest Gothic period, had long since succeeded in forming and training nearly everywhere skilled practitioners and intelligent executors of the art of construction? Were not these very same schools practiced in subjecting architectural forms to the test of reason? Had they not been particularly successful at opening up the minds of architects and workers and familiarizing them with the numerous problems and obstacles that always confront the builder? We are well aware that such sentiments as these will not be favorably received by those accustomed to judging the various forms of art according to their own sentiments or prejudices. In any case, it is not to such as these that we are addressing ourselves. We are rather addressing ourselves primarily to architects, to those who have already familiarized themselves at length with the resources and difficulties involved in the practice of our particular art of building. Certainly, artists trained in the study of an art in which everything is foreseen, everything is calculated—an art that, if anything, sins by its very excesses in always examining everything before acting and in always seeking the most practical possible means of execution; one, in short, in which the materials are at one and the same time both the masters of the forms employed and the subjects of the principles adopted—these artists cannot fail to develop open minds and be prepared to utilize whatever innovations the times demand.

It would take us too far afield from our present subject to try to explain here how there came to be formed, at the end of the twelfth century, a powerful new school of builders who were lay people; how this school came to be protected by the episcopate, which wanted to see the importance of the monasteries diminished; how this school enjoyed the sympathy of the people out of which it had arisen; how it embodied and reflected a wholly new and modern spirit of research and progress; how it came to be accepted by the secular feudal nobility because the latter could not find among the monks the builders who could build the habitations it wanted to have erected; and how this school, we maintain, seizing upon all these favorable circumstances that had thus presented themselves, managed to organize itself quite efficiently and to acquire thereby an unusual degree of independence. It is enough merely to point to all of these facts here in order that their importance might be appreciated; they add up to something new in the history of the arts. We have already taken note earlier of the point at which builders had arrived by about the year 1160. We have seen how they were constrained in successive steps to modify the Romanesque vault—which had been nothing else but an adulterated kind of Roman vault anyway—and introduce the wholly new kind of vault called the *ribbed vault.* Once this great step had been taken, though, there still remained much to be done. The very first result of this innovation was to oblige builders henceforth to proceed to erect their constructions by beginning with the vaults. Once this procedure came to be followed, nothing else was ever left to chance afterward, as it had so often been with their predecessors of the Romanesque period. This new method of proceeding, strange in appearance, consisted of designing the building on the ground on the basis of the vaults that were to be projected above. It is actually an eminently rational way of proceeding. What is the principal end in view when a vaulted structure is planned? To cover a given surface. What has to be done to achieve this? Establish the vaults on firm supporting structures. What is the principal object here? The vault itself. The supporting points or structures are merely means. Roman builders had been deflected from their own proper plans for their vaulted structures by the form and extent of the vaults they constructed. We speak here of a general principle only. An examination of a building plan from the late Roman Empire will not always reveal whether a given part was to be vaulted with a barrel vault, a groined vault, or a spherical dome; in many cases, any of the three are shown in exactly the same way on the plan.

This was no longer true in the twelfth century. Not only did the horizontal plan indicate the number and the form of the vaults; it indicated their diverse members as well, such as transverse arches, lateral arches, and ogival (or diagonal) arches. The nature of these various members dictated in turn the disposition of the vertical points of support, as well as their diameter and their relative height. From this it has to be concluded that, in order to trace a definitive ground plan and then to proceed to the execution of the construction, it was first necessary to make sketches of the vaults, of their *rabattements,* and of their imposts; and to know exactly what the forms and dimensions of the arch stones had to be for the various arches that were to be included. The first Gothic builders became accustomed so quickly to this method of planning a building from the top down that they used it even when constructing buildings that were not to be vaulted but merely to be roofed with planks or framed roofs. Nor did they fare so badly with this top-down method, either, as we shall see further on.

The first condition for preparing a building plan around the end of the twelfth century was to know whether the building in question needed to be vaulted, and, if so, how it needed to be vaulted. As soon as the number and direction of the arches of these vaults were known, it was then necessary to sketch the imposts on the capitals; for it was the sketch of these imposts that gave the form and dimensions of the abacuses and of the capitals themselves, as well as the number, strength, and location of the necessary vertical supporting points or structures.

Let us suppose that we have in figure 27 a room to be vaulted having inside measurements of 12 meters of width and composed of bays of 6 meters from axis to axis. Adopting the system of ribbed vaults spanned with a transverse arch, and following the method that the builders of the end of the twelfth century followed, we would have a basic procedure of tracing the lower bed of the imposts of the archs resting on points *A* and *B;* this was necessary in order to get the strength of the arch stones. We accept that these arch stones must have, in order to cover a room of that size, 40 centimeters of width and height; and we recognize that the various arches of a vault were almost always put together with

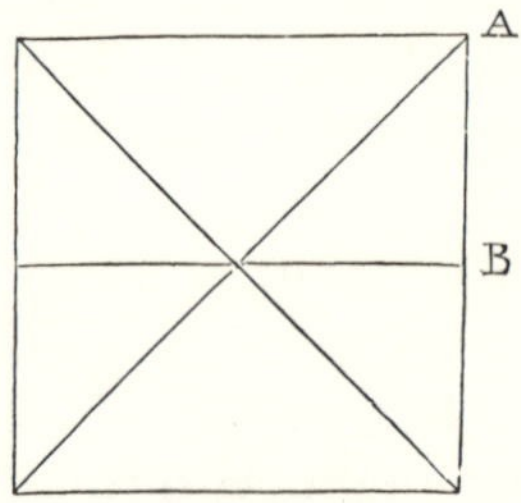

Figure 27

arch stones that were similar as to dimensions and as to form as well. We also recognize that the lateral arches, originating much higher than the transverse and diagonal arches, supported by columns, often exceeded the level of the imposts of these arches. Finally, we recognize that in tracing the bed of the imposts of the transverse and diagonal arches, we must take into account the crossing of the column carrying a lateral arch, as we must also take into account the lateral arch itself. Let figure 28 be the detail of the horizontal trace of the arches originating at *B;* at this point only one transverse arch and two lateral arches spring. The latter,

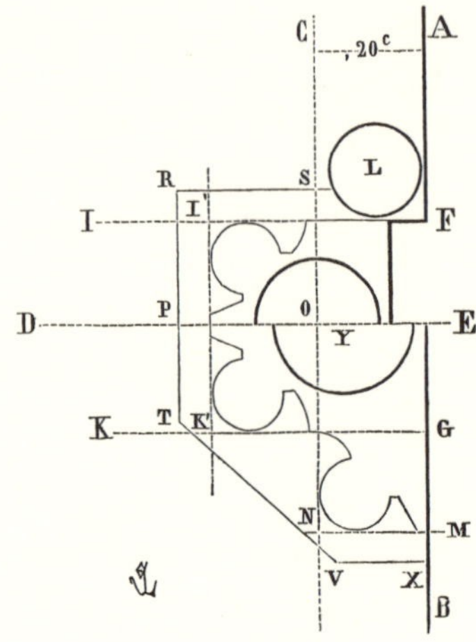

Figure 28

the lateral arches, govern here, for the transverse arch must be disengaged from the lateral arches from its very point of origin. Let *AB* be the surface of the wall; the lateral arch, customarily, has a projection half of the width of the diagonal arch or the transverse when these two arches have a comparable section, and half of the diagonal arch when these arches have a different section. In the present case, the lateral arch has 20 centimeters of projection from the surface of the wall. At *C* we draw a line parallel to *AB*. Since the axis of the transverse arch is *DE,* and points *F* and *G* are each 20 centimeters from that axis, we draw two parallel lines, *FI* and *GK,* which give us the width of the transverse arch. Carrying 40 centimeters from *F* to *I,* we get the height between the intrados and the extrados. We are then able to trace the appropriate profile in the square *FI'K'G,* and this is the lower bed of the impost. Where the column carrying the lateral arch rises above the level of this bed, as indicated at *L,* as is sometimes the case—as, for example, in the church of Nesle (Oise)—the lateral arch springs from the capital supporting the transverse arch; in that case, carrying from the axis *DE* 40 centimeters on the line *AB* gives us the point *M,* and we inscribe the profile of the lateral arch in the parallelogram *EONM*. It is understood that this lateral arch will penetrate a few centimeters into the wall. Once this lower bed of the impost has been found in the way we have indicated, it is then necessary to trace the abacus of the capital, of which the profile must form a projection around the springing of the arches. If the lateral arch is carried on a column rising to its point of origination, as marked at *L,* the abacus *PRS* goes back squarely to be absorbed against the column, *L,* of the lateral arch. If, on the contrary, the profile of the lateral arch goes all the way down to the capital of the transverse arch, the abacus assumes the figure *PTVX* on the horizontal plan. In order to trace the column under the capital, in the first case, from the summit of the right angle, *R,* of the abacus, we draw a line of 45 degrees; this line comes to meet the axis *DE* at a point, *O,* that is the center of the column; to this is given a diameter such that the projection of the abacus on the surface of this column must be greater than the radius of the column. There then remains, between the column and the surface, *AB,* of the wall, an empty space that needs to be filled with a pilaster concealed by this column and by the column of the lateral arch. In order to trace the column under the capital, in the second case, we take a center *Y* on the axis *DE* in such a way that the projection of the abacus on the surface of the column will be greater than half its diameter; in this case, the capital will be a pendant or corbel and will be more flared under the lateral arch than under the face of the transverse one.

Let us take from figure 27 the springing, or origination, point, *A,* of the two lateral arches, of the two diagonal arches, and of the transverse arch. Let *AB* (figure 28-II) be the surface of the wall, and *CD* the guiding line of the diagonal arch. We trace the

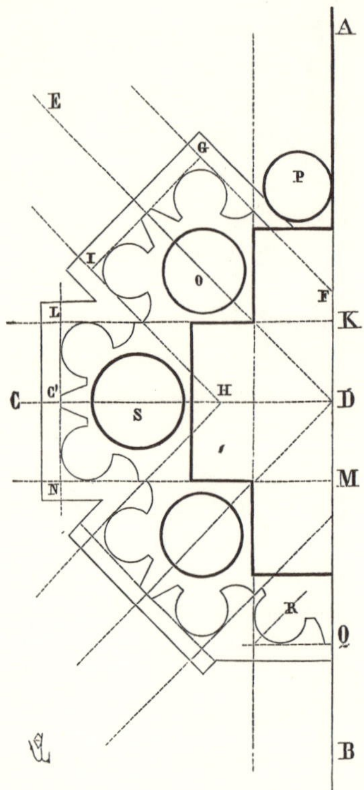

Figure 28-II

projection of the lateral arch in the same manner as above. The diagonal arches govern the transverse arch. From each side of the line *DE* we go out 20 centimeters and draw two parallel lines, *FG* and *HI;* this gives us the width of the diagonal arch. From point *H,* the meeting point of the line *HI* with the axis *CD,* we take 45 centimeters, that is, little more than the height of the arch stones of the diagonal arch, and then we draw the perpendicular *IG,* which gives the face of the diagonal arch. In the parallelogram *FGIH,* we trace the appropriate profile. From the two sides of the axis *CD,* taking the same 20 centimeters, we draw two parallels *KL* and *MN.* From the point *H,* carrying 40 centimeters on the axis *CD* from *H* to *C,* we draw a perpendicular line *LN* to that axis, which gives us the face of the transverse arch, so we inscribe this profile. At *P* we suppose that the column supporting the lateral arch will go beyond the point of origination, or springing, of the transverse and diagonal arches. At *R* we accept as we did before that the profile of the lateral arch will fall vertically on the abacus of the capital. In order to trace this lateral arch, in this last case, we go 40 centimeters on the line *AB,* from point *M* to point *Q;* and at this point *Q,* drawing a line perpendicular to the line *AB,* we have the parallelogram inscribing the profile of the lateral arch; the abacuses of the capitals are traced parallel with the faces of the arches, as our figure shows. From the summits *G* and *L,* drawing lines at 45-degree angles, we meet with the axis *DE* at *O,* which is the center of the column supporting the diagonal arches, and with the axis *CD* at *S,* which is the center of the column of the transverse arches. We trace these columns in conformity with the rule established above. Behind these isolated pillars appear the returns of the pilasters that reinforce the wall; the lateral arch, *R,* is sprung on a face of these pilasters, which carry a capital just like the columns.

Often the lateral arches do not come down to the abacus of the capitals of the great arches; nor do they have a supporting column coming all the way up from below; instead they originate on a smaller column resting on the lateral projection of the abacus, as indicated in figure 29, both on the ground plan and in the illustration. In this situation, the abacuses of these smaller lateral columns are cut in such a way that their oblique face, *CD,* is perpendicular to the guiding line, *B,* of the diagonal arches; they are divided into two equal parts by that guiding line.

With all of this, it is still necessary to recognize that only gradually did builders decide to project the forms, direction, and members of their vaults down onto the ground plans of their buildings. For a long time they continued to maintain monocylindrical piers at the ground-floor level. From the end of the twelfth century on, though, what preoccupied them was constant and rigorous observation of a principle of construction that up to that time had not been considered a necessary principle of construction at all. The principle was that of the equilibrium of forces; it had now been substituted for the principle of inert stability, which had been so successfully practiced by the Romans but which the Romanesque builders had unsuccessfully attempted to maintain in their huge vaulted edifices composed of several naves. Recognizing the impossibility of giving to isolated, freestanding piers a foundation strong enough to resist the thrust of the vaults, the builders of the twelfth century decided to cut clean; they decided to look elsewhere for their means of resistance. They no longer accepted that freestanding piers should be anything but vertical points of support, maintained not by their own foundations but by the laws of equilibrium. Employed on that basis, the piers needed only to be strong enough to resist pressure from a vertical direction. Even when a principle such as this becomes accepted, however, there still remains a certain period of time during which it is first being applied when there is still considerable indecision and trial and error. It never happens that old traditions are simply abandoned from one day to the next.

Figure 29

In devising the ribbed vault constructed on a square plan and lying across transverse arches, the builders looked for other points of support spaced at right angles to the principal thrusts and hence against every other pier. In figure 27, point *A* carries the burden and receives the thrusts both of a transverse arch and of two diagonal arches, while point *B* carries the burden and receives the thrust only of a transverse arch. This system of vault construction, adapted during the second half of the twelfth century, required builders to raise under point *A* stronger piers than under point *B,* and to give to the arch stones of the principal transverse arches falling on point *A* a width and thickness greater than those given to the arch stones for the diagonal arches and for the secondary transverse arches. It is worth remarking about the original Gothic vaults, as we have already indicated, that the stones of all the arches generally present the same section.

The pointed equilateral arch was so aptly dictated by the need to diminish thrusts and to resist loads that we see in the original Gothic structures such broken arches adopted only for the transverse arches and the lower archivolts, while the semicircular arch was preserved for use in the bays of the windows, for the ornamental arcades of the galleries, and even for the lateral arches, all of which carried only weak loads and did not have great width or span. The cathedral of Noyon, the original vaults of which were constructed around 1160,* had lateral arches, typical of that era, which were semicircular arches. Similarly, the cathedral of Sens, which was built around the same time, was furnished with semicircular lateral arches,** while, at the same time, the transverse arches and archivolts were pointed equilateral arches. The same thing is true of the abbey church of Vézelay, constructed at the end of the twelfth century; the lateral arches were constructed as semicircular arches. In the case of these edifices, and of the cathedral of Sens in particular, the piers under the combined loads of the diagonal arches and the transverse arches present an elaborate horizontal section composed of engaged fascicular columns;

*These original vaults were rebuilt in the thirteenth century under the great nave except for the original lateral arches, which were left in place. [Author's note]

**These lateral arches were reworked at the end of the thirteenth century, as can still be recognized in the bays of the apse. [Author's note] under the load of the single transverse arch, however, the piers are twin monocylindrical columns placed perpendicularly to the axis of the nave. At Noyon the intermediate transverse arches were originally placed on a single column, before the reconstruction of the vaults. However, the nave of the cathedral of Sens is much wider than that of the cathedral of Noyon, and, in general, its construction is much sturdier. This disposition of vaults, consisting of two bays for each vault and concentrating the loads and the thrusts on every other one of the piers, permitted builders from the very beginning to limit the placing of their flying buttresses against every other pier only. It is quite probable that this was the case for the cathedrals both of Sens and of Noyon, as it was for the cathedral of Paris. The fact that these first two cathedrals were redone in the thirteenth century, however, makes absolute certainty on this point impossible. What we can be quite certain of, however, is that at the end of the twelfth century builders fell back upon the flying buttress because they had to; they tried to avoid making this decision as long as possible; they still mistrusted this device and had not yet come to see both its strengths and its advantages; they still regarded it as a kind of auxiliary feature or as a resource to be resorted to only when absolutely necessary, and, indeed, sometimes, only afterward, as insurance, or when they belatedly recognized that they could not get along without it. The best proof we can offer for what we are saying here is what happened a few years later. Architects definitively adopted a new system based on the equilibrium of forces; they used this system on buildings with three naves, regularly opposing the thrusts of vaults with flying buttresses. But by then they were also using flying buttresses even for arches that had little or no thrust. They also replaced the flying buttresses of the twelfth century, which had probably been both insufficient for the purpose they were expected to serve and badly placed as well. They replaced them with flying buttresses that were both new and well designed from the standpoint of resistance to pressure.

Before going further we need to indicate to the reader something about the construction procedures that were followed, as well as something about the nature and dimensions of the building materials employed. We saw at the beginning of this particular article how the original Romanesque builders did their masonry work; it consisted of rubble fillings enclosed within dressed freestone facings or facings of dressed small building stones. The

Gothic builders of the twelfth century modified some of the procedures that the Romanesque builders had used. Since they were constructing edifices that were greater in extent as well as raised up higher than those of the Romanesque period, and, at the same time, since these builders were trying to diminish the thicknesses of their piers and walls, they needed on the one hand to develop a mode of construction that was more homogeneous and resistant; and, on the other hand, they needed to avoid the expense of the vast manpower that the hoisting up of a large volume of heavy materials would have required in the case of buildings that were already being raised up to great heights. They therefore generally dropped the use of courses of large stones in construction (except in very particular cases or in the case of exceptional buildings); and they typically used courses of small building stones. They came to prefer the small building stones to the large freestones. As much as possible the greater part of the stones they used for wall facings or for the arch stones of archivolts, transverse arches, and diagonal arches were of small enough dimensions to be hoisted up into place on a man's back and laid down by a mason like our ordinary small building stones. Once this method came to be adopted, the use of these courses of small building stones came to exemplify structures that were very well constructed in the technical sense and possessed a judicious blending among all the elements of their construction. It amounted to a kind of middle way between the old Roman procedure of laying down courses of large dressed stones and the procedure of using rubble stones faced with revetments of brick or small building stones. In adopting the use of courses of small building stones for very large edifices, the builders of the twelfth century had too much good sense simply to lay them down in low and shallow courses, without mortar, as was the case with certain Romanesque edifices. The Gothic builders separated their courses with joints and beds of thick mortar (one to two centimeters thick) in order to establish a firm bond between the interior mass of the masonry and the facings. This was the former Roman method and it was an excellent method. It will be understood that, as in figure 30, if courses of stones without mortar are laid down in front of a mass of masonry consisting of rubble stones and mortar, this mass will come to be compressed as a result of the drying of the mortar under the load it is carrying; in that case, a vertical breakage will occur behind the facing at *AB* because the volume of the unmortared courses of stones piled surface to surface upon each other is unable to give anywhere; the facing will thus soon fall down as a result of the rupture. In figure 30-II, however, care has been taken to lay down a bed of thick mortar between each course or layer of stones, and hence not only will the fused or joined mass of masonry hold the stone course in place; it will permit these courses to undergo compression equal to the compression undergone by the mass of masonry inside.

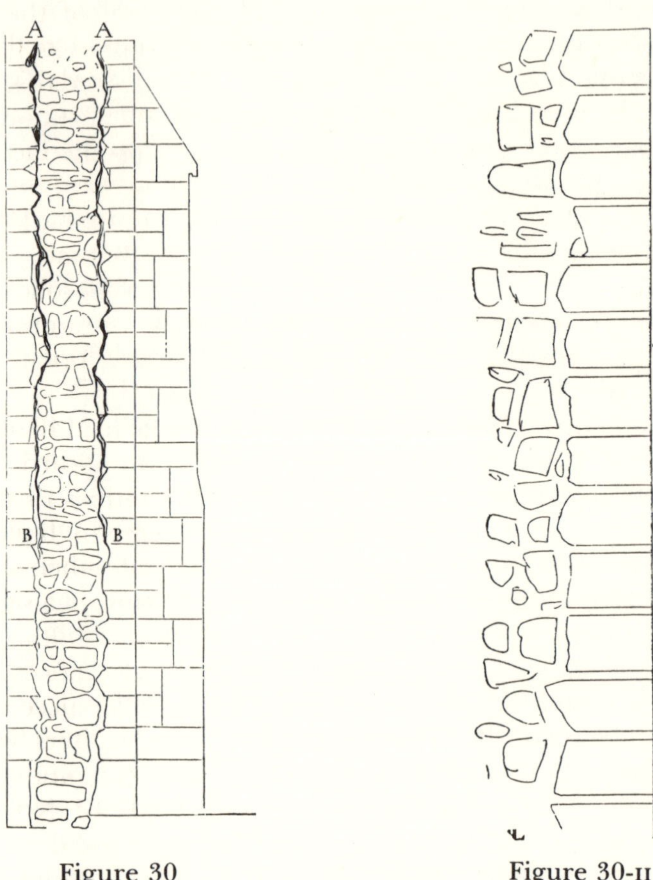

Figure 30 Figure 30-II

The original Romanesque builders, especially in those regions where large and hard building stones were available, for example, in Burgundy, Franche-Comté, Alsace, or along the Rhône and the Saône, did not fail to ape the Roman use of courses of large stones in construction; they laid down square stones that were both wide and tall, virtually flagstones or paving stones, in fact, in front of their wall fillings. However, they generally paid dearly for trying to make their construction look like something other than it was. In the majority of these buildings ruptures and breakages occurred between the facings and the fillings of the walls; longitudinal cracks and splits manifested themselves, which at the very least meant serious trouble; too often they meant ruin. These kinds of damaging effects occurred more frequently and dangerously the higher the buildings were. Better advised and taught in the hard school of experience, the architects of the twelfth century adopted a method using very low courses or layers of stone separated by thick beds of mortar; they adopted this method as much for reasons of economy and facility of execution as they did to avoid the defects of homogeneity between the facings and the fillings that we have described. The thick beds of mortar not only had the effect of compressing and binding the facings to the fillings; the mortar itself was made out of rich lime, and thus reached its consistency slowly, while awaiting perfect solidification. The entire construction thus had time to settle without undergoing any deformation and without causing any breaks in the masonry.

The buildings that were constructed between 1140 and 1200 in the Île-de-France, Beauvoisis, Soissonnais, the Picardy, Champagne, and Normandy provinces employed courses of masonry so small that it never fails to cause surprise. For the buildings in those areas were already starting to be vast in scale; their structure was complicated (even though they already possessed a significant lightness and airiness). To employ dressed small building stones as one's principal construction material in vast edifices such as these was really quite an audacious innovation; to succeed in the enterprise pointed to the existence of some builders who had become highly skilled in their profession. If we examine with care the twelfth-century portions of the cathedrals of Noyon and Senlis, and of a great number of the churches in the departments of the Oise, Seine, Seine-et-Oise, Seine-et-Marne, Marne, Seine-Intérieure, etc., we will be amazed at how the builders dared to raise up buildings to such great heights while employing means of construction that seem so fragile. Yet the stability of such buildings had by then become assured. If a fair number of them nevertheless had to undergo alterations of some kind, this was almost always as a result of particular accidents such as fires, lack of maintenance, or later loads or burdens placed upon them. Of all the buildings in this particular category, the cathedral of Noyon, built between 1150 and 1190, is one of the most excellent as well as one of the best preserved. Except for the columns, the large capitals, the imposts, and a few other exceptional features, the entire edifice is composed of small building stones without great resistance.

It is possible to get a good idea of this building from figure 31, which shows a part of the interior twin bays of the nave. The isolated small columns of the first gallery level, those of the small upper triforium, and those separating the high windows are all monoliths made out of hard stone laid up against the grain. The small triple columns, *A*, which, however, before the rebuilding of the vaults in the thirteenth century, received the transverse arch of the intersection of the diagonal and lateral arches, are composed of large pieces laid up against the grain and held with spaced clamps to *T*. The columns were set in place after the entire construction had been compressed; for that reason these columns are nothing but decoration; they carry nothing. The foundation of the capital and the impost—both engaged in the masonry—suffices to maintain the arch stones of the transverse arch. At *B* we have an indication of the point of origination, or springing, of the old diagonal arches of the great ribbed vault; and at *C*, that of the lateral arch behind the diagonal ones. It is worth remarking that here, as in the majority of the churches built at that time in the neighboring provinces of the Île-de-France, and, notably, in the Beauvoisis, the piers that carry the springing of the diagonal and transverse arches are very much stronger than those that support merely a simple crossing transverse arch. In other words, as the plan reproduced here indicates, the piers, *D*, are composed of a bundle of joined columns, while the intermediate piers, *E*, are monocylindrical columns at the ground-floor level with a bundle of small columns, *A*, resting on them and extending upward. The extreme lightness of this kind of construction, as well as the facility with which all the materials of which it is composed were cut and fashioned, raised up, and put in place, explain how, even with slender resources, the twelfth-century builders could already think of constructing buildings of vast compass raised high above the level of the ground. Today we have gotten into the habit of using hulking, enormous masses of stone in constructions that are themselves of minor importance; we have gotten into the habit, in other words, of putting in place structures with ten times the

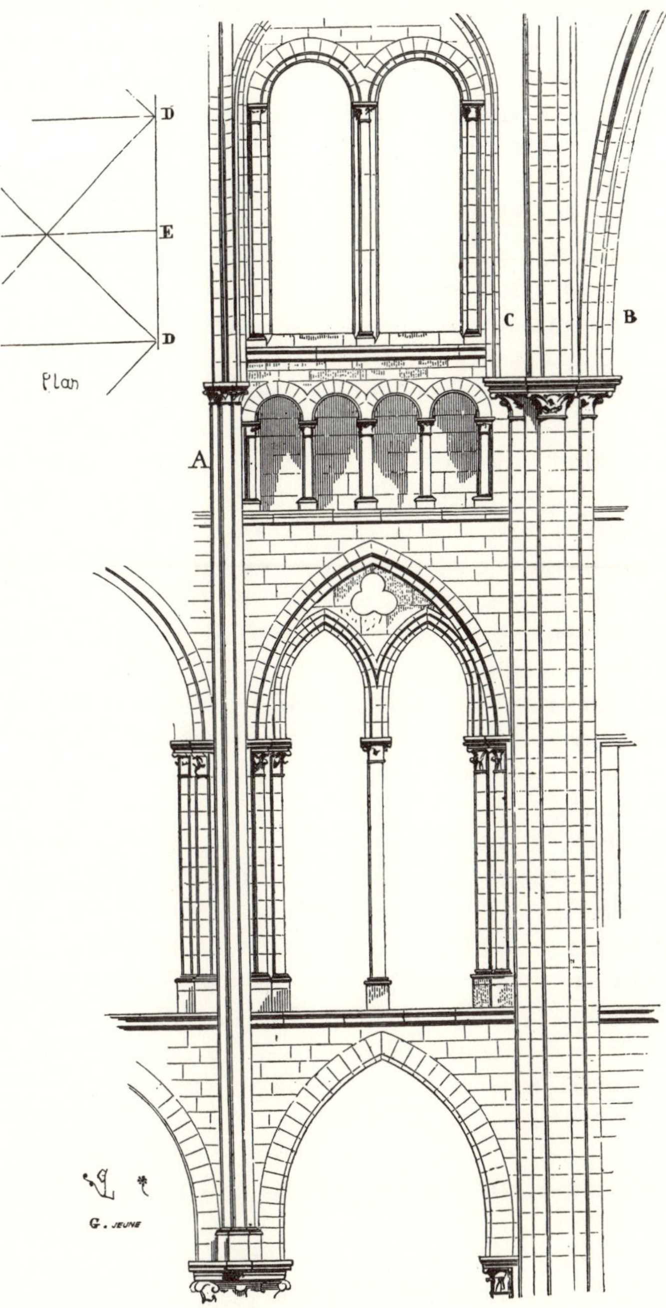

Figure 31

resistance that is necessary. We would never have dared to undertake the building of a cathedral of the scope and dimensions of the cathedral of Noyon with the exiguous means that the Gothic builders had at their disposition. We would expend fabulous sums in order to equal what in the twelfth century builders were able to accomplish with comparatively minimal resources. We would find this kind of construction expensive because we are now unwilling to employ the kinds of construction materials and procedures then in use. Despite all this, the cathedral of Noyon has been in place for seven centuries, and, if it continues to be appropriately maintained, could well last at least another five hundred years. Twelve hundred years, in fact, seems to be a reasonable span of time for a building to last. The great social revolutions to which humanity is always prone will take appropriate pains to see that buildings are eventually destroyed even if they are constructed with the idea of having them last for an even longer period.

Beyond the advantages of economy and ease in the procurement of materials, as well as ease in the execution of the work, the type of construction using smaller individual components was eminently in accord with the ideas of the architects of the twelfth century. These light buildings feature ground plans with a remarkably reduced patio between solid structure and open space. These structures were subject to oblique pressures, and hence the law of the equilibrium of forces is what governed them, in place of the old Roman law of inert stability; it was also essential that all their members enjoy a certain elasticity. Where builders less well versed in the new architectural principles attempted to reproduce the mere common forms of the new architecture of these lay artists of the twelfth century, without understanding the reasons that these forms had developed as they had, and where these less knowledgeable builders also tried to use larger individual components, lacerations quickly occurred that shattered the total equilibrium of their buildings. If the arches were not completely independent one from another; if at some point materials of great height were used, while, next to them, small stones of standard dimensions were used; if the various parts were too rigid or too tightly embedded in the masses of masonry; or if the materials were too heavy—in all these cases, the resistance provided was as likely as not to cause breakages or cracks. Indeed, in all these cases, the solid portions of the construction could have the effect of crushing or dragging down the weaker portions. We need to take note of the fact that, in these kinds of buildings, the piers of a weak horizontal section received the entire load; precisely because of the small surface of their foundations, these piers became more compressed than, for example, the walls (since the latter carried no load, and had even been relieved of the weight of the roof and the upper masses of masonry by the lateral arches).

If, in this system, there was a complete, rigid solidity or interdependence between the vertical points of support that carried the loads and the corresponding structural fillings, enclosing walls, and walls that did not enclose, then breakage was almost inevitable. If, on the other hand, the builders took the trouble to ensure that everything that carried a load maintained its own independent function, could move independently, and could be freely compressed; and that the accessory parts were merely enclosing walls independent of pressure or thrust—then breakage could not occur. In these latter cases, the state of disconnectedness actually favored the longevity of the construction rather than being harmful to it.

The Romans who had opposed thrusts with passive resistance alone nevertheless had recognized perfectly this principle of disconnectedness—the principle of a freedom among all the parts of a vaulted construction destined to carry actual loads and among those parts not destined to carry any load. The great ancient Roman baths were actually masterpieces of this type of composite construction. The entire system was based upon piers that carried vaults; walls were merely partitions, which could have been added as an afterthought; these walls could have been removed without harming in any way the solidity of the basic framework or skeleton of the building. The principles upon which this system was based were very simple and very natural. Why not always make use of them then? In fact, the Gothic builders carried these principles much further than the Romans ever had; the Gothic builders did so, as we have several times remarked, because they had adopted a system of construction where every force in play was an active force; where inert resistances acting through compact masses were simply nonexistent.

Once they had decided to erect such great buildings with such light materials and with functional parts occupying so little of the total surface, opposing oblique thrusts with obstacles of active rather than passive resistance, the Gothic builders of the twelfth century did not require a great deal of time before they learned the lesson that they still had to find some inert stability somewhere. If they then decided to erect flying buttresses against the walls at the points where the arches exerted their thrusts, these flying buttresses needed an immobile foundation if they were to fulfill their function properly. This foundation proved to be the external buttresses—the outside vertical piers where all the thrusts eventually ended up. However, to give to these buttresses a horizontal section broad enough to preserve the immobility of their mass at a great height would have been to encumber the outside of their buildings with huge masses of heavy masonry, which would have intercepted both light and air and would have been very expensive. Builders no longer possessed the recipe for the Roman mortars that had served as the principal effective agent for massive Roman construction. Moreover, any piers that the builders might have been able to erect would have lacked the necessary cohesion. The problem was thus to substitute for the inert resistance provided by the strong Roman points of support a force that was just as resistant but was derived from some other principle. The means the builders hit upon to solve this problem was to load down the points of support destined to receive thrusts with weight sufficient to resist the action of the thrusts. It is not necessary to be a builder in order to understand that a prismatic or cylindrical support composed of layers superimposed one on the other up to a height more than twelve times its diameter cannot stand, unless it is loaded down at the top. The Gothic builders believed they had found in this well-known law of statics the means to erect structures on very slender points of support so long as the latter were charged from above with weights capable of making them rigid enough to resist both contrary and oblique thrusts.

Let us take a pier, *AB,* as shown in figure 32, acted upon by two contrary oblique thrusts, *CD* and *EF,* acting from different heights. The stronger thrust, *CD,* is 10 on a scale; the weaker thrust, *EF,* amounts to 4 on the same scale. If we charge the head of the pier, *B,* with a weight equivalent to 12, not only will the thrust *CD* be canceled out, but, *a fortiori,* so will the thrust *EF,* and the pier will therefore maintain its equilibrium and uprightness. Since they were not able to charge the piers of their naves with a load sufficient to cancel out the thrusts of the great vaults, the builders decided to oppose the thrust *CD* with a flying buttress, *G.* From that point, the weight *BO,* augmented with the pressure

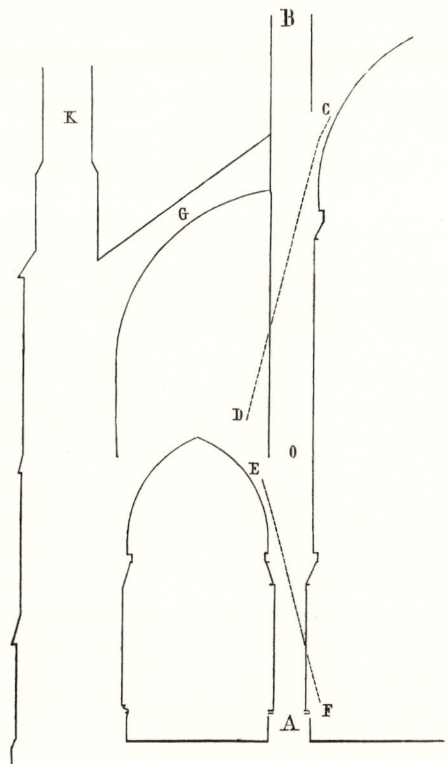

Figure 32

CD, becomes 15, and then, for example, the thrust of *EF* is canceled out. If the flying buttress *G* opposes the thrust *CD* with a resistance equal to its oblique pressure and thus completely neutralizes it, then the thrust *CD* becomes a vertical action on the pier *AB,* and there is no need to maintain the oblique action of the flying buttress against the exterior buttress. However, if this oblique action amounts to 8 on our scale, it is not augmented by the totality of the thrust *CD,* but only by a small part of that thrust; it is 10 on the scale, or perhaps 12 in certain cases. The external buttress, by its own mass, provides a resistance of 8, and hence it suffices to charge it with a weight amounting to 5 in order to maintain the general equilibrium of the building.

We must be very careful not to imagine that we can resolve these questions of equilibrium with algebraic formulas. Such formulas were constantly modified in practice by reason of the materials employed, the height or thickness or each layer of stones, the quality of the mortar, the resistance of the ground, the action of various external agents, and the amount of care taken in the course of the construction. Formulas are good for the purpose of demonstrating the knowledge of the one who formulates them, but they are almost always useless to the true practitioner of the art of construction, who allows himself to be guided by his instinct, his experience, and the observations he himself has made, as well as by the innate "feel" any true practitioner has about the right thing to do in any particular circumstance. We cannot ever hope to make builders out of those to whom nature has denied this innate quality of having a "feel" for construction, although we can help develop the instincts of those who do possess it. It is not really possible to teach either common sense or right reason, but it is possible to learn how to make use of the former and pay close attention to the latter.

The study of Gothic construction is useful because this study cannot be conducted through the mere consideration of abstract formulas; the latter are always neglected in the actual execution of any work by an experienced practitioner; to accord to error the confidence that truth alone ought to inspire is perhaps the least possible danger here.

Even though Gothic construction is not subject to absolute formulas, though, it is the slave to certain principles. All of its efforts and improvements tend toward the conversion of its principles into general laws. Indeed, this is the result that actually is attained. What are these principles? They include equilibrium; forces of compression and consolidation opposed to forces of separation and dispersion; stability obtained by loads that reduce the diverse forces acting obliquely by transforming them into vertical weight; and, as a consequence, the reduction of the horizontal sections of the supporting points or structures. These are the principles in question, and they remain, in fact, the principles of modern construction. By the latter, of course, we do not mean those types of construction that blindly seek to reproduce buildings originally erected in conditions very different from those of our own civilization, serving needs very different from our own; we mean those that respond to our contemporary needs as well as to our social system. If the Gothic builders had disposed of the same kind of cast iron in large segments that we do, they would no doubt have seized upon the use of this material, confident that it would enable them to construct supporting structures as slender and at the same time as firm as possible; perhaps they would have used cast iron more skillfully than we do. All their efforts tended toward the equilibrium of forces; they came to consider supporting points or structures as nothing more than vertical members of a total framework maintained in place not by the solidity of their own foundations but rather by a complete neutralizing of the oblique forces acting on them. Do we build otherwise in those of our constructions where practical needs silence the habit and routine that would frown on this type of construction? If there is one thing that should surprise us today, it is to observe, constructed at one and the same time and in one and the same city, houses, markets, railroad stations, and commercial buildings all standing up on their vertical supports and covering large internal spaces, yet with scarcely any appreciable foundations beneath their functional parts—all of them side by side with massive edifices constructed out of enormous blocks of stone piled one on the other in order to cover comparatively minimal inside spaces and to carry horizontal beams that exert no oblique pressure at all. Does not such a surprising spectacle as this indicate that architecture today has gone off the tracks? Does it not appear that it has reached a point where it is practiced virtually in isolation from the real needs of today? Even from our own genius of today? Indeed, does not architecture actually seem, by its practice, to be complaining about or even denying these modern needs and this modern genius? Can the time be far off when the public, impatient with an architecture that continues to scorn its own public—a public that, after all, has its own preferences, which certainly do not include great concern for maintaining classical traditions—will come to classify the architect along with the archaeologist as someone capable of nothing beyond perhaps enriching our museums and libraries with their scholarly lucubrations or diverting small coteries of initiates with sterile discussions? By contrast, we cannot repeat too often that Gothic-type construction, in spite of its defects, its errors, its experiments—indeed, perhaps because of all these things—remains an eminently useful subject of study; it constitutes the surest kind of initiation into a modern type of art that does not yet exist and that is still seeking its proper way. The reason for this is that Gothic construction lays down true principles to which we must still adhere even today. It dared to break with the tradition of antiquity; it remains endlessly fecund in its applications. It is not of great importance whether or not a pinnacle happens to be covered with ornaments that are not to the taste of this or that school of art, if that pinnacle possesses its own reason for being, if it performs a necessary function, and if it allows us to take up less space on the public thoroughfare. It is not of great importance if a broken arch seems shocking to the narrow partisans of antiquity, if this type of arch turns out to be more solid and more resistant than the semicircular arch, and if it spares us the necessity of piling up huge blocks of stone. It is not of great importance whether columns have 20 or 30 different diameters, if those columns suffice to hold up our vault or our ceiling. The beautiful, in the case of an art that is necessarily one both of convention and of reason, is not eternally linked to a single form; the beautiful can reside wherever form becomes an integral expression of a satisfied need and a judicious use of the available building materials. So what if the crowd only descries the external adornments of Gothic architecture, and notices at the same time that this particular type of decoration is not exactly a type of adornment typical of our own times? Does this mean that the principles that went into this type of construction are incapable of any further applications? It would be just about as valid to assert that a geometric treatise was valueless because it was printed in Gothic type and that the students studying it and learning things such as that "angles opposite to the apex are equal to each other" were in reality acquiring knowledge that was nothing but foolishness and were being led astray—all because it was printed in Gothic type. The truth is, however, that if we can still teach geometry from books written in the past, we can also teach construction from the successful practice of it in the past. Indeed, we must necessarily seek principles of construction where they have actually been realized, namely, in buildings that have actually been built. As for the particular textbook in stone that we call "Gothic," however strange its style and its varieties may appear, it is at least as worthy as any such practical handbook, especially when we consider the degree to which it was governed by reason.

There is no other architecture in which we will find so many ingenious and practical features devised to deal with the many obstacles and difficulties that faced the original Gothic builders in the midst of a society whose particular needs were extremely if not excessively complex. Gothic construction was not, as was the construction of antiquity, something all of a piece, fixed and absolute in its ends and its means; instead it was supple, free, and of an inquiring, problem-solving nature, just as the modern mind is. The principles of Gothic construction allowed it to make use of all the different kinds of building materials supplied by nature or industry according to the qualities that these materials possessed. Gothic construction never allowed itself to be stymied by difficulties; its principal characteristic was to be ingenious. This word tells all: ingenious. The Gothic builders were subtle craftsmen; they were ardent and indefatigable workers; they constantly made use of their native reasoning powers; they were free and easy in the procedures they followed; and they were always avid in seizing upon new things or new ways to go. All these characteristics—whether we consider them good qualities or defects—certainly put these builders squarely in the camp of modern civilization. They were not monks subject to fixed rules or traditions; they were laity in the habit of subjecting everything they touched to firsthand analysis; they recognized no law beyond reason. Nor did the faculty of reason as they understood it even necessarily bow before the laws of nature; for if they were of course obliged to accept the laws of nature, they did so only to transcend them by opposing them one with another. If this is a defect, is it fitting for us to be reproaching them for it?

It is to be hoped that we will be pardoned for this digression; it has been necessary to help understand the meaning of a type of construction of which we are also presenting many concrete examples. Our readers will more readily appreciate the efforts of the Gothic builders, and the reactions those efforts have provoked, if they also understand the general tendencies and the independent spirit of the Gothic builders, and understand how patiently they labored in a society that was just beginning to be formed. Perhaps readers will discover, as we have, that these builders were actually bold innovators whose audacity was that of the modern outlook itself—distracted somewhat, in their case, though not stifled, by habit and routine, exclusivist doctrines, and the kind of prejudices that accompany attachment to a ready-made system.

At the beginning of this article we saw the extent to which ancient Roman construction was uniformly excellent, wise, coordinated; it resembled the social constitution of the Roman Empire itself; once it was set upon a path it marched forward with a sure step, following the same invariable laws of construction and employing the same means of execution up until the time of the late empire. All this was good and admirable; but it was also incapable of transforming anything. It was a principal strength of the Romans to have been able to maintain their social constitution in the face of the most obvious symptoms of dissolution. The same thing was true of Roman architecture. Under the last pagan emperors, taste deteriorated, and so did execution. However, the construction remained the same; the Roman building was still a Roman building. Except for the spherical vault resting on pendentives, which appeared in Byzantium at a time when the Roman Empire was hastening to its end, there was no further progress in Roman construction, no transformation of anything, no new effort of any kind. The Romans built the way bees construct their hives; the result was a marvel, yet today's hives are no different from those of the days of Noah. If we presented the architects of the Baths of Titus with castings, wrought iron, sheet metal, wood, and glass, and then asked them to construct a covered market out of them for us, they would reply that it was impossible to construct anything out of such materials. The modern genius, though, is something else again: if we asked a typical modern man to build us a room with a twenty-meter opening out of cardboard, he would not simply tell us that the thing was impossible; he would try to do what was asked; he would invent some means to lend greater rigidity to cardboard; and we can be fairly sure that he would ultimately construct the desired room.

The Roman drew the plans of his building with great good sense; he established all the necessary bases; and then he proceeded with great assurance to carry out his prearranged task. He suffered no disquietude in the course of his execution of the work; he was certain in advance of what the result of his efforts would be. He had taken all the necessary precautions; he went securely about his construction work. Nothing could disturb or deflect him; he had already forestalled all possible eventualities. His building would go up on unshakable foundations, and he could sleep soundly during the entire process. What could possibly have been lacking to him? The proper place to build? He simply took it over. Building materials? He could get them from anywhere; if nature failed to provide them, he would manufacture them. Did he ever lack manpower, transport, or money? No, he appropriated them as needed; he was the master of the world, after all. The Roman was indeed a superhuman kind of being; he possessed something of the measured grandeur that we ascribe to the divinity. Nothing could stand in the way of his power. He built as he wished, where he wished, at a place chosen by him, and with the help of manpower blindly subject to his will. Why would he go out of his way to create difficulties for himself? Why would he bother to invent machines to raise water up to great heights when he could simply follow rivers back to their sources in the mountains and then pipe water into the city, and this across whatever distance, by means of a natural slope? Why, in short, would the Roman choose to struggle against the regular order of the things of this world? For this world, in effect, both human and material, belonged to him.

The error of the early Middle Ages was to believe that it was still possible in the state of anarchy into which society had fallen by then to replicate exactly what the Romans had done. Thus, while this transitional era was still trying to drag itself along after the Romans, what powerlessness! What poverty! Then the spirit of modern society began to emerge; instead of the vain desire to try to revive a dead civilization, there emerged a spirit of antagonism among men and a combative attitude against material nature itself. Society itself was broken up; the individual was thrown back upon his own responsibility. All existing authority was constantly being challenged, because all existing powers were constantly fighting with each other; each existing power found itself victorious only by turns. Discussions went on, as well as searches; new hopes were constantly being raised. From the debris of antiquity it was not at first the arts that were exhumed but rather philosophy, the knowledge of things. Already in the twelfth century, it was to the Greek philosophers that elite spirits went to look for their intellectual weapons. As a result this society, even though it still remained so miserable and imperfect, was nevertheless still functioning in the real world that existed around it; its natural instincts served it well; it extracted from the remains of the past that which could enlighten it and help it make progress. The clergy fought vainly against these tendencies. In spite of all the feudal power the religious arm possessed, it was itself actually drawn in to the new movement; everywhere there grew up a spirit of examination, discussion, and critical analysis. In that era everything that tended to diminish one power was likely to be upheld by some rival power. The national genius profited enormously from these rivalries; this genius was still in the process of formation; it became emboldened. Always dominated materially, it made itself independent morally; it followed its own path, picking its way among the battles that were constantly going on around it between powers that were not enlightened enough to demand from the intelligent people who were then emerging anything other than a material submission. Many writers before us have pointed out, with greater authority than we can claim, how political history, the history of the powers that be, as customarily written, presents only one narrow aspect of the total history of peoples. Illustrious authors of our own day have shown that it is not possible to understand the life of peoples, their development, and the causes of their various transformations as well as of their progress, without digging deeply into all aspects of their lives. And it is quite true that a history that comprehends all of the members of a particular society has never been written. Around the midpoint of the Middle Ages, though, there arose a class that was vital, active, and intelligent, a class that, at the same time, was not involved in all the wars, the politics, and the trade that customarily went on and attracted so much attention. This new class assumed an important place of its own in the society of its time; it consisted of artists and artisans constituted into corporations. Because of society's continuing need for the services their corporations had to offer, these artists succeeded in obtaining extensive privileges. However, they tended to work in silence and not to call undue attention to themselves; they did not work under the vaults of the cloisters but rather in their own ateliers or workshops. They sold their material labor, but they retained their own innovative and independent outlook. These artists managed to be quite united among themselves and hence they made progress together; they lived in a society that was happy to take advantage of their intelligence and their hands even while it had little comprehension of the liberal spirit that animated them.

If only others would undertake the task of describing the achievement of these original artists and artisans! Up to now it has hardly been told anywhere else but by us here. Yet the achievement of these artists and artisans was wonderful, and should excite general sympathy; it dealt with questions of order of the most elevated kind; an understanding of it would perhaps throw light on some of the basic questions being raised in our own day, and not without reason, by some of the most clear-sighted among us. To know the past well, we believe, is the best and surest way to prepare for the future. Of all the classes of society, the class in which the ideas, tendencies, and tastes vary the least is certainly the working class, the class that produces things. In France the working class demands more than merely to have its daily bread; it demands the satisfaction of being able to maintain its own self-respect; it insists on maintaining its own individuality too. It actively desires problems to be solved, for its intelligence is more active than its hands. If it has to be occupied materially, it also wants to be occupied morally. The French working class wants to understand what it is doing and why it is doing it; it also wants society to be grateful to it for what it does and to express that gratitude. Everybody knows this to be true of our soldiers; it is the very thing that has contributed to their long predominance. Why should not the same characteristics be recognized also in our workers? Speaking merely about our subject of construction, we can affirm that our manpower has deteriorated in quality in precisely those eras when individual work has been subordinated to some kind of classical "rules," rules imposed arbitrarily from above. And when our manpower deteriorates, social crises are not slow to follow in France. Of all the industries, the construction industry generally demands the largest number of hands; it also demands from each worker a high degree of intelligence. Masons, stonecutters, limeburners, carpenters, joiners, metal-workers, roofers, painters, sculptors, cabinetmakers, and tapestry makers, along with all the subcategories of these arts and crafts, constitute an innumerable army of workers and artisans. Obliged to work under a single, unified direction, these workers and artisans are generally disposed to submit to such direction provided it is intelligent—just as they are disposed to throw off their discipline when the direction they are given works at cross-purposes with their own nature and characteristics. Our workers and artisans generally neither listen to nor follow leaders unless the latter know where they are going and what they want. The question that is always in their mouths as well as in their eyes is *Why?* It is not necessary to spend much time at a construction site in order to discover with what mocking indifference our workers work on things whose reason for being they do not understand—or with what application they will work on those whose utility they do understand. A stonecutter will not treat the part of his stone that he knows will be hidden from view with the same care that he devotes to the part whose function he understands. Nothing the superintendent of a construction site can say or do will change this. This may be deplorable; but it is something that can be quickly verified on any construction site. In France *appearances* count above all; it is an all-too-common weak point of ours. Moreover, there is no help for it; one might as well try to make use of it to some advantage. It is said that we are Latins. Perhaps this true of our language. With regard to our manners, morals, tastes, national character, genius, and suchlike, we are in no way Latins. And this was just as true in the twelfth century as it is today. Cooperation in a common effort is active, devoted, and intelligent in France whenever it is known and understood that such cooperation, in however small a degree, will be recognized and appreciated. When, however, this recognition and appreciation are not accorded, and individual efforts become lost in the shuffle, cooperation then becomes correspondingly languid, soft, and lackadaisical. It is important for our readers to understand this trait of our national character, so long misunderstood, if they are to understand properly the true meaning of some of the examples we have been presenting in this work.

In order to become truly knowledgeable about an art of which both the original resources and the practical means of execution have long since been forgotten, it is necessary to try to enter into the spirit of those who were the practitioners of that art. Once that has been done, everything follows; everything hangs together; the point of it all becomes clear. We do not attempt or pretend to conceal the defects of the system we describe. It is in no way our intention to enter a plea here in favor of Gothic construction; our intention has been to provide a simple exposition of both the principles and consequences of this type of construction. If we have succeeded in making ourselves understood, no sensible architect, after having read with attention what we have had to say here, will ever be able to reach any other conclusion except that of the utter unprofitableness, not to use a stronger term, of merely creating *imitations* of Gothic art. At the same time, this discerning architect will not fail to understand the very great utility of studying this unique type of art, so intimately connected to our national genius.

We intend to pursue an examination of our great religious edifices, in the first place, because they are the most important of all the Gothic structures; but secondly because they developed so rapidly at the end of the twelfth century, and because the principles in virtue of which they were erected are applicable to every other type of construction. We now know what the successive phases were through which the construction of vaulted edifices had to pass in order to move from the ancient Roman system of vaulting to the medieval Gothic system of vaulting. To put this another way, we now understand the difference between an architectural system of passive resistances and one of active resistances. Between 1150 and 1200 there were built in the French royal domain, and in the neighboring Beauvoisis and Champagne, the great churches of Notre-Dame de Paris, Mantes, Sens, Senlis, Noyon, and Châlons-sur-Marne; and of Saint-Remy de Reims (choir only). All of these churches were built in accordance with the new principles that had been adopted by the lay school of architects flourishing at the time; and all of them have continued in the centuries since to preserve a perfect stability in all of their principal elements.

RESTORATION
"le mot et la chose"

RESTORATION, s.f. Both the word and the thing are modern. To restore an edifice means neither to maintain it, nor to repair it, nor to rebuild it; it means to reestablish it in a finished state, which may in fact never have actually existed at any given time. The idea that the constructions of another age can actually be restored is an idea that dates only from the second quarter of our own century, and it is not clear that this kind of architectonic restoration has ever been clearly defined. Perhaps this is an opportune occasion for us to get a clear idea of exactly what is meant and what ought to be meant by a *restoration*. For it would seem that many ambiguities have come to surround the meaning that we assign and ought to assign to this particular activity.*

We have said that both the word and the thing are modern; and, in fact, neither any civilization nor any people in history has ever carried out restorations in the sense in which we understand that term today.

*We have translated the entire entry "Restoration" from vol. 8, 14–34. [Editor's note]

In Asia, in the past as still today, whenever a temple or a palace fell into ruin or decay as a result of the ravages of time, either it was simply rebuilt or else another one was built in its place. This does not mean that the ancient edifice itself even had to be destroyed; that was normally left to the action of time itself; time would surely not fail to wear it down little by little as if the edifice belonged to time. The Romans rebuilt; they did not restore. The proof of this is that there is not even a Latin word that corresponds to our word *restoration* in the sense in which we understand the word today. *Instaurare, reficere, renovare*—none of these words means "to restore" but rather "to reestablish" or "to rebuild anew." When the emperor Hadrian set out to reinstate in good condition a number of the monuments of ancient Greece and Asia Minor, he went about it in a way that today would have surely stirred up against him all the archaeological societies of Europe; and this was the case even though Hadrian had some credentials in the matter of antiquarian knowledge. Nevertheless, the reestablishment of the Temple of the Sun at Baalbek cannot be considered a restoration; it is rather a rebuilding done in accordance with the principles that obtained at the time of the rebuilding. The Ptolemies, who prided themselves on their archaism, nevertheless did not respect the forms of construction of the ancient Egyptian dynasties, but instead went about the reconstructing they did in accordance with the manner current in their own day. Similarly, the Greeks did not do restorations—that is to say, they did not reproduce the old forms of the buildings of theirs that were falling or had fallen into ruin and decay; they believed themselves entirely justified in putting the stamp of the present moment upon whatever buildings needed to be rebuilt. To erect a triumphal arch such as the Arch of Constantine using fragments taken from the Arch of Trajan was neither a restoration nor a reconstruction; it was an act of vandalism, a resort to barbarian plunder. To cover the architecture of the Temple of Fortuna Virilis in Rome with stucco was, again, not anything that we could consider a restoration; it was rather a mutilation.

The Middle Ages no more had any idea of restoration than antiquity did. Far from it. Did a broken capital have to be replaced on a twelfth-century building? It was replaced with a capital of the thirteenth, fourteenth, or fifteenth century, as the case might be. Given a whole row of crockets along a frieze, if a single one was missing it would be replaced with an ornament of the style in vogue at that time. It is for this reason that, in times before the attentive study of styles had been developed up to the point where it is today, replacements of this type were merely considered aberrations, and sometimes as a consequence false dates were assigned to parts of an edifice that should rightly have been considered interpolations in an existing text.

We might even say that there is as much danger in restoring a structure simply by reproducing an exact facsimile of everything found in it as there is in substituting later forms for those originally existing in the structure. In the first kind of case, the sincerity and good faith of the artist can result in serious errors that come about because he puts his seal of approval, so to speak, upon what is in fact an interpolation. In the second kind of case, the substitution of an earlier form for an existing one known to be a typically later form obliterates any possible traces of the earlier repair of a defect, the cause of which, if known, might have signaled the presence of an exceptional architectural disposition. We will explain all of this in due course.

Our era, and our era alone, since the beginning of recorded history, has assumed toward the past a quite exceptional attitude as far as history is concerned. Our age has wished to analyze the past, classify it, compare it, and write its complete history, following step-by-step the procession, the progress, and the various transformations of humanity. A fact as novel as this new analytic attitude of our era cannot be dismissed, as some superficial observers have imagined, as merely some kind of temporary fashion, or whim, or weakness on our part. The entire phenomenon is exceedingly complex. Cuvier, by means of his studies of comparative anatomy, as well as of his geologic research, unveiled to the public almost literally from one day to the next a very long history of the world that had preceded the reign of mankind. People were captivated by Cuvier's revelations and eager to travel down the new path he had charted for them. Then philologists discovered the origins of European languages, all of them coming ultimately from the same source. Ethnographers, for their part, oriented their work in the direction of the study of races and of their various aptitudes. Finally, the archaeologists came on the scene, and, studying artistic productions from India through Egypt and on through Europe itself, they compared, discussed, and distinguished among these various productions, uncovered their origins and charted their interrelationships, and, following the same analytic method, eventually succeeded in classifying them according to certain general laws. To consider all this activity as a mere temporary fashion or fantasy, or as indicating some kind of moral malaise, is to treat lightly a scientific phenomenon of very considerable significance. To treat it thus lightly is equivalent to holding that the discoveries in the natural sciences since the time of Newton have also amounted to nothing more than insignificant productions resulting from human caprice. But if the new analytic phenomenon as a whole is indeed significant, why should not its individual manifestations and details also be significant? All of these researches lead into one another and are mutually supportive. Europeans of our age have arrived at a stage in the development of human intelligence where, as they accelerate their forward pace, and perhaps precisely because they are already advancing so rapidly, they also feel a deep need to re-create the entire human past, almost as one might collect an extensive library as the basis for further future labors. Is it reasonable to characterize such a vast effort as this as mere whim or ephemeral fantasy? How can anyone possibly hang back and continue to be blind to the meaning of it all? How can anyone consider modern research and study to be nothing but useless encumbrances? On the contrary: should not the discrediting of old prejudices and the discovery of forgotten truths rank among the most effective methods of ensuring true progress?

If our age succeeds in doing nothing else but transmitting to future ages our own new analytic method of studying history (whether in the material order or in the moral order), it will deserve the gratitude of posterity. Actually, all this is really well known already. Our age has not in fact been content just to cast a superficial glance backward. The retrospective work being carried out today also relates to future problems and will provide help in facilitating the solutions of such problems. Synthesis follows analysis.

In spite of all this, though, the fact is that our modern investigators of the past, our archaeologists patiently exhuming debris down to its smallest components and thereby rediscovering arts that supposedly had been lost forever, are today obliged to overcome many prejudices concerning their work. These prejudices continue to be maintained by large numbers of people for whom every new discovery, every sighting of a new horizon, appears to represent somehow a loss of our own traditions; in fact it probably represents an all-too-convenient kind of intellectual quietism. The story of Galilee is eternal. Occasionally history may advance beyond this level, but we always find it again on the same steps that humanity, with effort, climbs. We may remark in passing, however, that those historical epochs characterized by significant progress in general have also generally been noted for the attention they gave to at least a partial study of the past. The twelfth century in the West represented a veritable renaissance in the political, social, and philosophical spheres, as it also did in literature and the arts. At the same time, there were indeed those who contributed to this renaissance through their study of the past. The same phenomenon occurred in the sixteenth century. Archaeologists do not therefore have to be too concerned about the fact that there are those who would like to call a halt to their work. Not only in France but in Europe as a whole, their work is much appreciated by a public quite eager to accompany them on their journeys back into the past. That these archaeologists sometimes have to turn away from their usual preoccupation with the dust of the past in order to launch themselves into polemics to defend their work is not even necessarily all to the bad: for polemics can engender new ideas; polemics can motivate more attentive study of problematic questions. To contradict the solutions that people suppose are the only valid ones is an action that can help lead to better solutions. Let us not be too harsh, therefore, on those who appear to be immobilized in their contemplation of the present, or who appear to be simply decking out their prejudices when they appeal so quickly to "tradition." In reality, they are the ones who are missing out on the riches that have now been exhumed from the past. They may imagine that all humanity dates only from the time of their own births, but this illusion of theirs should prompt us to compensate for their blindness by insisting all the more strongly on the validity of the results of our research.

There are, however, some veritable fanatics among researchers, who diligently seek certain kinds of treasures that they happen to prize, but who refuse to allow anyone else even to try to search for things they do not consider treasures and have therefore neglected; they apparently see the past as a kind of raw material suitable only for monopoly exploitation. They declare haughtily that humanity only produced works worth preserving in certain historical periods, which they themselves, of course, have succeeded in identifying; they arrogate to themselves the right to excise entire chapters from the history of human achievement. They thus set themselves up as censors of the archaeological profession, saying: "That layer is unhealthy. Do not dig there. If you should dare to uncover anything there, though, we shall not fail to denounce your work to your contemporaries as corrupting." It was not too many years ago, in fact, that those who were working to make better known the arts, literature, and customs of the Middle Ages were treated in exactly this fashion. If the fanatics who thus attacked them have since diminished in number, those who remain are, if anything, even more passionate in their attacks, and they have today adopted a clever tactic calculated to influence people who are not accustomed to looking very deeply into things. This is the vein in which they carry on: "You are studying and calling to our attention the arts of the Middle Ages. You must want us all to go back to the Middle Ages! Meanwhile, though, you are neglecting the study of antiquity. If you had your way, there would soon be *oubliettes** again in all our prisons as well as torture chambers attached to all our courts of justice. You speak about all the good work performed by the monks in the Middle Ages. You must therefore want to take us back and place us under a regime of monks. You must favor paying tithing, too. You must favor a debilitating asceticism. You tell us all about feudal castles. You must therefore oppose the principles of '89! If we listened to you, we would soon have the *corvée*** back again." The most amusing thing about such fanatics (we insist on the word) who tax us with accusations such as these is the further epithet they often apply to us: the epithet *exclusive.* Very probably they lay this charge upon us because we do *not* exclude the study of the Middle Ages. On the contrary, we actually allow ourselves to be partial to and to recommend this kind of study.

At this point the reader may well be wondering what all this has to do with the title of this article. We shall explain in due course. In France, architects are never in much of a hurry. Toward the end of the first quarter of the present century, literary studies of the Middle Ages had become quite serious and sophisticated.

**Oubliette:* windowless medieval dungeon cell, reachable by trapdoor, where prisoners were left to be "forgotten"; from *oublier,* "to forget."

***Corvée:* an obligation to perform feudal service, particularly work on roads. [Translator's notes]

At the very same time, though, architects were still seeing in Gothic arches nothing at all beyond the notion that they represented *an imitation of German forests!* This was actually an accepted and even venerable phrase at one time. The architects of the time, though, considered the ogival, or pointed, arch to be a symptom of what they considered a "sick art." The pointed arch was a "broken" one; therefore, it also had to be one that was "sick." This reasoning was considered conclusive. The churches of the Middle Ages—which had, of course, in any case, been devastated by the French Revolution and had often been abandoned as well as darkened by time and eroded by the humidity—gave the appearance of being nothing else than so many empty coffins. It was their appearance that prompted the kinds of remarks made by Kotzebue, so often echoed elsewhere by others.* In fact, the interiors of Gothic structures must have inspired nothing but sadness at the time (which was perhaps understandable considering the state to which they had been reduced). The spires of Gothic churches penetrating through the mist did inspire a few romantic phrases, of course; writers spoke of stone *lace,* of *bell turrets* erected atop buttresses, of *elegant* little columns joined together to enable them to support vaults at *frightening* heights. All these features were supposed to represent nothing but the *piety* (some said fanaticism) of our *fathers;* such features pointed to a situation half-mystical and half-barbarous, in which nothing else but a capriciousness of spirit must have reigned. However, there is no point in dwelling further on this kind of banal nonsense; it was very much the rage in 1825, but it is now only to be found in articles in journals that are behind the times. However that may be, we do find these same kinds of empty phrases in a number of the collections that appeared with the help of the Museum of French Monuments, particularly that of Sommerard. It seems that a number of artists had,

*We refer to the *Souvenirs de Paris en 1804* of August von Kotzebue (French translation, 1805), concerning the author's visit to the Abbey of Saint-Denis. We can discern here the dawning of admiration for old buildings that was to characterize the Romantic era. The author wrote: "Leaving the subterranean part, we mounted up into the solitary enclosure where time had begun to wield its scythe. An old man (for there is always an old man amid such ruins) hoped someday to see the abbey restored. This hope was based on a few words that Bonaparte himself had allowed to slip. Since the necessary repairs would be extremely costly, it would be out of the question for the moment." [Author's note] curiously, actually decided to look into some of the debris of "the centuries of *ignorance* and *barbarism*." Their research was surely both timid and superficial at first; they were no less subject to sharp remonstrances for all of that. As various grave personages solemnly opined, people were actually making drawings on the sly of some of the constructions erected by the "Goths." Actually, some of those involved were not really artists and hence were not subject to the iron rod of academic discipline. Consequently, some of them did some remarkable work, especially when we consider the time when this work was done.

In 1830 Monsieur Vitet was named inspector general of historical monuments. This sensitive writer brought to his new responsibilities no broad knowledge of archaeological research, which, indeed, nobody possessed at the time anyway. What he did bring, though, was a critical and analytic spirit, which first of all ensured that some light would henceforth finally penetrate into the history of our ancient monuments. In 1831 Monsieur Vitet submitted to the minister of the interior a lucid and methodical report on the inspection trip that he had carried out in the northern departments; this report revealed for the benefit of the enlightened the existence of treasures that had been unknown up to then. Even today this report of Monsieur Vitet's has to be considered a masterwork among these types of studies. We may perhaps be permitted to quote a few extracts from it.

> I realize [Monsieur Vitet wrote] that many considered to be authorities in the matter will consider it a singular paradox if anyone tries to speak seriously about the sculpture of the Middle Ages. According to these experts, there scarcely was any such thing as sculpture in the true sense between the time of the Antonines and that of Francis I; the sculptors of the time between were considered nothing but crude and uncultivated masons. In order to appreciate the falsity of this prejudice, however, it is only necessary to have eyes. It is also necessary to be able to give the benefit of a doubt where this is called for, because, in fact, we have to recognize that at the end of the centuries of barbarism there did arise in the Middle Ages a great and beautiful school of sculpture which was heir to the methods and even to the

> style of ancient art. Even so, this medieval school was also already a modern school, modern both in its spirit and in the effects it produced. Like all schools of art, it underwent its own phases and revolutions; it passed through its own childhood, maturity, and decline. . . .
>
> . . . We must consider ourselves fortunate whenever we are able to find in some protected place which has escaped the hammers of destruction some examples of this noble and beautiful sculpture.

And as if to counter the influence of the usual sepulchral phraseology employed whenever monuments of the Middle Ages were in question, Monsieur Vitet expressed himself thus on the subject of color in architecture:

> The fact is that recent travels and other experiences that cannot be challenged no longer permit us to be in doubt about the degree to which ancient Greece used colors in architecture; paintings sometimes covered even exterior walls. Yet on the basis of a few discolored pieces of marble, our scholars over the past three centuries have led us to believe in an ancient architecture that was entirely colorless and cold. The same thing has occurred with respect to the Middle Ages. What happened is that at the end of the sixteenth century, thanks to Protestantism, pedantry, and a few other things, our imaginations have become less lively and less natural; our imaginations became dulled so to speak. People began whitewashing lovely painted churches. A taste for bare walls and bare wainscoting took hold. If some interior decorations still continued to be painted, it was on a small scale, "in miniature," as it were. Since things have been this way for roughly the last two or three centuries, we have concluded that things must always have been this way, and that our monuments from the past always stood in the same colorless and denuded state in which we see them today. If you examine them carefully, however, you will quickly discover some bits and fragments of their

> former coloring; wherever the whitewash is chipped off, you will discover the original paint. . . .

Because he had been so singularly impressed by the ruins of the castle of Coucy, Monsieur Vitet included as a conclusion to his report on the monuments of the northern provinces he had visited the following request to the minister of the interior—a request that today can only strike us as most pointedly apt:

> Concluding what has been said regarding these monuments and their preservation, Mr. Minister, allow me to say a few words about what is perhaps the most valuable and impressive monument of all those about which I have been speaking, a monument that I would propose to attempt to restore. It would be a restoration for which not so much stones and cement would be required as sheets of paper. The aim would be to rebuild or, rather, to reinstate this great fortress of the Middle Ages in its totality as well as in its finer details, and to reproduce its interior decoration up to and including its furnishings. The idea would be, in a word, to give it back its form and color and, if I may dare to say it, its original life. This is the idea that came into my mind when I entered the enclosure of the castle of Coucy. Both its immense towers and its colossal donjon seem in some respects to have been built yesterday. Even in its dilapidated parts, though, what impressive vestiges of paintings, sculptures, and interior arrangements are to be found! What documentation for the imagination they are! They represent stages on the road to a true discovery of the past. This is true even without reference to the old plans and drawings of du Cerceau which, although not very accurate, can still be of great help.
>
> Up to now this type of work has only been carried out on the monuments of antiquity. I believe, though, that the same type of work can yield even more results when applied to the monuments of the Middle Ages; for with the latter we are dealing with indications based upon more recent facts and we are

> also dealing with monuments that are more nearly intact. What is merely conjecture with respect to antiquity becomes something approaching certitude where the Middle Ages are concerned. The restoration I have in mind, for example, if placed opposite the castle as it is in its present state, would encounter, I believe, very few nay-sayers.

The program that was traced out so sharply some 34 years ago by this illustrious critic is one that we have actually seen realized in our day, and not merely on a few sheets of paper or in a set of fugitive drawings; we have seen it actually realized in stone, wood, and iron in the case of a castle no less interesting than the Coucy—namely, the castle of Pierrefonds. Many things have happened since the 1831 report of the inspector general of historical monuments. Many aesthetic debates have emerged; but the seeds planted by Monsieur Vitet have now borne real fruit. He was the first to become seriously concerned about the restoration of our ancient monuments; he was also the first to come up with any practical ideas on the subject, just as he was the first to introduce critical analysis into the kind of work that was required. He opened the doors; other critics and scholars followed and, after them, artists then began to throw themselves into this work.

Fourteen years later the same critic, still engaged in the work that he had begun so auspiciously, wrote the history of the cathedral of Noyon. It was in this remarkable work that he described the various stages through which scholars and artists specializing in these types of studies had been obliged to pass:[1]

> In order to understand the history of an art, it is not enough to determine the diverse periods through which it has passed in a particular place. It is necessary to follow its development in all the different places where it has been produced, to indicate the various forms that it has successively assumed, and to draw up a comparison between all of its varieties, not only in each nation but in each province of a particular country as well. . . . It has been in view of this double aim, as well as in this spirit, that all of the research has been undertaken in the past twenty

years on the subject of the monuments of the Middle Ages. Already at the beginning of this century several scholars in both England and Germany furnished us with good examples by means of the essays they produced on the subject of the buildings in their two countries. No sooner had their work penetrated into France, particularly into Normandy, than it began to stimulate lively imitations. A taste for this kind of work was propagated rapidly through Alsace, Lorraine, Languedoc, Poitou, and, indeed, in all of our provinces. Now practically everywhere there is similar work going on, whether research, the gathering of materials, or the preparation of them. Fashion, which so often intrudes into everything that is new, sometimes to its detriment, has unfortunately not always respected the analytic and scientific aspects of this developing work, and in some instances it has even been responsible for compromising its progress. People of fashion have too often wanted to take immediate advantage of what has been done; they have called for foolproof methods of dating whatever structures might happen to be in question. On the other side of the coin, some scholars, carried away by their zeal, have sometimes fallen into a dogmatism destitute of any real proofs but bristling nevertheless with peremptory assertions; this has only served to increase the doubts of those whom they wished to convert to their views. In spite of all these obstacles, though—obstacles that were inherent in the development of any really new discipline—authentic workers in the field continue to carry on their work with patience and moderation. Fundamental truths have been established. A new science now actually exists and only remains to be consolidated and extended. Pruning of some untenable notions is required, of course; failure to carry out this pruning could cause embarrassment. Certain incomplete demonstrations need to be brought to a logical conclusion. Much remains to be done, in fact; but the results obtained to date are such that the definitive achievement of the goal cannot be in doubt.[2]

It has been necessary to quote at length the greater part of this text in order to show how much progress its author made in the study and appreciation of the arts of the Middle Ages, and how great was the light that he was able to spread around him amid the darkness that had reigned up to then. Monsieur Vitet showed clearly that the architecture of the Middle Ages was a complete and integral art, possessing its own original laws and its own reasons for doing things the way it did. Monsieur Vitet wrote further: "The only possible excuse for treating these truths as illusions and for adopting a stance of disdainful skepticism with regard to them has been a simple failure of critics even to open their eyes."[3]

It was at that point that Monsieur Vitet stepped down from his post as inspector general of historical monuments. Since 1835 the responsibility for these functions has been entrusted to one of the most distinguished figures of our era, Monsieur Mérimée.

It was under the patronage of these two godfathers, Vitet and Mérimée, that the first nucleus of young artists desirous of becoming completely knowledgeable about the forgotten arts of the Middle Ages received their formation. It was under their wise inspiration, always tempered with a severely critical spirit, that the first restorations were undertaken. At first they were carried out with certain reservations; later they were carried out in a more venturesome spirit, and they also became more extensive. From 1835 to 1848, Monsieur Vitet presided over the Commission on Historical Monuments. During that period a large number of buildings in France, dating both from Roman antiquity and from the Middle Ages, were studied; they were also preserved from ruin. It is necessary to emphasize that a program of restoration was an entirely new thing at the time. Leaving aside entirely the restorations carried out in earlier centuries—which were nothing but substitutions—our era from about the beginning of this century witnessed a number of attempts to present a true idea of an earlier art by means of the production of certain compositions. These compositions were really the products of fantasy. But at least their authors imagined they were really producing the ancient forms. Monsieur Lenoir in the Museum of French Monuments, which he himself had organized, attempted to classify in chronological order all the historical remnants that had been saved from destruction. It has to be conceded that the imagination of this celebrated conservator played a more active role in his efforts than did any real knowledge or any real critical spirit on his part. Thus, the tomb of Abelard and Heloise, today reinstalled in the Cemetery of the East,* was composed of ornamental arcades and small columns taken from the lower part of the abbey church of Saint-Denis: of bas-reliefs taken from the tombs of Philip and of Louis, brother and son of St. Louis; of keystone masks taken from the chapel of the Virgin of Saint-Germain-des-Prés; and of two statues dating from the beginning of the fourteenth century. Thus, too, the statues of Charles V and Jeanne de Bourbon, taken from the tomb at Saint-Denis, were placed above sixteenth-century wainscoting taken from the Château of Gaillon and crowned by a late-thirteenth-century aedicule. The room described as "fourteenth-century" was decorated with an ornamental arcade from the rood screen of the Sainte-Chapelle, while thirteenth-century statues were placed against pillars from the same edifice. For lack of any authentic statues of Louis IX and Marguerite of Provence, statues of Charles V and Jeanne de Bourbon that had once decorated the portal of the church of the Celestines in Paris were pressed into service to represent this king who was a saint and his wife.** Since the Museum of French Monuments was destroyed in 1816, the confusion was only magnified when many of these same monuments were afterward transferred to Saint-Denis.

By the will of the emperor Napoleon I, who was ahead of his times in almost everything, and who understood the importance of restorations, the church of Saint-Denis was not only supposed to serve as the burial place for the new dynasty; it was also supposed to serve as a kind of living museum illustrating the progress of art in France from the thirteenth to the sixteenth centuries. The emperor set aside funds for this restoration. The initial restoration efforts corresponded so little to his expectations, however, that he personally reproached the architect commissioned to direct the work, to such a point that the latter is said to have died from the distress this caused him.

The unfortunate church of Saint-Denis served, in fact, as the

*Père-Lachaise Cemetery. [Translator's note]

**As a result of this substitution, almost all the painters or sculptors charged with representing these personages always thereafter gave to St. Louis the visage of Charles V. [Author's note]

cadaver on which the very first artists attempting to carry out restorations operated. Throughout a period of some 30 years it had all possible types of mutilations inflicted upon it—to such an extent that its stability was threatened. After considerable expense, and after major alterations of the church's original dispositions, as well as the ruin of many of the beautiful monuments it contained, this costly experiment was finally terminated. It became necessary to go back to the overall restoration program proposed by the Commission on Historical Monuments.

We must now provide an explanation for this restoration program. It is being followed today in both England and Germany (both of which countries preceded us in the serious theoretical study of ancient monuments). Italy and Spain have also accepted the same kind of restoration program in principle; they, too, want to introduce critical analysis into the preservation of their ancient monuments.

The program in question requires first of all that all buildings or parts of buildings constituting historical monuments be restored in the style that belongs to them, not merely in appearance, but in basic structure. There are few buildings, especially those constructed during the Middle Ages, that were built overnight, though; or which, even if they did go up rapidly, did not undergo notable modifications later, by either additions, conversions, or partial changes of one type or another. It is therefore essential, before any repair work actually begins, to ascertain exactly the age and character of each part of the building, and then to write up an official report on all these things based on solid documentation, a report that may include written notes as well as drawings and illustrations. More than that, in France each province had its own style; each had a particular school of architecture whose practices and principles it is always necessary to understand. Information collected about a monument in the Île-de-France, accordingly, cannot serve as the basis for restorations in Champagne or Burgundy. The differences between the various schools persisted for a long time; these differences may be determined by following certain rules, which, however, are not regularly followed. Thus, while the art of that part of Normandy watered by the Seine is very close to the art of the Île-de-France in the same era, the Norman art of the Renaissance differs in essential ways from that of Renaissance Paris and its environs. In several southern provinces, the architecture styled "Gothic" was never anything but a foreign importation. Thus, a Gothic edifice in Clermont may have come from one particular school, while one in Carcassonne dated from the same era may have come from a completely different architectural school. The architect in charge of restoration must have exact knowledge not only of the styles assignable to each period of art, but also of the styles belonging to each school. It was not merely during the Middle Ages that such differences as these occurred; the same phenomenon appears in the monuments of Greek and Roman antiquity. Roman construction from the age of the Antonines in the south of France differs in many respects from contemporary construction in Rome itself. Nor can the Roman construction on the east coast of the Adriatic be confused with that of central Italy, of Asia, or of Syria.

Limiting ourselves here to questions of the Middle Ages, though, we must take note of the many difficulties and obstacles in the way of any authentic restoration. Often buildings or parts of buildings dating from a certain era have been repaired, sometimes more than once, and sometimes by workers who were not native to the province where the buildings were constructed. Many difficulties can arise from this kind of situation. Both the earliest parts and the modified parts of the edifice need to be restored. Should the unity of style simply be restored without taking into account the later modifications? Or should the edifice be restored exactly as it was, that is, with an original style and later modifications? It is in cases like this that opting absolutely for one or the other of these restoration solutions could be perilous. It is in fact imperative not to adopt either of these two courses of action in any absolute fashion; the action taken should depend instead upon the particular circumstances. What would these particular circumstances be? We cannot list them all. It will suffice if we identify a few of the most important of them in order to bring out the element of the critical analysis always required in work of this kind. Ahead of everything else—ahead of any specific archaeological knowledge, for example—the architect responsible for any work of restoration must be an able and experienced builder, not in general but in particular. He must be knowledgeable about the methods and procedures of the art of construction employed at different times and by different schools. These various methods and procedures of construction have only a relative value, of course; not all of them are equally good. Many of them had to be abandoned, in fact, because they were not very good.

Thus, for example, let us take a building constructed in the twelfth century without gutters for its roof drains, which had to be restored in the thirteenth century and at that time was equipped with gutters producing combined drainage. The crowning is now in bad condition and has to be completely rebuilt. Should the thirteenth-century gutters be abandoned in order to restore the cornice of the twelfth century (of which the elements are all still present)? Certainly not. The cornice with gutters from the thirteenth century needs to be reestablished and its form retained—for it would be impossible to find a twelfth-century model with gutters that could be used. To construct an imaginary twelfth-century model with the idea of preserving the integral architecture of that particular epoch would be to construct an anachronism in stone. Let us take another example: the vaults of a twelfth-century nave were destroyed as a result of some kind of accident and were then rebuilt later, not in their original form but in the typical form of the time of the rebuilding. But now these later vaults, too, are threatening to collapse; they need to be rebuilt. Should they be reconstructed in their later, remodeled form, or should the earlier, original vaults be reestablished? The latter. Why? Because there is no particular advantage in proceeding in any other way. Yet there is a distinct advantage in giving back to the structure its original unity. In this second case, it is not a question, as it was in our earlier example, of maintaining or preserving a rebuilt feature that was a necessary improvement on an earlier but defective model; it is rather a question of reminding ourselves that the earlier restoration or rebuilding was carried out in accordance with the practice of that time; all rebuilding was done in accordance with the style and practice then current. However, we want to follow a contrary principle; we hold that an edifice ought to be restored in a manner suitable to its own integrity. Let us, however, go on to consider yet another important point: suppose the rebuilt vaults, even though they are alien to the original structure, happen to be of remarkable beauty, and, at the time they were installed, they also made it possible to construct glasswork employing stained glass that is of equally remarkable beauty; moreover, when the modified vaults were added they were fashioned in such a way that the exterior construction of the building now also has great intrinsic value. Should all of these valued features now be done away with merely in order to restore the construction of the nave to its primitive simplicity? Should the beautiful stained-glass windows go into storage? And should exterior buttresses and flying buttresses be left in place if, the building having been restored to its original condition, they now no longer have anything to support? Our answer on all three counts in this modified example must be: Certainly not. It is easy to see from these kinds of examples that the adoption of absolute principles for restoration could quickly lead to the absurd.

Another case: it is necessary to provide new underpinning for the detached, isolated pillars of an edifice; they are being crushed under its weight because they were made out of material that was too fragile and their foundations are defective. At various times in the past a number of these pillars have already been replaced, and sections have been added to the structure that were not part of its original plan. In restoring these pillars, do we need to copy exactly the various sections as they now exist? And should we stay with the original dimensions of the foundations, which have turned out to be too weak? The answer is no in both cases: we should restore all the pillars in accordance with the original model, and we should then place them on larger foundations in order to prevent the kinds of accidents that made our restoration efforts necessary in the first place. However, some of the pillars have already seen their sections modified as a result of plans to change or transform the building as a whole. From the point of view of art, some of these planned changes or transformations have been very important; we may think, for example, of those that Notre-Dame de Paris underwent in the fourteenth century. In providing new underpinnings to a structure of this kind, therefore, must we destroy all traces of an earlier project that was not entirely carried out, especially when the traces indicate the existence of a particular school? The answer is no. We should reproduce them in their modified form in this case, for the modifications they have undergone can illuminate points in the history of art. Another example: in a thirteenth-century edifice, such as the Cathedral of Chartres, for example, where drainage was managed by means of weather molding, it came to be believed that this drainage could be better regulated by adding gargoyles to the gutters, and so this was done in the fifteenth century. However, these gargoyles are now in poor condition, and they need to be replaced. Should we, in the name of the unity of the structure, substitute thirteenth-century gargoyles for them? Again the answer is no: for we would be destroying thereby traces of an original disposition that appear to be quite interesting. In this case, we would once again insist on restoring the later features (though always maintaining their style, of course).

Yet another example: between the buttresses of a nave chapels were added subsequent to the original construction. The walls under the windows of these chapels and the pillars of their bays were not connected in any way with the older buttresses, and for this reason it is easy to see that the chapels were indeed constructed later. Now it has become necessary to reconstruct both the exterior facings of the buttresses, which have become eroded, and the fastenings of the chapels. Do we have to tie together in our restoration these two features, each of which was constructed at a different time, just because we are restoring both at the same time? The answer is no. We would want to be careful about keeping entirely distinct the apparatus of each of them, and we would restore them separately; thus, it would always remain clear that the chapels had been added in between the buttresses at some point after the latter had been firmly in place.

The same principles apply to the restoration of those parts of a structure not visible to the human eye. We must scrupulously respect all traces or indications that show additions or modifications to a structure.

There exist in France certain cathedrals, among those rebuilt at the end of the twelfth century, that were not provided with transepts. For example, there are the cathedrals of Sens, Meaux, and Senlis. In the fourteenth and fifteenth centuries, however, transepts were added to these naves, taking up the space of two of their bays. These modifications were more or less skillfully and adroitly carried out, although for trained and practiced eyes, many traces of the original dispositions do remain. It is in cases such as these that the restorer must be scrupulous to a fault; indeed, he must accentuate the traces of the original dispositions rather than attempt to conceal them.

There are also situations where it is necessary to rebuild from scratch portions of structures of which no trace whatever remains any longer, whether because of construction needs imposed on earlier builders, or because of mutilations that occurred in the past and that now need to be repaired. In these cases the architect responsible for the restoration must really feel himself into the style of the school or movement concerned to which the structure belongs. A certain kind of pinnacle of the thirteenth century will be a distinct blemish, for example, if you simply transfer it without further ado, even to another structure of the same century. A profile adopted from a small building will not fit if it is simply applied mechanically to a larger one. It is in fact always a gross error to imagine that an architectural member of the Middle Ages can be enlarged or reduced in size with impunity. In this architecture each member is designed on the scale of the structure to which it belongs. To attempt to alter the scale is to deform the member. In this regard, it is worth mentioning that the majority of new "Gothic" structures built today do attempt to reproduce known structures, but usually on the wrong scale. This or that church will be modeled on the Chartres, for example, or upon the church of Saint-Ouen in Rouen. This way of proceeding is the exact contrary of the practice of the masters of the Middle Ages, who always had specific reasons for proceeding the way they did. The resulting defects in these new structures are jarring in the extreme and preclude these buildings from having architectural value. When it is a question of the restoration of old buildings, though, such defects are really dreadful. Every building raised up in the Middle Ages possessed its own scale relative to the whole; this scale, in turn, was always subject to the dimensions of the human being. It is therefore necessary to think twice before simply proceeding to supply missing parts to any structures built in the Middle Ages; it is first necessary to acquire a true sense of the scale adopted by the original builder.

There is another overriding condition that must always be kept in mind in restoration work. It is this: both the methods and the materials of construction employed by the restorer must always be of superior quality. The restored building needs to be given a longer lease on life than the one that is near expiration. No one can deny that the scaffolding, struts, and supports employed in construction, like any necessary clearing or removing of parts of the masonry, just might possibly have disturbed the fundamental structure in such a way as to provide a potential for possible accidents that could be highly unfortunate. It is therefore prudent simply to assume that any building that has been in place over time has lost some part of its strength as a result of such possible disturbances in the past as those we have indicated. It is necessary, therefore, as a matter of principle to compensate for this probable weakening that has occurred, by the use of new building materials of maximum strength, by devising improvements in the structural system where possible, by the use of chain bond or other ironwork to strengthen the structure, and, in general, by providing greater resistance to the construction by every possible means. It ought to be superfluous to have to mention that the choice of building materials is one of the most important of all factors in restoration. Many buildings threaten to fall into ruin only because of the mediocre quality of the materials out of which they were originally constructed. Every stone that has to be removed should be replaced with a stronger and better stone. Every system of fastening that has to be removed should be replaced with a continuous new system of fastening in exactly the same place as the old. It is impossible to attempt to change the equilibrium of a building that has been in place for six or seven centuries without running grave risks. Buildings, like people, settle into certain habits, which we must accept. If we may be permitted to express ourselves in such a fashion, buildings have their own *temperaments.* Buildings must be carefully studied and understood before any attempt is ever made to work on them. Indeed, all of the following have their own individual temperaments: the construction materials employed, the quality of the mortar used, the ground and the subsoil, the general structural system with particular regard both to the vertical support system and the horizontal joining system, the weight, the greater or lesser concretion or fusing of the vaulting, and the greater or lesser elasticity of the masonry. In some buildings the vertical support system may be completely inflexible as a result of the way the columns were installed; this is often true in Burgundy, for example. In the buildings of Normandy and Picardy, though, the aspect of these same structural features is wholly different; in these latter provinces columns were fixed on small, low foundations. Given these differences in construction methods, underpinning or foundational support that works in one place could cause unfortunate accidents in others. It is possible without damage, for example, to provide new underpinning to piers resting entirely on low foundations. This same undertaking attempted where the columns are inflexible, however, will cause breakage. When attempting to provide new underpinning in this latter kind of case, it is necessary to cram mortar into the joints with the help of iron plates and sharp hammer blows in order to prevent the slightest depression from occurring. In some cases it is even necessary to remove individual columns when providing new underpinning to the foundations; these columns then have to be replaced after the new underpinning has been completed and has had time to settle.

It is clear that the architect responsible for restoration needs to know the style and forms of the building he is working on, as well as the school of architecture to which it belongs. Even more, the architect needs to know the structure, anatomy, and temperament of the building. He needs to know these things because, before everything else, his task is to make the building *live.* He needs to develop a feel for it and for all of its parts almost as if he himself had been the original architect. Once he has acquired this kind of knowledge of his building, he must then have at his disposition several alternative methods of carrying out the work of restoration. If one method fails, he needs to be able to fall back upon another, and even upon a third, if necessary.

We must never forget that the buildings of the Middle Ages were not constructed in the same way as were the buildings of Roman antiquity. In the latter type of construction, structure was created by using various means of active strength and applying them to members representing passive resistance. In the construction of the Middle Ages, however, the idea was that every architectural member should function actively. If a vault exerts pressure, then its buttress or flying buttress needs to exert counterpressure. If a springer or impost becomes overburdened, merely shoring it up vertically will never suffice; it is necessary to provide for the diverse thrusts that press upon it from different directions. If an arch becomes deformed, it is not sufficient merely to center it, since any given arch serves at one and the same time as an abutment for other arches exerting oblique pressures. If you remove any weight from a pier or pillar, you have to compensate for the pressure it was exerting where it was. In a word, it is not merely a question of positioning inert forces exerting only vertical pressures downward, but of creating countervailing forces exerting opposing pressures, placed in such relation to each other that equilibrium is achieved. The removal of any part whatever from this kind of structure tends to disturb its equilibrium. If all the various kinds of problems and troubles facing the restorer disorient the builder who has not come to appreciate the need for conditions of equilibrium in this kind of architecture, these same problems actually provide a stimulus to the restorer who has taken the trouble to know intimately the building he is responsible for restoring. His work amounts to conducting a kind of warfare; he must carry out a series of tactical maneuvers, each of which must be modified each day on the basis of constant observations of the successive effects that are being produced. We have actually observed, for example, how attempts to shore up the underpinning of buildings can cause towers and belfries resting on four points of support to shift the burden of their weight from one point of support to another; and we have seen how the axis of the horizontal projection of such towers could be changed by several centimeters in the course of a 24-hour period.

These are effects that the experienced architect is apt to make light of, but only on condition that he have ten different ways of dealing with the many possible accidents that could result from the different situations he faces—indeed, only on condition that he can inspire his workers with the conviction that he knows what he is doing, and that he can work without exhibiting fears, anxieties, gropings, or hesitations; he must be able to operate in this fashion in order to prevent the kind of panic on the part of his workers that would preclude effective responses to unfortunate happenings when they occur. In the very difficult situations that often arise in the course of restoration work, the architect should have been able to foresee even the most unexpected kinds of happenings; he should already have figured out in advance what to do, so that, acting without haste or alarm when the unexpected does occur, he can prevent disaster. In the sort of work we are talking about, our French workers are eminently capable of understanding the purpose of the maneuvers they are asked to execute; they will be dedicated to their work and will exhibit confidence in carrying it out to the extent that they have noted the composure and foresight of their chief. By contrast, these same workers can be refractory to the extent that they perceive doubt or hesitation in the orders they are asked to carry out.

Restoration work understood as something both serious and practical is something that belongs to our own time, and it does our time honor. Restoration has forced architects to expand their knowledge and develop exciting new methods, which are both expeditious and sure; it has put them in closer touch with construction workers and has enabled them to provide instruction to these workers; it has also enabled them to form clusters of the most skilled of these workers, everything considered, and the latter can now be found at important work sites both in Paris and in the provinces.

As a result of contemporary restoration work, important arts and industries have been newly revived.* The quality of contemporary masonry has improved. Improved use of building materials has become more widespread. Architects given responsibility for restoration work have had to locate new quarries or, if necessary, reopen old ones. Sometimes they have done so in remote villages lacking nearly everything else. They had had to organize ateliers of workers. Rather than being able to find where they were all the resources of large urban centers, they have often had to improvise their own resources, train their own workers, and establish regular methods of working in everything from bookkeeping to management of work sites. In this fashion, unused materials have been put back into circulation; regular work methods have been introduced into departments that did not have them before; centers of skilled workers have been able to send out such workers far afield; ordered habits for solving construction problems have become the norm in communities that before were hardly able to build the simplest kinds of houses. French administrative centralization has its virtues and advantages; we do not deny it; it has served to cement the political unity of the country. But there is no point in trying to deny its disadvantages either. Continuing to speak here only about architecture, we may note that centralization has not only robbed the provinces of their own architectural schools; it has also robbed them of their own particular methods and even of their crafts and industries, since the latter often went along with their architectural schools. Also, many capable workers left home to congregate in Paris or in two or three other large centers. So much was this the case that, 30 years ago, even in the principal towns of each department, there were not to be found architects, contractors, heads of ateliers, or even

*It has been at restoration work sites that a number of arts and industries have been newly revived, following the low estate to which they had fallen by the beginning of this century: fine forged ironworking, figured lead working, woodworking understood in terms of structural arrangement, glazing, and mural painting. It would be interesting to tally up the number of ateliers that have been created or revived as a result of restoration work and to which the detractors of that work have themselves come to seek the skilled workers or knowledge of new methods to be found there. It will readily be understood why we do not venture to delve further into this subject. [Author's note]

skilled workers capable of either directing or executing works of any importance. If proof is needed for this statement, we have only to look at some of the churches, town halls, markets, hospitals, and the like that were constructed between 1815 and 1835, or, at any rate, we can look at those that are still standing in many provincial towns (for many of these constructions had a very short life span). Nine-tenths of all these buildings evince a sad ignorance of the most elementary principles of construction; we need not advert to their style at all. In matters of architecture, in other words, centralization led to something resembling barbarism. Little by little all knowledge, traditions, methods, and ability to execute construction procedures disappeared from the peripheral areas of the country. Even if there had been in Paris an architectural school dedicated to useful and practical ends and capable of sending out artists able to direct construction work anywhere, the provincial schools would still not have been any less doomed. But such a school in Paris would at least have sent out architects who would have merely maintained architecture at the same uniform level in all the various departments, as is in fact the case with the work performed by the national service of roads and bridges. The school of architecture in Paris, however, was preoccupied with other things; its thoughts were reserved for training laureates for the French Academy in Rome, for example. Its students were generally good-enough draftsmen, but they basically lived in a dream world and were not really capable of directing actual work sites in nineteenth-century France. These members of the elect, once they returned to their native soil after a five-year exile, during which they had worked at making graphic restoration studies of a few ancient monuments, never really came to grips with the real practical problems of their profession; rather than work in the provinces, they always preferred to remain in Paris, waiting for someone to confer upon them some work worthy of their talents. If some of them ever did return to their own departments, it was usually to occupy senior positions in the largest cities. Secondary localities thus lacked even the possibility of acquiring any solid artistic knowledge or of realizing any real artistic progress. Municipal construction works were as likely as not to be directed by land surveyors or by officials in the national service of roads and bridges, that is to say by the schoolmasters who were principally geometricians. The very first persons who finally began to think of trying to save from ruin those historical edifices that had come down to us from the past, and which by any standards were among the most beautiful things in the country, acted only out of aesthetic motivations. These artistic pioneers were appalled by the destruction that threatened some very remarkable constructions; each and every day these priceless treasures were victims of a kind of casual vandalism that operated with the blindest indifference. The pioneers could not have foreseen, however, at least in the beginning, the considerable results that their work was eventually to have, even from a purely practical point of view. Nevertheless, they quickly recognized that the more their work was carried out in isolated localities, the more likely it was to have widespread and beneficent effects. After they had been at it for a few years, localities where once quarries had ceased to be worked, and where scarcely a stonecutter, a carpenter, or a smith capable of fashioning anything more complicated than a horseshoe was any longer to be found, were suddenly once again supplying such skilled workers to all the neighboring regions. They were excellent workers, masters of methods that were both economical and sure. Good contractors and meticulous stoneworkers appeared; such workers as these naturally brought principles of regularity and good order into public works. Some of their work sites were to see the majority of their stonecutters go on to become the principal stoneworkers for a large number of different ateliers. Fortunately, even though hidebound habit and routine so often reign at the top in our country, it is also often possible, if one is persistent and careful enough, to circumvent the deadening influence from the top somewhere farther down the line. Our workers are intelligent, and they therefore recognize the supremacy of the intelligence. Just as they can be indifferent and negligent at a work site where the pay is their only recompense, and strict disciplinary rules the only recognized standard, so they can be, by contrast, both alert and involved whenever they sense that a knowledgeable and methodical leadership, sure of what it is accomplishing, is in charge—or, especially, whenever they see that same leadership taking the trouble of explaining to them the advantages or disadvantages of this or that method of working. Self-respect always provides the most effective motive for working for those who are engaged in the manual trades; and by addressing itself to their intelligence and their reason, effective leadership can be sure of getting everything that is needed out of them.

Indeed, has it not been quite remarkable how those architects who dedicated themselves to the restoration of our ancient monuments came to follow week by week the progress of these workers, and how as a result they came to love the work being performed? It would be rank ingratitude on our part not to mention in these pages the dedication and disinterested efforts that so often characterized the laborers at our work sites, and also the alacrity with which they helped us to overcome difficulties that sometimes seemed insurmountable, as well as the cheerful nonchalance with which they were even able to face real dangers once they themselves understood the end in view to be achieved. We find all these qualities in our soldiers. Why should we not also find them in our workers?

The works of restoration undertaken in France, at first under the direction of the Commission on Historical Monuments and later under that of the government service for so-called *diocesan* buildings, not only succeeded in saving from ruin many works of undisputed value; these restoration works also rendered a service of immediate utility. Through its work the Commission on Historical Monuments conducted a significant campaign against the dangers of administrative centralization with respect to public works; it performed for the provinces something that the Ecole des Beaux Arts was never able to do for them. Considering what the results have been—and we are very far from exaggerating their importance—we can surely stand by tranquilly while certain of our contemporary doctors attempt to lord it over the art of architecture, even though many of them may never have placed one brick on top of another themselves. Yet they have nevertheless dared to decree from the heights of their ivory towers that the artists who have devoted a good part of their lives to a painful and even dangerous kind of work, a work from which they have derived neither profit nor great honor, are—not really architects! These doctors may well go on attempting to condemn these dedicated artists to this kind of ostracism; they may well ensure that these dedicated artists are never given any responsibility for architectural work considered by them more honorable and productive (it is certainly less difficult). However, their present disdain as well as their lofty pontificating will be long forgotten while the buildings that have now been saved from ruin, and which are surely among the glories of our country, will go on standing for centuries more to come, testifying thereby to the dedication of a few who were more interested in perpetuating that glory than they ever were in their own private interests.

We have been able to give only some slight indication, and that in a very general way, of the difficulties that face the architect responsible for doing restorations. As we said earlier, we could describe only the broad lines of the kind of overall restoration program called for as a result of all the critical analysis of the problems of restoration. The real difficulties, though, are in no way merely material difficulties. Since all the edifices whose restorations have been undertaken actually have a purpose and in some way continue to be used, it is impossible to be merely a restorer of ancient dispositions that are no longer of any practical use to anybody. Once it leaves the hands of the architect, a building has to continue to be as suitable for its assigned purpose as it was before its restoration was undertaken. Too often, archaeologists of a speculative bent fail to take such practical questions as these into account; they are therefore capable of blaming an architect rather harshly for what they consider his caving in to present exigencies—as if the building he was responsible for restoring somehow belonged to him personally, or as if he was never under any obligation to carry out the program of restoration that was given him.

These, then, are the kinds of circumstances that usually present themselves to the restorer; the sagacity of the architect must show up, precisely, in how he works in the circumstance given to him. He is always under the obligation to reconcile his role as a restorer with his duty as an artist to deal creatively with unforeseen circumstances and necessities. The fact is that the best of all ways of preserving a building is to find a use for it, and then to satisfy so well the needs dictated by that use that there will never be any further need to make any further changes in the building. It is clear, for example, that the architect responsible for transforming the beautiful refectory of Saint-Martin-des-Champs into a library for the Ecole des Arts et Métiers [*sic*], if he was going to respect the construction at the same time as he was restoring it, had to organize the bookshelves and compartments in such a way that there would never again be any necessity to alter the dispositions of the room.

In such circumstances, the best thing to do is to try to put oneself in the place of the original architect and try to imagine what he would do if he returned to earth and was handed the same kind of programs as have been given to us. Now, this sort of proceeding requires that the restorer be in possession of all the same resources as the original master—and that he proceeds as the original master did. Fortunately, though, the art of the Middle Ages, which seems so limited to those whose knowledge of it consists only of a few pat formulas, is, on the contrary, once it has been properly understood, so subtle and so flexible, so varied and so liberal in the means of execution it permits, that there is no program of restoration that cannot be carried out. This architecture is based on principles, not on formulas. It exists for all time, and is capable of satisfying all possible needs, just as a developed language is capable of expressing any and all ideas whatsoever without ever doing violence to its own grammar. It is the grammar of this architecture that one must come into possession of; therefore, it is imperative that this grammar be mastered.

We concede that we are necessarily on a kind of slippery slope once we have granted that restoration is something else besides literal reproduction. Still, there remain certain courses of action that must not be followed except in the most extreme circumstances. It is also necessary to concede that some other courses of action are sometimes imperatively demanded by necessities to which we cannot just say *non possumus.* It would be understandable if an architect refused to install gas pipes in a church in order to avoid mutilation as well as to preclude possible accidents arising out of any attempt to install them; it would be understandable because the building can always be lighted by other means. If the same architect objected to a central heating installation on the grounds that this type of heating was not in use in the churches of the Middle Ages, however, then the whole thing would be merely ridiculous. There can be no reason to oblige the faithful to catch cold merely on account of archaeology! Nevertheless, this type of heating would require the construction of chimney flues. Faced with this problem, the architect should proceed exactly as the master of the Middle Ages would have proceeded if faced with the same or a similar problem. Today's architect most certainly should not attempt merely to conceal what in effect would be a new architectural member. The master of the Middle Ages, far from attempting to disguise any needed function, always attempted instead to clothe each member in dress most suitable for it, while, at the same time, always considering each member yet another motif for decoration. Similarly, to reject, for example, iron construction when a roof has to be rebuilt on the grounds that the medieval masters never built such iron frameworks would be a grave mistake, in our opinion; for an iron framework would preclude the terrible possibilities of fire that, so often, have literally been fatal for some of our historical monuments. But in these cases does the architect not have to take into account the dispositions of a building's supporting points or structures? Does he not have to change the conditions of weight distribution? If the wooden framework to be replaced weighs down equally on the walls, does the architect not have to look for an iron framework structure presenting the same advantages? He does indeed; he especially has to ensure that his new iron roof does not weigh any more than the wooden roof being replaced. This is the most important thing. There have been all too many instances where there has been cause to regret overloading these ancient buildings; in cases where their upper parts have been restored with materials heavier than those employed in the original building, disasters have occurred. Omissions and negligence in such vital areas have been the cause of more than one such disaster. We cannot repeat too often that the constructions of the Middle Ages were calculated with scientific precision; these buildings really are delicate *organisms.* There is nothing excessive or superfluous about them, any more than there are any features that serve no purpose. If you make a change in any part of such a delicate organism, the other parts are automatically changed as well. There are those who consider this a defect in this kind of architecture. For our part, we believe it is something that has been unfortunately too often neglected in modern construction. In modern construction we can often remove more than one member without compromising the whole. But what purpose should exact science and calculation serve in matters of construction if not to bring into play exactly the strengths that are required in any given case? Why have columns at all if we can simply remove them without compromising the solidity of the work? Why have walls 2 meters thick, if walls 50 centimeters thick, reinforced from point to point by buttresses measuring a square meter each, provide a stability that is entirely sufficient? In the construction of the Middle Ages, each part of a structure fulfills a specific function and exerts a specific type of action. The architect must strive to understand the value of each function and of each action before ever attempting to undertake any restoration work. As an adroit and experienced professional performing an intricate operation, he must not lay his hand on any organ until he has entirely understood its function and until he also foresees the possible consequences, both immediate and future, of the operation he is about to perform. If his idea is just to act casually or at random, it would be better if he did not act at all. It is better just to let the patient die than to kill the patient.

Photography, which every day is assuming a more important role in scientific and scholarly pursuits, seems to have come along just in time to be of enormous help in the great work of restoration of our ancient edifices that is today preoccupying all of Europe from one end to the other.

When architects had at their disposition only the ordinary means of design, including even the most exact of these means, such as the camera lucida, it was very difficult for them to avoid certain omissions in their work. At the same time, it was very easy for them to neglect various traces or indications, which were sometimes hardly even noticeable. Moreover, even after the work of restoration was completed, the exactitude of their layouts and drawings of this or that state of the edifice could always still be challenged. Photography, however, has the advantage of making possible an exact and irrefutable presentation of a building in any given state; it provides documentation that can continually be referred back to, even after the work of restoration has covered over some of the damage that came about as the building was falling into ruin. Photography has also motivated architects to be even more scrupulous in the respect they must accord to the smallest remaining fragment of an ancient disposition; it has enabled them to come to a more exact appreciation of the structure of a building; and it has provided them with a permanent justification for the restoration work they carry out. It is impossible to make too great a use of photography in restoration; very often one discovers on a photographic proof some feature that went unnoticed on the building itself.

In restoration there is one dominant principle that cannot ever under any pretext be put aside; this principle is that every single trace indicating an architectural disposition must be taken into account. Before satisfying himself that he has reached the point where he can actually begin issuing orders to his workers, the architect has to be sure that he has discovered both the best and the simplest combination of steps to be taken in conformity with the architectural trace he happens to be considering. To decide upon a particular disposition *a priori* without being in possession of all the available information that ought to dictate the disposition called for is to plunge into the hypothetical, and, in restoration work, nothing is more dangerous than the hypothetical. If you have the misfortune of adopting at a given point a certain disposition that in fact deviates from what is really called for—that is, the structure's original disposition—you will be drawn by a series of necessary logical deductions down a wholly false path, which you will no longer be able to abandon; and the farther you go in the same direction, the farther away you will find yourself from the true path. In view of all this, if you happen to be the one responsible for restoring an edifice already partly in ruins, you must, before beginning to do any actual restoration work at all, excavate everything, examine everything, and bring everything together, including the smallest fragments, taking care to note exactly where they were discovered. You can begin your actual restoration work only when the purpose of everything in all this debris has been determined and everything has been put into its proper logical place, like pieces of a jigsaw puzzle. If this kind of careful preparation is not carried out, you will be in for all kinds of unpleasant disappointments later: this or that fragment discovered after your work is finished will provide the demonstration that you were in error. In the case of the fragments turned up in excavations, you must take account of the cut of the stones and their joints as well as of the bed or layer where they were laid down; for each kind of carving or chasing was done in order to produce a certain effect at a given height. Even the way certain fragments behave in falling will provide you with indications of the place they occupied in the structure. In those perilous cases of reconstruction of parts of an edifice that have been demolished, the architect must be present at the excavations. Moreover, the excavations themselves must be confided only to experienced excavators. Then, when trying to put the whole thing back together again, the architect must to the extent humanly possible replace the ancient debris as it was, however it might have been altered over time; this effort will represent the guarantee both of his sincerity and of the exactitude of his research.

We have now said enough to make comprehensible the difficulties that an architect responsible for restoration will encounter if he takes his job at all seriously—that is, if he wants not only to appear as a sincere artist but to carry out his work with the consciousness that he has left nothing to chance and, most of all, that he has not attempted to deceive himself.

STYLE

the manifestation of an ideal
based on a principle

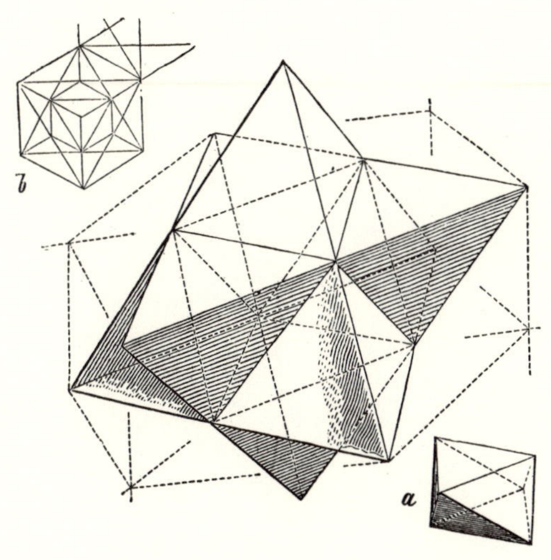

STYLE, s.m. There is *style;* then there are the *styles.* Styles enable us to distinguish different schools and epochs from one another. The styles of Greek, Roman, Byzantine, Romanesque, and Gothic architecture differ from each other in ways that make it easy to classify the monuments produced by these various types of art. It would have been truer to speak of form: the Greek form, the Romanesque form, or the Gothic form, and not use the word *style* to distinguish the particular characteristics of these types of art. However, usage has rendered its judgment, and thus we do in fact speak of the Greek style, the Roman style, and so on.*

This is not primarily what we are concerned with here, however. In several entries of the *Dictionary,* we have brought out the differences of style that enable us to classify the architectural works of the Middle Ages both by schools and by epochs.

We will speak here of *style* only as it belongs to art understood as a conception of the human mind. Just as there is only *Art* in this sense, so there is only one *Style.* What, then, is style in this

*We have translated the entire entry "Style" from vol. 8, 477–501. [Editor's note]

sense? It is, in a work of art, the manifestation of an ideal based on a principle.

Style can also be understood as mode; that is, to make the form of an art appropriate to its objective. In art, then, there is *absolute style;* there is also *relative style.* The first dominates the entire artistic conception of an object; the second can be modified depending upon the purpose of the object. The style appropriate for a church would not be appropriate for a private dwelling; this is relative style. Yet a house can reveal the imprint of an artistic expression (just as can a temple or a barracks) that is independent of the object itself, an imprint belonging to the artist or, more precisely, to the principle that he took as a starting point: this is *style.*

In the arts—in particular, in architecture—vague definitions have engendered many errors, allowed many prejudices to develop, and caused many false ideas to become entrenched. Someone proposes a particular word, and everybody then attaches a different meaning to it. Reasonings that never should have been brought together in the first place all get laid down on the same shaky foundations; they fail to advance the questions; they simply burden indecisive spirits and nourish slothful ones.*

*As an example of what I mean, I cite one of those words so beloved of art amateurs but one on whose meaning they have never been able to agree, and this for the very good reason that it is devoid of sense. There is no art critic who, in speaking of painting, fails to invoke the word *chiaroscuro.* What is *chiaroscuro?* If it refers to the distribution of lights and shades within a painting, why not simply speak of *modeling,* a word that covers the transitions between lights and shades perfectly? If it refers rather to the particular tone of the painting, as some critics appear to admit—that is to say, to the particular harmony adopted by the painter, if not with respect to color, at least with respect to the distribution of light—why not just say "harmony of light" or "harmony of color," phrases understandable by everybody? Instead a vague—indeed, a strictly meaningless—word is preferred. This passes for great technique, but nobody ever bothers to explain it. None of this would be so terribly unfortunate, of course, except that this kind of nonsense word can create great uncertainty in young artists. We have actually known painters who work to achieve *chiaroscuro,* which is something indefinable, something beyond evaluation, something indeed we know not quite what—such painters are both wasting their time and allowing their judgment to be debased. [Author's note]

No creative work that issues from the human brain, whether in the domain of literature or in that of the arts, can truly live unless it possesses what we call style.

Style belongs to mankind; it is independent of the object. In poetry, for example, there is the thought or the impression; then there is the manner of expressing it, of making it penetrate into the soul of the hearer: this is style. There can be a hundred witnesses to an event, yet in reporting it only one of them makes a profound impression on his hearers. Why? Because of the *style* in his narration. The style belongs to the narrator; yet, in order to have any effect, it must be style in a general sense, style that affects everyone. Ten painters paint, under identical conditions, a portrait of the same person. The portraits even resemble one another. Yet only one of them strikes those who know the subject personally as truly rendering not merely his physical traits but his true physiognomy, his way of being, his spirit, his jovial or melancholy temperament as the case may be. The painter of this one painting has style.

We return to our original definition: *style is the manifestation of an ideal based on a principle.* In the example we just gave, even if the physiognomy, character, and demeanor actually belong to the subject of the portrait, the operation of becoming penetrated or imbued with these same qualities and attributes—in such a way that they are not overtly expressed as individual qualities and attributes—this operation belongs to the artist himself. It is the consequence of the artistic principle to which the artist submits. We call this operation an "ideal" because it is essential that the artist fashion an integral, indivisible whole out of the various qualities and attributes of the subject he is dealing with; in accomplishing this, he may soften and attenuate certain traits, while placing other traits in sharp relief. We may be pardoned if we choose a rather banal example of the faculty we are talking about in order to make it understood: a *caricature,* if it is a good one, always has style in the sense we mean. In a caricature, the artist selects the most salient aspects of a physiognomy and exaggerates them well beyond the point of verisimilitude. All peoples who are truly artistic have produced caricatures; and these caricatures are nothing else but an unrestrained expression of the faculty that artists and poets possess. We must appreciate how narrow are the differences between an absolute realism achieved by photographing an object, an "idealism" achieved by reducing that object to caricature, and the pedantry and platitude that result from treating the same object in accordance with the rules of a supposed classicism behind which refuge is sought. The impression that any object produces on various artists itself varies as a result of the faculties of each artist; any artistic expression of it will accordingly also vary. But only artists who possess style will succeed in making the spectator feel what the object made them feel. The poet, the painter, or the sculptor may experience feelings that are sudden, vivid, and clear; these feelings, aroused by externals, are merely a kind of imprint. Before this particular imprint can assume the form of art it must undergo a sort of gestation in the brain of the artist; the artist must assimilate it little by little, and re-create it as a work of art that he brings into being with the help, precisely, of style. If this faculty of assimilation is lacking in the poet, painter, or sculptor, his works will arise out of a sensation or feeling that is blunted, and hence he will fail to produce any effect.

For the architect, as for the musician, however, the psychology is different. These two types of artist do not take from an object or phenomenon of nature a feeling or sensation of their own that is then transformed by them into a work of art. Rather, the work of art must issue from out of their own intelligence; the work of art must arise in embryonic state in keeping with their possession of the faculty of reasoning. It is then their task to develop it by nourishing it with observations that they have borrowed from nature, science, or earlier artistic creations. If the architect is an artist he will naturally assimilate the wherewithal for such nourishment, which he will seek wherever he can find it, the better to develop his conceptions. If he is not an artist, his work will be nothing but an accumulation of borrowings whose origin will not be difficult to recognize. His work, in other words, will lack style.

Style is for a work of art what blood is for the human body: it develops the work, nourishes it, gives it strength, health, and duration; it gives it, as the saying goes, the real blood that is common to all humans. Although each individual has very different physical and moral qualities, we must nevertheless speak of style when it is a question of the artist's power to give body and life to works of art, even when each work of art still has its own proper character.

It is not necessary for us here to attempt to appreciate the degree in which painting, sculpture, and poetry are imitative arts directly inspired by objects outside ourselves of which we are the witnesses. It is only necessary to say here—what no one is likely to dispute, it seems to us—that architecture is not an imitative art in the sense in which we are discussing it. Exterior objects can only have a secondary influence on the development of architecture. Architecture as an art is a human creation. Such is our inferiority that, in order to achieve this type of creation, we are obliged to proceed as nature proceeds in the things she creates. We are obliged to employ the same elements and the same logical method as nature; we are obliged to observe the same submission to certain natural laws and to observe the same transitions. When the first man traced in the sand with a stick a circle pivoting upon its axis, he in no way *invented* the circle; he merely discovered a figure already existing. All discoveries in geometry have resulted from observations, not creations. The angles opposite the vertex of a triangle did not have to wait to be discovered by somebody in order to be equal to each other.

Architecture, this most human of creations, is but an application of principles that are born outside of us—principles that we appropriate by observation. Gravitational force existed before we did; we merely deduced the statics of it. Geometry, too, was already existent in the universal order; we merely took note of its laws, and applied them. The same thing is true of all aspects of the architectural art; proportions—indeed, even decoration—must arise out of the great natural order whose principles we must appropriate in the measure that human intelligence permits us to do so. It was not without reason that Vitruvius said that the architect had to be in possession of most of the knowledge of his time, and for his part he put philosophy at the head of all knowledge. Among the ancients, of course, philosophy included all of the sciences of "observation," whether in the moral order or in the physical order.

If, therefore, we succeed in acquiring some little knowledge of the great principles of the universal natural order, we will quickly recognize that all creation is developed in a very logical way and, very probably, is subject to laws anterior to any creative idea. So much is this the case that we might well claim: "In the beginning, numbers and geometry existed!" Certainly the Egyptians and, after them, the Greeks understood things that way; for them, numbers and geometric figures were sacred. We believe that the style the Egyptians and Greeks achieved—for style is never lacking in their artistic productions—was due to the religious respect they had for the principles to which universal creation itself was the first to be subject, that universal creation which itself is style *par excellence.*

In questions of this order, however, we need to bring forward some simple and obvious demonstration. We are not here concerned with philosophy; we are concerned with bringing some great and fundamental principles within our grasp—simple principles, in fact. Style is able to enter into architectural work only when it operates in accordance with these fundamental principles.

There are those who appear to be persuaded that artists are simply born with the faculty to produce works with style and that all they have to do is to open themselves to a sort of inspiration of which they are not the masters. This idea would appear to be too broadly general in its sweep; it is, nevertheless, favored by the fuzzy-minded. It is not an idea, however, that ever seems to have been favored or, indeed, even admitted in those epochs that knew best how to produce the works of art that have been most noted for their style. On the contrary, in those times it was believed that the most perfect kind of artistic creation was the consequence of a profound observation of the principles on which art can and must be based. (It was, of course, also granted that artists did possess artistic faculties.)

We will leave it to poets and painters to decide whether what we call inspiration can or cannot get along without a long and profound observation of nature. As far as architecture is concerned, however, this particular pursuit is compelled on its scientific side to observe the imperatives that rule it; it is obliged from the very first to seek the elements and the principles on which it will be based, and then to deduce from them with an utterly rigorous logic all the consequences that follow. It happens to be the truth that we cannot pretend to proceed with a power greater than that possessed by universal creation itself, for we act at all only by virtue of our observation of the laws of that creation. Once we have recognized that nature (however we suppose nature herself to have been inspired) has never so much as joined two single atoms together without being subject to a completely logical rule; once we have recognized that nature always proceeds with mathematical exactitude from the simple to the complex, without ever abandoning its first principles—once we have recognized these things, we will surely have to be allowed to smile broadly if we then find an architect waiting for an *inspiration* without first having had some recourse to his reason. Even if we go no further, we must still say that only human reason allows us to achieve a pale human imitation of the relentless march of logic that was followed in the creation of the world. No doubt our world is itself a minuscule grain of dust with respect to all creation. Nevertheless, it is the world we live in; it is the world we perceive and observe. However insignificant an object it may be in the total immensity of creation, we can nevertheless recognize that, in forming it, nature did not reason things out too badly. May we be pardoned for this digression—which is only apparently a digression—since what we are going to say is intimately connected with our architectural art, and particularly with our art as it was practiced during the Middle Ages. The basic problem nature had to resolve was this: "Given a spherical mass more or less in a state of molten liquefaction, how can it be solidified on its surface by cooling, that is, by contraction, by condensation, a little bit at a time, in a way that will result in the formation of a homogeneous and sufficiently resistant crust around the spheroid, which will otherwise remain in fusion?"

It is a fact that before this problem was ever posed, geometry already had to exist, for the problem's solution turned out to be entirely in accordance with the laws of geometry. Let us note in passing, by the way, that nature never discovers the undiscoverable or the absurd; nature never attempts to square the circle. However, nature does dispose of means that we, too, have succeeded in appropriating for our own use by dint of careful observation of nature's laws. For nature as for us, a circle remains a circle; and if the problem is to cover a spheroid with a resistant crust, that is, with a kind of solid pavement, then nature will proceed as we, too, would have had to proceed—namely, by juxtaposing bodies suitable for the purpose. The question, then, was to find, with no opportunity for trial and error, what unique kind of body was suitable for this particular purpose. On what kind of model could be found the absolute properties of resistance that were necessary? When nature is at work, successive deductions follow in accordance with an inflexible logical order: nature traces a circle and inscribes in it the only geometric figure whose shape cannot be modified, a figure of which both the sides and the angles are equal to each other—namely, an equilateral triangle. Given a sphere rather than a circle, however, what turns out to be required, by induction, is a pyramid; for the four faces of a pyramid are all equilateral triangles. Now we have a solid whose shape cannot be modified and whose properties are the same no matter which one of its four sides are in question. Here, then, is the solid, now conveniently discovered: equal sides, equal angles, equal resistance. On this model nature will form the solid crust of the incandescent sphere; for this particular solid is in fact quite adaptable to this function.

Two equilateral triangles possessing a common base form a rhombus (as can be seen in *A*, figure 1): equal sides, obtuse angles *a* (120°), acute angles *b* (60°). With the help of six such rhombuses (as shown in *B*), the rhombohedron *C′C* is obtained. This is a body composed of two pyramids *e*, of which the four faces are equilateral triangles, of which, in turn, the middle part *g* possesses a common base *f*, on which two opposed pyramids arise and of which the faces are again equilateral triangles.

We can see here how, with the use of a single figure, the equilateral triangle, a body is obtained with properties capable of

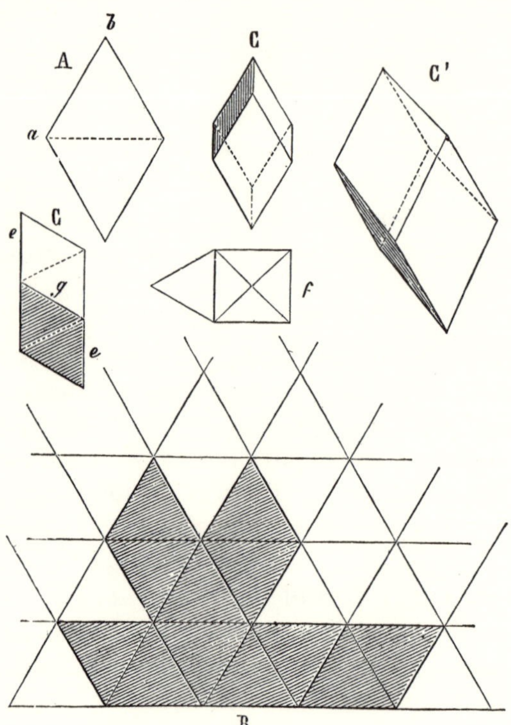

Figure 1

prodigious extension. Let us take first of all the body *C:* does it not present the eye with the junction of six equal parts capable of being attached to three networks that cut into or penetrate each other, thus lending itself to the covering of curved surfaces? Now four such rhombohedrons penetrating each other constitute two pyramids composed of equilateral triangles also penetrating into each other—that is to say, they constitute a solid in the form of an eight-pointed star; each of the like points of this star is itself a pyramid composed of equilateral triangles (see figure 2). This solid, of which the middle part *a* is that of the rhombohedron, inscribes the projection of the six points of the bases of the two pyramids penetrating each other in the hexagon *b;* it inscribes the points of the star in a sphere and in a cube (see figure 3). It is not necessary for us to insist on all these various elements. But the resulting body, composed out of a single basic figure, the equilateral triangle, has extensive properties.

If, now, we take the trouble of examining the first crystallized geologic layer, namely, granite, we will discover that it is entirely composed of juxtaposed rhombohedrons (see *a,* figure 4). Wherever we find basaltic eruptions that have become contracted in solidifying, we will find that they yield prisms with hexagonal sections *b,* and these, of course, are derivative of the rhombohedral form.

Now, the reticulated faces of the rhombohedron lend themselves to providing a covering for a spheroid better than cubes ever would. The meeting planes of these rhombohedrons are not perpendicular to the curve of the earth, as the meeting planes of cubes would have been; cubes would have formed a juxtaposition of truncated pyramids with square bases. The rhombohedral planes, however, since they are not perpendicular to the curve of the earth, provide better resistance to pressure, whether from within or without. It should be clear that bodies disposed in the manner of those shown in *C* will not be able to hold in a molten core *X,* with a tendency to escape, as well the bodies disposed as shown in *D.* This latter disposition, of course, is precisely that of granitic rhombohedrons. We need not linger any longer on these geologic formations. It has, however, been necessary to help make better understood how the very first creative datum of the globe that we inhabit—and, quite certainly, the other similar globes spread across space, for an equilateral triangle on Saturn cannot be any different from the one we have here—proceeds in accordance with the rigorous application of a principle, the only principle, indeed, that could apply. If we were to follow through and examine all the phases of creation in our own world, both organic and inorganic, we would quickly find it to be the case that, in all of nature's various works, however different they may be in appearance, the same logical order proceeding from a fundamental principle is followed; this is an *a priori* law, and nature never deviates from it. And it is to this natural method that is owing the "style" with which all of nature's works are imbued. From the largest mountain down to the finest crystal, from the lichen to the oaks of our forests, from the polyp to human beings, everything in terrestrial creation does indeed possess style—that is to say, a perfect harmony between the results obtained and the means employed to achieve them.

This is the example that nature has provided for us, the example we must follow when, with the help of our intelligence, we presume to create anything ourselves.

What we call imagination is in reality only one aspect of our human mind. It is the part of the mind that is alive even while the body is asleep; it is through that same part of the mind that, in dreams, we see spread out before us bizarre scenes consisting of impossible facts and events that have no connection one with the other. This part of ourselves that is imagination still does not sleep when we are awake; but we generally regulate it by means of our reason. We are not the masters of our imagination; it distracts us unceasingly and turns us away from whatever is occupying us, although it seems to escape entirely and float freely only during sleep. However, we are the masters of our reason. Our reason truly belongs to us; we nourish it and develop it. With constant exercise, we are able to make out of it an attentive "operator" for ourselves, able to regulate our actions and ensure that our accomplishments are both lively and lasting.

Thus, even while we recognize that a work of art may exist in an embryonic state in the imagination, we must also recognize that it will not develop into a true and viable work of art without the intervention of reason. It is reason that will provide the embryonic work with the necessary organs to survive, with the proper relationships between its various parts, and also with what in architecture we call its proper proportions. Style is the visible sign of the unity and harmony of all the parts that make up the whole

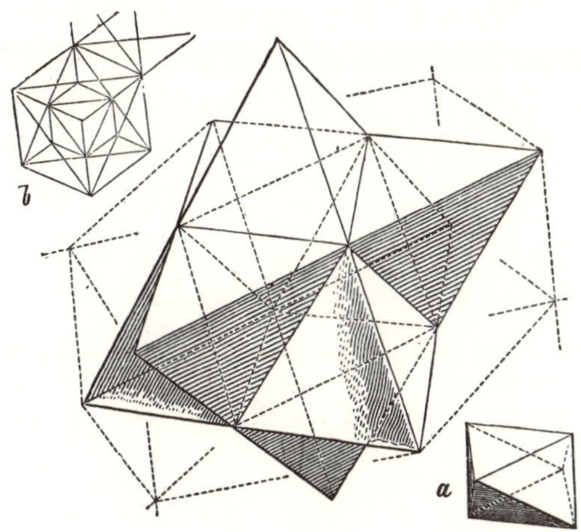

Figure 2

Figure 3

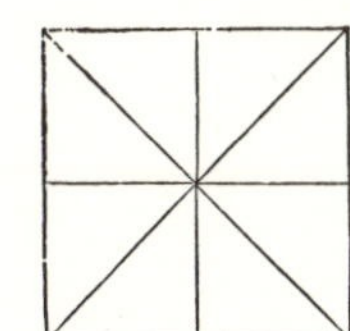

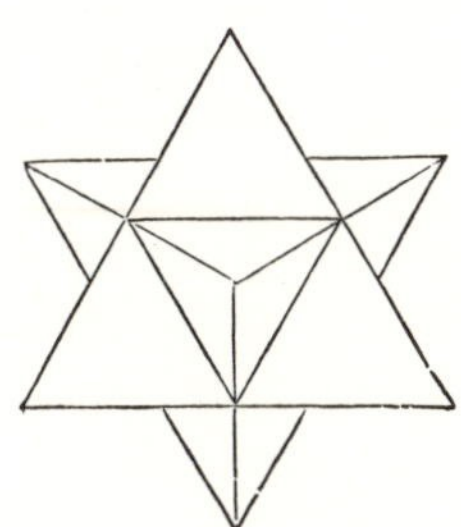

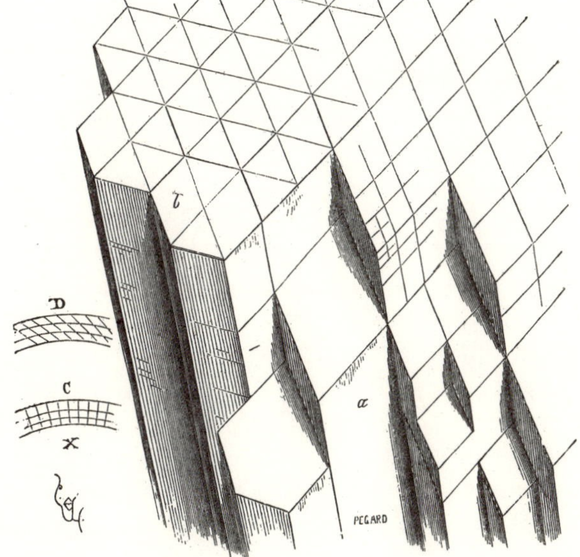

Figure 4

work of art. Style originates, therefore, in an intervention of reason.

The architecture of the Egyptians, like that of the Greeks, possessed style because both architectures were derived by means of an inflexible logical progression from the principle of stability on which both were based. One cannot say the same of all the constructions of the Romans during the Roman Empire. As for the architecture of the Middle Ages, it, too, possessed style once it had abandoned the debased traditions of antiquity—that is, in the period from the twelfth to the fifteenth centuries. It possessed style because it proceeded according to the same kind of logical order that we have observed at work in nature. Thus, just as in viewing a single leaf it is possible to reconstruct the entire plant, and in viewing an animal bone, the animal itself, it is also possible to deduce the members of an architecture from the view of an architectural profile. (See the entry "Trait.") Similarly, the nature of the finished construction can be derived from an architectural member.

If, when at work, the creative force of nature could obtain an integrated result only by combining parts; if, without speaking of higher organisms, the crust of the earth had to be formed by a juxtaposition of crystallized bodies formed according to a unique pattern; and if the results obtained were based strictly upon the proper combination of all the parts—then it is all the more incumbent upon us in fashioning our own creations to employ our raw materials in accordance with their form and their qualities. For we humans must inescapably make use of already existing raw materials, fashioning them for our purposes. We can, of course, force our raw materials, for example, metals—up to a certain point. We can force them into assuming certain arbitrary forms. Nevertheless, we are finally obliged to accept wood and stone for what they are and as nature has fashioned them already; certain laws dictated the formation of these natural materials. We are therefore obliged to conceive of a structure for them that accords with their qualities. Style is possible only under certain conditions. This is the case because the nature of the materials is already fixed: they will take on the form of art only as a consequence of the harmonious adaptation of their particular properties with the artistic end in view; moreover, every use of materials must be proportional to the object. Proportions are relative, not absolute. This does not mean they are relative as to number. Rather, they are relative with respect to the materials employed, to the object, and to what is to be made out of it. In architecture it is not possible to establish a fixed formula such as that 2 is to 4 as 200 is to 400. Although you can place a lintel 4 meters long on posts 2 meters high, you cannot do so with one 400 meters long on pillars 200 meters in height. When the scale changes, the architect must also change his mode of operating. Style consists precisely in choosing the mode that best accords with the scale of the work, taking the word *scale* in its broadest sense. The Greeks, of course, did not accept what we call scale. (See the entry "Echelle.") They did accept the relationship of numbers. But then they built only relatively small buildings.

If the masters of the Middle Ages accepted a single module related to the human dimension, they nevertheless modified the proportionate scale of their work in harmony with its dimensions, its structure, or contexture; what followed from this were diverse appearances, which nevertheless had style because they were based on the application of a true principle.

A comparison will help us appreciate the profound difference between the architecture of the Middle Ages and that of Greek antiquity at its prime. The Greek column, which served as the basis for vertical support, had no other function except to support the horizontal beam members or entablatures; it was a part of the classical Greek *order,* and was always found in an identical proportional relationship with the members it supported. If the beam, lintel, or entablature was greater in volume, it stood to reason that the column supporting the particular member would be strengthened in the same proportion, except that there was, of course, a limit to the dimensions a member might assume. Once the arch was admitted, though, and following it, the vault, a column could no longer simply be part of an order; its function had to be dictated by the nature of the structure being constructed. Since the use of horizontal members did not permit intercolumniation of more than a certain width—for horizontal members longer than ten meters cannot be supported—it was logical to utilize columns of a thickness proportionate to their intercolumniation and thus also to their height. The capacity of an arch being almost unlimited meant that it would been illogical to fix the thickness of columns in accordance either with their height or with their intercolumniation. It is for this reason that, in the architecture of the Middle Ages, it was the weight and function of what they supported that determined the relative proportions of the columns; if these proportions were correct, the column then had style.

Nothing is more satisfying or more nearly perfect than the Doric order of the Parthenon. Artists who could achieve such true proportional relationships among the various parts of the structure must surely have benefited from many long efforts devoted to the end in view. Nevertheless, the structure is limited both in its scope and in its use. In order to transcend the limitations of this type of structure, what was required was another type of structure. This other type of structure would become possible by utilizing the arch and the vault. The use of these elements, in turn, would create a new relationship between blank spaces and functional spaces, and, therefore, it would create an entirely new system with different harmonics. To believe that the beautiful is irrevocably linked to one artistic form, that beauty is, as it were, married to that form, and that all other artistic forms must therefore stand in a false relationship with the beautiful as well as with artistic style—this is a pedantic, schoolmasterish idea, one that may very well seem plausible within the four walls of a classroom but cannot hold up when exposed to the fresh air. Nature never becomes either suspended or stopped, and the limits that certain kinds of mentalities pretend to be able to place upon what is to be considered beautiful—to possess style!—must inevitably remind us, if we may be pardoned the comparison, of the point on the dial of a barometer reading "set fair," although the needle does not stop there any more often than it does on any of the other barometer points. A tempestuous sky or a wind in the woods or on the sea, clouds broken up by a storm, a heavy fog—all these phenomena have their own kind of beauty, every bit as much as does the deep blue of the sky on a hot summer day. At the point where we find ourselves, then—and looking only at questions of art—style as well as the beautiful, we must insist, resides not merely in forms, but in the harmony of a form with reference to an end in view, to a result to be achieved. If a form clearly delineates an object and makes understandable the purpose for which that object was produced, then it is a beautiful form. It is for this reason that the creations of nature are always beautiful in the eyes of the observer. The correct application of a form to its object and to its use or function, and the harmony that necessarily always accompanies such a correct application, can only evoke our admiration, whether we observe it in a stately oak tree or in the smallest of insects. We will discover style in the mechanisms of the wings of a bird of prey, just as we will discover style in the curves of the body of a fish; in these cases style clearly results from mechanisms or curves so aptly designed that flight results in the one case and swimming in the other. It hardly concerns us if someone points out that a bird has wings in order to be able to fly or that this bird is able to fly only because of its wings; the fact is that the wings are a perfect machine, which produces flight. This machine represents a precise expression of the function that it fulfills. We other artists need go no further than this.

If, therefore, we happen to come upon architectural works in which the same condition of harmony obtains between the form, the means, and the object, we naturally declare: "These works have style." We are wholly entitled to speak in this fashion. What, indeed, could style possibly be if it did not arise out of these very qualities? Can style really reside merely in a given form, regardless of the object, the methods employed, or the end in view? Would style somehow be the "soul" of this particular form, inseparable from it? Can such things be? Let us take a highly organized being, a living animal; if we change its habits and surroundings, it can lose the natural harmonic quality of its style. A bird of prey imprisoned inside a cage becomes an awkward, sad, and deformed kind of creature, even though it still has the same instincts, appetites, and qualities. The same is true of a column on a monument; by itself it is nothing but raw form. Is it likely that, if you removed it and put it somewhere else, separated from the causes that brought it into being in the particular proportions it has, it would retain the style and claim that characterize it as part of the ensemble for which it was built? This charm, this style, arises out of the proper context of a particular object—both the ensemble of which it is a harmonious part and its total surroundings. Suppose we rebuilt the Parthenon on the hill of Montmartre—the Parthenon, with its proportions, its silhouette, its proud grace, but without the Acropolis, the sky, the horizon, the sea off Attica, indeed, without the people of Athens! It would still be the Parthenon, no doubt. It would be like the lion in the zoological garden. Now suppose we simply extracted from the Parthenon its Doric order and reproduced it somewhere else along a wall with windows. What name could we give to such a barbarous fantasy? What would happen to the style of the Greek monument under these circumstances? Could not what we are saying here about the Parthenon be true of all such kinds of more or less random borrowings? Does the style of an edifice crumble along with its various members? Does each member possess independently a part of the style of the whole? No: when we build with bits and pieces picked up here and there—in Greece, in Italy—belonging to styles of art remote from our times and our civilization, we are really engaged in collecting body parts and members of cadavers. When we remove these members from the bodies to which they belonged, we cut them off from the source that gave them life. Out of such we cannot fashion work that lives.

In the created order that surrounds us, and is there at our disposition, so to speak, everything that we touch or arrange or change loses its style—unless we reintroduce into the work a style of our own arising out of our own minds, the stamp of which we then place upon the disorder we would otherwise be producing. When we make a garden of the type called "English," we take away the true aspect of nature, which always possesses its own inner logic, and substitute for it our own fancy; style disappears as a consequence. If, however, we lay out a garden according to a plan reflecting human genius, making use of natural products as our materials; if we invent an order that did not exist in nature, rectilinear avenues, for example, or quincunxes, or symmetrical cascades intermingled with architectonic forms—in these cases we may have destroyed nature's own style; but we will have substituted for it a style arising out of our own genius, on the basis of principles that we have laid down in advance. Should we make use of human creations rather than those of nature, adopting mere parts of them as we would stones from a quarry or trees from the forest, we will again, *a fortiori,* be removing the original style from those human creations. In order for style to reappear, it is necessary that a new principle animate the materials with its own breath of life.

This is the way the masters of the Middle Ages understood things to be. They had at their disposition a type of Romanesque art that had descended from the architecture of the Roman Empire, even though it had been purified by a Greco-Byzantine contribution. This type of art did not lack grandeur nor, indeed, even originality. Occidental peoples had succeeded in fashioning a practically indigenous product out of it. After the great impetus that had been given to this style of art in the wake of the first Crusades, however, it had reached a certain relative perfection and had come to lack further inspiration. It operated within the confines of a fairly narrow circle; this was because it was based on no new, whole, or absolute principle. This type of art had limited itself to studying forms without occupying itself with their content. It is true that improvements in construction were realized; there were even innovations in the methods of construction. But the basic structural principles of this architecture remained unchanged. Ornamentation might achieve greater elegance; architectural profiles might be more delicately traced. But this improved ornamentation rested upon no new observations; and the profiles did not clearly indicate their function. Romanesque architects purified their taste; they constantly sought to perfect and refine their forms; but they failed to achieve style, because style results only from an idea linked to a generating principle aiming at a particular end in view. This generating principle was the utilization of materials by taking into consideration their particular qualities, while always allowing the function of the parts to appear—just as, in the case of the human body, we distinguish the skeletal framework, the points where the muscles are attached, and the seat of the various organs . . . the form is solely the result of this use. The consequence is that the ensemble of the entire monument, along with each of its parts, perfectly serves the end in view; nothing is lost.

The art of the French school that arose toward the end of the twelfth century in the middle of a medieval civilization whose principal outlines were beginning to be clear, although confusion still persisted between old ideas and new aspirations, sounded with the clarity of a piercing trumpet fanfare amid the vague humming and buzzing of a crowd. People quickly gave their support to the nucleus of artists and artisans who were prepared to affirm the natural genius of a nation that had been suppressed up to then. The nobility, the clergy, and the bourgeoisie were all prepared to pour their treasure into programs of building new churches, palaces, castles, town mansions, public buildings, and houses, according to the newly adopted principle, meanwhile hastening to demolish earlier structures already in place. No one thought for a moment of hindering the new artists in the carrying out of their principles. Indeed, only artists without principles are hindered.

A principle is an article of faith; when, in addition, this principle is based on human reason, it can no longer be opposed with the same weapons that might be employed against an unreasoning faith. Just try to shake a geometer's faith in geometry!

The general phenomenon that produced our architecture of the Middle Ages, so endowed as it was with style, was all the more remarkable when we consider that, generally speaking, style finds its most vigorous expression in primitive art, becoming progressively more attenuated as the execution is perfected. It would seem, however, that our lay architecture of the twelfth century in no way possessed the character of primitive art, since its point of departure came from an art in decline, namely, Romanesque art. But we must be careful not to confuse the form of an art with its basic principle. If there were transitions in form between the Romanesque and the Gothic, there were none in structural principle.

With the introduction of a new structural principle, style will arise out of adherence to a law that is unimpeded by exceptions. In proceeding thus, art acts in the same fashion as nature does, style in nature being the corollary of principle.* All this is very simple in the case of primitive civilizations, where everything human has its own style: religion, customs, manners and morals, arts, and dress are all imbued with a distinct flavor deriving from direct and unsophisticated observations. The mythology of the Vedas, like that of the ancient Egyptians, arose out of this kind of direct observation; and these mythologies are accordingly penetrated with a style *par excellence.* Those arts that were an expression of these mythologies similarly possess style. Something quite out of the ordinary, however, is the case of a complex civilization made up of a confused mixture of the debris of an earlier civilization which then turns out to be able to bring to new birth types of artistic expression possessing a style that had been extinguished for centuries. For such a phenomenon to be realized a powerful effort was obviously required, indeed, a great movement of minds along with a fundamental change of outlook. Moreover, to us it seems evident that this great movement of minds was confined to a single class in society. It was neither found in nor appreciated by the other classes, and it is this fact that explains why, even

*We have sufficiently brought out elsewhere the novelty of the new structural principle established by the lay French school of the twelfth century, and hence it is not necessary to dwell upon this here. In any case, this new structural principle can be expressed in a single word: *equilibrium.* [Author's note]

today, the lay inspiration of this art is unknown to most people. The art that was due to this new school of laymen involved a sort of initiation into a number of truths whose existence was barely suspected; it involved a return to a more primitive state, as it were. It took place amid the disorder and collapse of confused traditions; it involved the planting of new seeds in soil that was already teeming with other crops, but they were tangled and broken ones, some of them rotting on top of the others. At first the young plant could barely be seen. Cultivated as it was with great persistence, though, it soon grew to overshadow all the others. It had its own aspect and bearing, just as it produced its own fruit and flowers. For a long time it provided a cover over all the sad debris of the other plants, which at that point were lying in its shadow.

The opinion we are expressing here regarding the formation of an art within a certain class of society without the other classes of society being directly involved may perhaps seem strange to some, almost as if the art in question had been practiced as a kind of Freemasonry. The obstacles to such a development would appear to be very great; it is not clear how the vigor of the principles of such an art could be maintained at one and the same time against the monastic establishments, which had maintained a monopoly on teaching up to that point; against a secular clergy, which tended to reach toward omnipotence; against a nobility that tended to be jealous; and against a lower class that was simply ignorant and vulgar or rude.

But it was precisely in the face of such antagonisms that men of principle were obliged to affirm their principles. At the end of the twelfth century, the feudal system in France was in a situation for which there was no parallel anywhere in Europe. In other countries the balance between power in society and the various social classes was less equal. Social antagonisms did not give rise to countervailing powers in a society engaged in a permanent struggle. In one place, old municipal traditions had been preserved; in another, pure feudalism still reigned, or else a kind of theocracy, or else a monarchy tempered with some civil-type liberties. In these diverse kinds of systems, art spoke a language that was more clearly understood than was the case in France. In the case of the almost republican institutions of the Italian municipalities, art was as much a public thing as it had been in ancient Greek city-states. If you were an artist or an artisan, you fulfilled a public function. Art was understood by everyone; it was honored, envied, sermonized about, or even persecuted, as the case might be. Under an absolute feudal regime, the artist was nothing else but a bondman liable to forced labor, a villein, or a serf obliged to carry out the orders or even the whims of the master who stood over him. In a theocracy tied to a hieratic order no artist could either develop or change; what had been the practice yesterday remained the practice today. In a country that enjoyed more liberal institutions, such as, for example, England, there existed among the various classes of society some frequent common interests, which made possible some mutual comprehension between the various classes. In France, however, there was, on the one hand, a feudal nobility that maintained its class prejudices, founding them on the right of conquest; on the other hand, there was another but contested power, which sought support sometimes from the nobility, sometimes from the communes, and sometimes from the higher clergy: this was the monarchy. There was also a population at large that had not completely forgotten its old tradition of municipal liberties; it was a class that was always ready to rise up; it was intrepid, industrious, pugnacious. Alongside this class, there was a secular clergy, which was jealous of the predominance of both the monastic establishments and the feudal nobility. The secular clergy saw itself as a kind of clerical oligarchy and dreamed of an alliance with the rising power of the towns; all this was to take place under a monarch without real power, even if he was surrounded with great prestige; he was to be a king who would be a sort of Venetian doge, ruling alongside a senate of bishops. But in such a society as this, who would be involved in the practice of the arts? Would it be the monastic establishments? It was not the least important area where they might possibly act. In the communes the old Gallic spirit was being revived. These communes were almost constantly in turmoil, constantly struggling with the feudal nobility. Though they were both industrious and rich, the bourgeois were divided into different bodies in accordance with the art or craft that they practiced. They also often had to meet and make their plans in secret because their meeting halls were always being dismantled or they were forbidden to hold their meetings in the public square. These groups became foyers of municipal liberties, and schools of lay artists were formed within them. When the day came that they were able to work independently, without reference to the monastic establishments, the bishops recognized in them a potential for helping the bishops carry out their projects in the face of the power of the abbeys and of the lay nobility; the bishops thus turned to these schools of lay artists in order to secure their help in building a worthy and proper monument to the city itself, namely, the cathedral. (See the entry "Cathédrale.") Who in that era would ever have been able to appreciate the extent of the sheer intellectual work that went into the development of art by means of the meetings of these bourgeois artists and artisans? They had been obliged to learn their arts and crafts literally in the shadows; when they suddenly were able to bring out their construction activities into the full light of day, their monuments seemed to be highly mysterious to everybody except themselves. And just as in an individual work of art style emerges only if the artist lives apart from the workaday world, so the expressions of the general style that prevailed among these artists were like a perfume arising out of the collective state of mind that was produced by a concentration of ideas and of tendencies belonging to a class of citizens who had been able to fashion for themselves their own world separate from the world around them.* The new school of lay art adopted absolutely and from the beginning its set purpose: its art would be established on the laws of equilibrium. These laws of equilibrium, of course, had not been observed in architecture up to that time. The other foundations of this art were geometry and the observation of natural phenomena. Everything was to proceed by way of a crystallization, so to speak; nothing was to deviate in its development from the strict path of logic. Anyone who wishes to substitute principles for traditions is obliged to study the plants of the field with minute care in order to derive from nature a type of ornamentation that is suitable for his needs. Any school that has studied natural flora minutely, and natural fauna as well, and that has succeeded by the application of logical method in

*There does not exist any example of an artist who has achieved in his work what is called style and who at the same time has simply lived the life of the world at large in the complicated and diffuse social situation of our modern societies. There is in true style something sharp and harsh, which is quickly diluted and attenuated as a result of contact with the world, such as the world has become over time. Thus it is that the quality most lacking in works of our time, even works often remarkable in other ways, is, precisely, style. What replaces it is *manner,* and all too often, manner is taken to be style, even among artists. [Author's note] creating out of stone an organism with its own laws similar to those of a living organism—this school does not have to be preoccupied with style; these methods, then as always, constituted the very essence of style. The day when artists go out looking for style, that is when art no longer has style. It is better to begin with an art that, in itself, is impregnated with style. Whenever an architecture is, by its very constitution, logical, true, and subject to a principle from which it does not for a moment deviate; whenever it is the absolute and exacting result of this principle—then any example of the work will always have style, even if the individual artist happens to be mediocre. Such an architecture will continue in future ages to be a subject of admiration for some, and of tiresome comparisons for others. Is it not precisely this latter sentiment to which we must attribute the disapproval that has so often been heaped upon the architecture of the Middle Ages? All its characteristics—its unity of style, its logical aims, its disdain for the traditions of antiquity, its freedom, the mystery of the interrelationship of all its parts—all these things have counted as so many reproaches against it in the minds of those for whom architecture is a kind of game played with forms borrowed from imperial Rome or Renaissance Italy, without any understanding of those forms. Many have found it easier to affect disdain for the architectural art of the Middle Ages than to attempt to study its principles and thus to understand how their application just might have constituted something wholly new in art. Instead, the sharpness of this style of architecture has been considered barbarous, and the science of its various combinations has been held to be nothing but the reign of confusion. The truth is, though, that the nature of these very reproaches is actually an indication of the very qualities that distinguish this kind of art. Nevertheless, it would probably be impossible ever to expect artists who think architecture is some kind of an exterior shell or cover, devoid of any ideas, meaning, or logical cohesion, and having no necessary relationship to its object, to understand and appreciate the work of medieval masters who never laid down a stone or a piece of wood or traced out a profile without being able to give a reason for what they were doing.

This is what our school of lay architects of the end of the twelfth century actually accomplished: they devised a structural system that was free, extensive, and applicable to every kind of plan, one that allowed the utilization of every kind of material, as it did every kind of combination, from the most complex to the simplest; they endowed that structural system with a form that was nothing less than a wholly organic expression of the system itself; they applied a type of decoration to the form that never clashed with it but rather always accentuated it, meanwhile explaining this type of decoration by means of combinations of profiles traced out according to a geometric method, a method that was nothing else but a corollary of the method employed by this architecture as a whole; they gave to this architecture (that is to say, to this new structural system endowed with an appropriate artistic form) proportions that were based on the simplest principles of stability, those principles, indeed, that are immediately grasped by the eye; then they enriched the whole with a type of ornamentation methodically derived from nature and based upon exact and delicate observations of plants and animals; they provided, finally, this organic, unitary architecture that they had thus created with a type of statuary that always went well with it without conflict or clash and, indeed, was always an integral part of it. This is only a summary of what this architectural school accomplished. Now, style is inherent in an architectural art when that art is practiced in accordance with a logical and harmonious order, whether in its details or as a whole, whether in its principles or in its form; nothing in such an architectural art is ever left to chance or fantasy. It is, however, nothing but fantasy that guides an artist if, for example, he provides a wall that has no need of it with an architectural order; or if he provides with a buttress a column already erected with a view toward carrying a load. It is fantasy that includes in the same building concave bays along with square bays terminating with horizontal beam members; or that inserts projecting cornices or ledges between the floors of a building where there are no roof drains; or that raises up pediments over bays opening on a wall; or that cuts into an upper story in order to make a door opening for the people or vehicles that must pass through the door; and so on. If it is not fantasy that leads to the construction of such things, so contrary to reason, then it must be what is commonly called *taste.* But is it a proof of good taste in architecture not to proceed in accordance with reason? Architecture, after all, is an art that is destined to satisfy, before everything else, material needs that are perfectly well defined; and architecture is obliged to make use of materials whose qualities result from laws to which we must necessarily submit.

It is an illusion to imagine that there can be style in architectural works whose features are unexplained and unexplainable; or that there can be style where the form is nothing but the product of memory crammed with a number of different motifs taken from here or from there. It would be equally valid to say that there could be style in a literary work of which the chapters or, indeed, even the sentences were nothing but a loose collection of words borrowed from ten different authors, all writing on different subjects.

Leaving aside these sad and costly examples of abuses, if we compare our architecture of the twelfth and thirteenth centuries with another type of architecture possessing style in the true sense, a style arising out of its own genius, namely, the architecture of imperial Rome, we will find that the living essence of style is more marked in the works of the Middle Ages: they possess a more perfect harmony; the link between their structure and their form is more organic, as it is between their form and its decoration.

Let us take an example. In Figure 5, *A,* we have the springing of a Roman groin vault on the capital of a column over a fixed vertical point. In the case of this architectural member, what is the reason for the entablature *B?* What purpose does it serve? It is all a matter of taste, it might be replied. For my part, though, my reason and consequently my taste are shocked to find between [this vault *A* and] the member that actually carries the load—the capital of the column, *C,* which is already sufficiently crowned and widened to carry the load—an entire arrangement of architrave, frieze, and cornice. I do not understand the purpose of such an arrangement; it is quite superfluous. What is the point of the projecting ledge *a* on the cornice? Could the impost of the vault, *b,* not be carried just as easily on the capital? If, on the other hand, these projections were supposed to carry the scaffolding needed to secure the masonry of the vault, then this indicates an undue emphasis on accessories that should never have been anything but provisional in the first place; headers placed in the vault at *d,* which could have been cut off after the construction was complete, could readily have served this function.

Besides, why expend so many apparent efforts to which the decoration seems to assign such great value merely in order to carry imposts on which the pressure is not vertical but oblique? This pressure penetrates into the mass of the masonry in such a way that the vault, by the very effect of its curves, does not appear

Figure 5

to the eye to be supported by these projecting members anyway. If, though, we then examine the springing of the vault according to the system adopted at the end of the twelfth century (as shown by *G*), do we not find that the load rests quite clearly on the fascicular column and on the common capital? Is there a single useless member here, a member whose function and reason for being are not immediately apparent? The problem to be solved is the same in both cases. Was it the Roman architect or the French master who solved the problem in the most satisfactory manner? If style results from the perfect accord between purpose and form, in which of these two examples can style be said to reside?

The particular Roman *arrangement* that we have reproduced here is, in fact, the one that lacks style. Whenever a Roman artist succeeded in producing work with style, it was always when he was not consciously seeking it: in the great Roman public works, for example, such as in a huge amphitheater where everything was sacrificed to a well-conceived plan; in the simplest of the baths (leaving aside the borrowed ornamentation); or in the broad porticoes built to shelter large crowds. Whenever the Roman attempted to play the artist in the Greek manner, however, appropriating an architectural order without understanding its original significance and then applying it uncritically to the springing of a vault, or employing it as a buttress along a wall, then the art of the Roman lacked the first characteristic of style, which is clarity. By clarity we mean the proper application of form to its object. Ruins that are truly Roman ruins, based on Roman ideas, possess style. If you were to restore most of these ruins, putting the orders back in place within their accustomed frameworks, supplying them with the ornamentation, the stringcourses, and the like that were removed by the barbarians or by the passage of time, you would find the style proper to these grandiose constructions being eclipsed in precisely the measure that you supplied them with features borrowed from another art, another order of ideas, or other structural principles.

Style is the consequence of a principle pursued methodically; it is a kind of emanation from the form of the work that is not consciously sought after. Style that is sought after is really nothing else but *manner.* Manner becomes dated; style never does.

When an entire population of artists and artisans is strongly imbued with logical principles in accordance with which form is the consequence of the object as well as its purpose, then style will be present in the works that issue from their hands, from the most ordinary vase to the most monumental building, from the simplest household utensil to the costliest piece of furniture. We admire this unity in the best of Greek antiquity, and we find the same kind of thing again in the best of what the Middle Ages produced, though the two types of art are different because the two civilizations that produced them were different. We cannot appropriate to ourselves the style of the Greeks, because we are not Athenians. Nor can we re-create the style of our predecessors in the Middle Ages, for the simple reason that time has moved on. We can only affect the manner of the Greeks or of the artists of the Middle Ages; that is to say, we can only produce pastiches. If we cannot accomplish what they did, we can at least proceed as they did by allowing ourselves to become penetrated with principles that are true and natural principles—just as they were imbued with true and natural principles. If we succeed in doing this, our works will possess style without our having to seek after it.

The thing that particularly distinguishes the architecture of the Middle Ages from those architectures of antiquity worthy of being considered types of art is the freedom of medieval architecture in its utilization of form. The principles that were accepted, although different from those of the Greeks and even of the Romans, may have been followed with a bit too much rigor; but form was nevertheless allowed a freedom and elasticity that had been unknown up to that time. To put the whole thing more exactly, form was moved onto a more extended field of operations, whether we are talking about structural methods, systems of proportion, or the use of details borrowed from geometry or from natural flora and fauna. Architecture in its organic aspect saw a more ample development; it was based upon a greater number of actual observations; it was more scientific and sophisticated, more complicated, and hence also more delicate. It constituted an organic whole already on the road to modernity, and thus it is rather strange that it should have once suffered rejection as something antiquated; it is equally strange that it should have been replaced by types of architecture that are actually considerably more remote from the modern spirit. In architecture, however, everything today is a contradiction. If we look at things as they really are, we will find that what is generally wanted is the easy way out, a path to be followed that allows us simply to slip right past principles based on reason without ever coming up against them.

For many people style in architecture is nothing but a kind of outer decorative shell or envelope. Even among artists we find many who sincerely believe they have achieved a work of style when they have superimposed upon a construction entirely modern in conception some ornaments or profiles borrowed from Etruscan, Greek, or even Gothic models—or ornaments or profiles borrowed from the Italian Renaissance. Certainly the traditions of an era anterior to our own are worth knowing, studying, and even imitating; but it is not in any of this that *style* manifests itself. Style resides much more in the principal lines of a construction, in the harmonious ensemble of its proportions, than in the garments with which architectonic works are clothed. The same is true of the work of a painter, where style manifests itself in the choice of lines, in the ensemble of the composition, and in the truth of the gestures represented; these are the important things, rather than a search for antiquated materials or an attempt to achieve exactitude in reproducing clothing and accessories. It is remarkable that this truth, recognized where painting and sculpture are concerned, is only grasped with difficulty where architecture is concerned. This example alone should prove to us how it is that the most elementary principles of architecture continue to remain generally unknown, and how the most natural of these principles have been distorted.

The Middle Ages represented distinct progress over the era of antiquity in certain important respects, and it is in these respects that we should follow the Middle Ages. The Middle Ages put the idea above every tradition or doctrine; the idea was pursued fanatically, often blindly, in fact. But to follow out an idea, even a foolish one, even one impossible of realization, is not to turn one's back on progress as such. Alchemists seeking the philosopher's stone opened up the road to the development of the science of chemistry. The nobles and free peasants who blindly rushed to the Orient following Peter the Hermit moved civilization a giant step forward thereby, especially in the arts. Even chivalry, so easy to mock, planted seeds that produced some of the best fruits of our own society. St. Francis of Assisi was a passionate lover of nature and of the created world; he spent hours contemplating a flower or a bird; he considered himself part of a created whole, and he did not separate the human from the rest of the universe. Antiquity produced nothing like this: neither among the Egyptians, nor among the Greeks, nor even less among the Romans were there ever any alchemists searching for the philosopher's stone; nor were there ever any warriors rushing into battle in the name of an idea; nor, certainly, was there ever anyone like St. Francis of Assisi! What is chiefly reflected in the art of ancient Egypt or of ancient Greece is the narrow egotism of ancient man. The art is perfect, complete, exact, clear, and finished. But this art has no *beyond* to it. If it moves us, it is because our imagination as moderns associates it with the things and events to which its surviving monuments bear witness. It is necessary to be educated in order to appreciate properly an ancient monument—that is, in order to experience an emotion in viewing it that has no reference to anything beyond what the object itself exhibits. The most modest construction of the Middle Ages, however, can set even the ignorant to dreaming. Let us be very clear about what we are saying here: we are not trying to make comparisons favorable either to one or to the other of these kinds of art; we are not engaged in any special pleading for one or the other. We are merely trying to bring out the qualities that truly do distinguish the two kinds of art and to identify those elements that truly bring out the particular style with which they are imbued. We may be sure that posterity will agree with us about style on the day when it is finally realized by all that style is nothing else but the natural savor or aroma of a principle, of an idea followed in conformity with the logical order of things in the world; style is not something sought after. Style develops as does a growing plant, in accordance with certain laws of nature; it is not some sort of spice that one takes out of a bag and sprinkles upon works that, by themselves, have no savor, that is to say, no style. From everything that has been said up to now, it should be clear that we have not been trying to lay down a set of rules by which the artists of the Middle Ages somehow injected style into their works. The style was there because the form they gave to architecture was the logical consequence of the structural principles they were following. All of this dictated (1) the materials to be used; (2) the way of putting these materials to work; (3) the aims to be achieved; and (4) the way of deducing the details of the work logically from the plan of the whole, a way similar to the natural order found in the case of created things, where the part is complete and self-contained like the whole and is constituted like it. Most of the articles in this *Dictionary* bring out both the logical spirit and the unity of principles that guided the masters of the Middle Ages. It is not their fault, though, if we have since identified unity with uniformity, and if our architects still persist in seeing nothing but disorder and confusion in an architectural organism whose features and logical connections they have in fact never studied. We say "organism," for it is difficult to assign any other name to this architecture of the Middle Ages, which developed and made progress in the same formative way that nature herself works—namely, by departing from a simple principle, which then becomes modified, perfected, and made more complex without ever damaging or destroying its original essence. All this was true up to and including the law of equilibrium of forces, which was brought into play in this architecture for the first time, and which almost transformed its constructions into living things. The law of equilibrium of forces opposes structural actions with inverse actions, pressures with counterpressures, overhangs with counterweights; it diffuses weight by spreading it out away from where it would tend to concentrate vertically; it provides each profile with a purpose related to the place that it occupies, and each stone with a function such that no stone could be removed without compromising the entire structure. Is this not, indeed, to give a work life insofar as it is given to us to give life to something with the work of our hands? No, it is nothing but science, ingenuity, some will object; it is not art at all. They are no doubt entitled to their opinion. But what is the art of architecture then? Is it nothing but a traditional form? A completely arbitrary one? If it is simply a traditional form, why one tradition rather than another then? If it is simply an arbitrary form, then it has neither principles nor laws, and this means that it is not even an art, but instead is merely the costliest and least justified of all possible fantasies.

That each stone of a building fill a useful and necessary function; that each profile have a precise purpose and that that purpose be clearly indicated in its line; that a building's proportions be derived from principles of geometric harmony; that ornamentation be based on natural flora, as observed truly and with imagination; that nothing be left to chance; that materials be employed in accordance with their qualities and that these qualities be indicated by the form they are given—does it follow from all of this that art is absent and science alone operative? We can admit, if you will, that the presence of all these material facts in no way constitutes an art. But is that the end of it? Would constructions fashioned along these lines be devoid also of ideas? And would these ideas be impenetrable and mysterious for all of us who are their children? The medieval lay masters were in fact the first to attempt to do what we do today, if not in architecture, so often forced as it is into an "academic" mold and hence so often backward, at any rate in industry, in naval construction, in major public works, and the like. The medieval lay masters wanted to master their materials, and to bend and fashion them in such a way that anything was possible. They vaulted huge spaces on slender points of support. They introduced light into their enormous covered spaces in such a way that this light itself constituted a kind of decoration, indeed painting. There were no longer walls but rather translucent tapestries. Forced by the conditions of their times to construct lordly manorial dwellings that could serve at the same time as fortresses, they were obliged to subordinate form to these two distinct necessities laid upon them. Yet they were still able to fashion a homogeneous art that was sufficiently flexible to fulfill both of these disparate requirements. The castles they built are both fortresses and habitations; this double function of theirs is clearly written on their front.

One of the marks of style is the adoption of a form that accords with each object. When an architectural work indicates clearly on its front the purpose for which it was constructed, then it comes very close to possessing style by that fact alone. When, in addition, it forms a harmonious whole with the structures that surround it, then it is pretty certain to possess style. Now, it is evident to those who have studied the varied constructions belonging to the period of the Middle Ages with which we are concerned here that, among the diverse expressions of the day, there did exist a harmony; there was agreement. The church did not resemble the town hall; nor did the latter resemble the hospice; nor did the hospice resemble the lord's castle; nor did the castle resemble the palace of the king—nor did any of these buildings resemble the dwellings of the bourgeois. The purpose of each of these various structures was plainly written upon it; yet at the same time there existed a link between all of them. They were all products of a social situation that was both the master of its own kind of artistic expression and, at the same time, never hesitated or faltered in its choice of a particular artistic language. Yet in that harmony what variety there was! Individual artists preserved their own personalities, even while they all spoke the same artistic language—and with what fecundity as each spoke it in turn! This was because the architectural laws they observed were not based upon accepted forms but rather upon accepted basic principles. For them a column was not an object that, by tradition, had to have a height that was a fixed number of times its diameter. Rather, it was a cylinder whose form had to be calculated in accordance with the weight it was expected to carry. For them a capital was not an ornament that crowned the shaft of a column but rather a projecting foundational feature placed on top of a column in order to carry the various members that the column was designed to support. For them a door was not a kind of bay with height equal to its width but rather an opening designed to admit the number of persons likely to be passing at the same time beneath its lintel. . . . But why go on insisting on the application of all these principles, which have so many times been spelled out in this *Dictionary*? All these principles amount to nothing else but sincerity in the use of form. Style enters into the execution of works of art in the degree that these works avoid departures from expressions that are true, clear, and appropriate. Finding the appropriate expression and being clear—these are eminent French qualities, which we possess in the plastic arts every bit as much as we possess them in the written or spoken word. Indeed, even the French architecture of the Renaissance, provided it was executed by competent hands—and in spite of the spurious elements dictated by the court or by fashion—even French Renaissance architecture preserved these same qualities of clarity and appropriateness; they are natural to us. The work of Philibert de l'Orme [Delorme] is proof enough. Here was a master architect who, in his portico in the Tuileries, adopted an order from antiquity joined to arcades by way of buttresses. He did not, however, design engaged columns; he used either pilasters or entire columns, the latter, projecting over the arcading of the portico, carrying balconies, juttings of a terrace over the garden, which served as kinds of watchtowers. The architect thus provided a justification for the use of his columns; the columns actually served a purpose, and were thus more than just a banal decoration. His order, of course, was not supposed to carry the unfortunate new floor level that has since been imposed upon it; surely the least defect of this latter feature is to render incomprehensible the entire disposition of the ground floor. Accepting the utilization of the order in this case, though, let us examine what kind of art and skill our master architect exhibited in utilizing it and endowing it with style—a style that, once again, arose out of an appropriate application of true principles. Philibert either could not or did not judge it appropriate to put up monolithic Ionic columns; instead he constructed the columns by placing one column drum on top of another. Moreover, he frankly revealed the structure of his construction. He separated the drums quarried in upper layers of Saint-Leu stone from those quarried in lower layers of marble; the effect was a number of rings circling the shaft like rings on a finger. On the marble drums he sculpted delicate designs, which scarcely stand out at all, thus indicating the delicate nature of the material. On the Saint-Leu stone drums he put fluting, and, beneath the capital, in order to effect a transition between the coldness of the shafts and the richness of the crowning, he fashioned laurel branches running up out of the fluting.

We accept the utilization of an order of antiquity when it is applied with as much sagacity as this, being subordinated to a structural mode imposed by the material being used. Art is not at all impossible in such a situation as this; invention is a distinct possibility. No one will challenge the elegance of the architectural piece under discussion, especially if we imagine it at least in spirit as being free of all the barbarous superfluities later imposed on it that tend to snuff out its life. If, however, we were to repeat this charming motif today, without reference to the reasons it was fashioned in the first place, style would disappear from the resulting product; it would be a pastiche that betrayed incomprehension of the original; it would be a vague and confused translation of language that was simple, logical, and clear. In order to possess style the work of an architect cannot dispense with ideas in its conceptual stage, any more than it can dispense with the intervention of reason in the course of its development. However, not all the splendors of the sculpture, its richness as well as its profusion of details, can make up for an initial lack of ideas or a lack of reasoning thereafter.

NOTES

INTRODUCTION

Pages 1–30

1. Frank Lloyd Wright, *An Autobiography,* New York, 97. This follows a passage in the late 1880s when he arrives in Chicago, and he says he got out of a church library Owen Jones's *Grammar of Ornament* and Viollet-le-Duc's *Habitations of Mankind in all Ages*: "I had read his *Dictionnaire,* the *Raisonné,* at home, got from the Madison city library." There has been some discussion as to whether or not Wright, who did not read French, was confused in his remembrance of these early readings and did not in fact mean the *Entretiens.* I am grateful to Narcisso Menocal for pointing this out to me.

2. There is no publishing history of the *Dictionnaire,* and few references to it in the published correspondence of Viollet-le-Duc. The best analysis to date is offered in the invaluable article by Françoise Boudon, "Le réel et l'imaginaire chez Viollet-le-Duc: les figures du *Dictionnaire de l'architecture,*" *Revue de l'Art* 58–59 (1983), 95–114. See also H. Lipstadt, "Architectural Publications, Exhibitions, and Competitions," in E. Blau and Edgar Kaufman (eds.), *Architecture and Its Image,* Montreal: Canadian Centre for Architecture, 1989, 109.

3. Ernest Beulé, "L'Enseignement de l'Architecture," in *Causeries sur l'Art,* Paris, 1867, 57.

4. The comment was actually made in relation to the dictionary of the decorative arts, which Viollet-le-Duc published in tandem with his more famous dictionary of architecture, the *Dictionnaire raisonné du mobilier français de l'époque carolingienne à la Renaissance* (6 vols., Paris, 1858–75). It comes from a letter of 1859 quoted in the preface to *Lettres inédites de Viollet-le-Duc receuillis et annotés par son fils,* Paris, 1902, v–vi, and in a subsequent review published in *Moniteur.*

5. Hubert Damisch, Introduction, *Viollet-le-Duc, L'architecture raisonné,* Paris: Hermann, 1978, 7–29. This essay is Damisch's virtuoso demonstration that Viollet-le-Duc's enterprise in the *Dictionnaire* could be analyzed by the methods of structuralism. The argument was made in much more strident terms by Damisch in, appropriately enough, the article "Structure et l'Art," *Encyclopédie Universalis,* Paris, vol. 17, 287–289. A thoroughgoing analysis and *mise en cause* of Damisch's claims is the subject of Philippe Boudon and Philippe Deshayes, *Viollet-le-Duc, Le Dictionnaire d'architecture, relevés et observations,* Brussels: Mardaga, 1979. It is not our purpose here to reanimate that debate over the relevance of structuralist linguistics to analyzing Viollet-le-Duc's method; rather we have preferred to situate the text in mid-nineteenth-century debates, so that the student of Viollet-le-Duc might temper any renewed efforts

to analyze the *Dictionnaire* by an awareness of the place it held in the polemics of Viollet-le-Duc's milieu.

6. We cannot undertake here a summary of the numerous attempts made to refute Viollet-le-Duc's theory of Gothic architecture, and in particular his theory of the structure of Gothic vaulting. Whatever position one takes, it is clear that these debates played a major role in the rapid decline of Viollet-le-Duc's reputation in the mid-twentieth century. The most famous of these is, of course, Pol Abraham's *Viollet-le-Duc et le rationalisme mediéval,* Paris, 1934.

7. As Robin Middleton has pointed out, Viollet-le-Duc moved around the time of the controversy over Ste.-Clotilde, from the pages of Didron's *Annales Archéologiques* to the pages of Daly's *Revue Général de l'Architecture.* See Robin Middleton and David Watkin, *Neoclassical and Nineteenth Century Architecture,* New York: Abrams, 1980, 357–358. After 1862, and with the passing of the editorial duties of the rival *Gazette des Architectes et du Bâtiment* into the hands of Viollet-le-Duc's followers, and eventually his son, this became for a number of years the official organ of the "*école rationaliste.*"

8. See note 4.

9. The *Entretiens* were translated in both England and the United States during Viollet-le-Duc's lifetime. In England, a self-styled disciple of Viollet-le-Duc, Benjamin Bucknell, published the *Discourses on Architecture,* London, 1877, while a translation entitled *Lectures on Architecture* was published in America by Henry van Brunt (Boston, 1875–81). On Bucknell, see Robin Middleton, "Viollet-le-Duc's Influence in Nineteenth-Century England," *Art History* 4 (1981), 203–219.

10. A complete repertory of Viollet-le-Duc's writings was prepared by Jean-Jacques Aillagon in the catalogue of the centennial exhibition held at the Grand Palais, *Viollet-le-Duc,* Paris: Réunion des musées nationaux, 1980, 395–404. The children's books, all of which have recently been reprinted, were published by Hetzel as part of his series, *Bibliothèque d'éducation et de récréation.*

11. The most succinct and accessible recent summary of Viollet-le-Duc's biography is Robin Middleton's entry "Viollet-le-Duc" in the *Macmillan Encyclopedia of Architects,* vol. 4, New York, 1982, 324–332. See also the classic essay by Sir John Summerson, "Viollet-le-Duc and the Rational Point of View," in *Heavenly Mansions,* London, 1949, 135–158.

12. See Barry Bergdoll, "The Legacy of Viollet-le-Duc's Drawings," *Architectural Record* 169 (mid-August 1981), 62–67. See also Bruno Foucart, "Viollet-le-Duc dessinateur, ou la passion de l'analyse," in *Viollet-le-Duc,* Paris, 1980, 338–340.

13. *Le voyage de Viollet-le-Duc en Italie.* Exhibition catalogue, Paris: Ecole Nationale Supérieure des Beaux-Arts, 1981.

14. Françoise Bercé, *Les premiers travaux de la Commission des Mon-*

uments Historiques, 1837–1848, Paris, 1979; and Laurent Theis, "Guizot et les institutions de mémoire," in Pierre Nora (ed.), *Les lieux de mémoire, II. La nation,* Paris: Gallimard, 1986, 568–592.

15. See "Restoration," p. 207, infra.

16. "De la construction des édifices religieux en France, depuis le commencement du Christianisme jusqu'au XVIe siècle," *Annales Archéologiques* 1 (1844), 179–186; 2 (1845), 78–85, 143–150, 338–349; 3 (1845), 321–336; 4 (1846), 266–283; 6 (1847), 194–205. Also, "Du Style Gothique aux XIXe siècle," in vol. 4 (1846), 325–353, which includes a full reprint of Raoul-Rochette's attack on the Gothic party. On this incident see Robin Middleton and David Watkin, *Neoclassical and Nineteenth Century Architecture,* New York: Abrams, 1980, 357–358. On the *Annales Archéologiques* consult especially Georg Germann, *Gothic Revival in Britain and Europe,* Cambridge: MIT, 1972.

17. One of the few parts of the dictionary translated into English in the nineteenth century, "Construction," appeared as the book by George M. Huss, *Rational Building; being a translation of the article "Construction,"* New York, 1895. The article "Restoration" also appeared in English as *On Restoration,* translated by Charles Wethered, London, 1875.

18. *Annales Archéologiques, op. cit.,* vol. 1 (1844), 181.

19. Ibid., vol. 2 (1845), 78.

20. Ibid., vol. 3 (1845), 325–326.

21. On this movement, see Barry Bergdoll, *Historical Reasoning and Architectural Politics: Léon Vaudoyer and the Development of French Historicist Architecture,* Ph.D. Thesis, Columbia University, 1986, esp. chapter 5; Robin Middleton, "The Rationalist Interpretations of Léonce Reynaud and Viollet-le-Duc," *AA Files* 11 (1986), 29–48; and most recently, David van Zanten, *Designing Paris: The Architecture of Duban, Labrouste, Duc, and Vaudoyer,* Cambridge: MIT, 1987.

22. *Annales Archéologiques, op. cit.,* vol. 6 (1847), 197.

23. On the academy's creation of an elite through the privilege of defining not only the doctrine but the very vocabulary of aesthetic discourse, see Jean-Pierre Epron, *L'Ecole de l'Académie (1671–1793), ou l'institution du goût en architecture,* Nancy, 1984; Werner Szambien, *Symétrie, Goût, Caractère,* Paris, 1986; and Barry Bergdoll, "Competing in the Academy and the Marketplace," in H. Lipstadt (ed.), *The Experimental Tradition, Essays on Competitions in Architecture,* New York, 1989, esp. 30–31.

24. Under the editorship of M. C. Bailly de Merlieux, the *Encyclopédie portative, ou resumé universel des sciences, des lettres, et des arts et une collection de traités séparés par une Société des Savans et de Gens de Lettres,* appeared in various editions as a small encyclopedia with individual volumes on specific subjects. E. Viollet-le-Duc had prepared two volumes, one on poetry (1828) and one on dramatic literature (1830).

25. Hugh M. Davidson, "The Problem of Scientific Order vs. Alphabetical Order in the *Encyclopédie,*" in *Irrationalism in the Eighteenth Century, Studies in 18th century culture* (Cleveland) 2 (1972), 33–49.

26. On Quatremère de Quincy in these years, see René Schneider, *Quatremère de Quincy et son intervention dans les arts,* Paris, 1916.

27. The publication history of Quatremère de Quincy's dictionary is complicated, and no full-scale study of this seminal and highly influential work exists. Begun in the mid-1780s as a three-volume work for Panckoucke's *Encyclopédie méthodique,* the work was not completed until nearly fifty years later when Quatremère issued a two-volume version of the work, revised and condensed, as the *Dictionnaire historique d'architecture,* Paris, 1832. Although illustrations were initially planned, these were never, for economical and practical reasons, inserted. Translations of some of its key articles have appeared in recent years, although the choice is often as illuminating about recent debates on architecture as it is about the essence of Quatremère de Quincy's theory. The article "Type" was published by Antony Vidler in *Oppositions* 8 (1977), 147–150, while more recently the articles "Architecture," "Character," "Idea," and "Imitation" were published in the London magazine *9H* 7 (1985), 25–39. In French, the articles "Architecture," "Construction," "Copier," "Imitation," "Invention," and "Type" are published in a supplement to a reprint edition of Quatremère de Quincy's 1823 publication, *De l'Imitation,* Brussels: AAM Editions, 1980. On Panckoucke's *Encyclopédie méthodique,* see George B. Watts, "Charles Joseph Panckoucke," in *Studies on Voltaire and the Eighteenth Century* 68 (1969), 71–205, and Robert Darnton, *The Business of Enlightenment: A Publishing History of the Encyclopédie, 1775–1800,* Cambridge: Harvard, 1979, especially the chapter "The Ultimate *Encyclopédie,*" 395–459. On Quatremère's theory of imitation, see most recently Sylvia Lavin, "Quatremère de Quincy and the Invention of a Modern Language of Architecture," Ph.D. Thesis, Columbia University, 1990.

28. See Paul Bénichou, *Le temps des prophètes: doctrines de l'age romantique,* Paris, 1977.

29. Robin Middleton, "Viollet-le-Duc's Academic Ventures and the *Entretiens sur l'Architecture,*" in *Gottfried Semper und die Mitte des 19. Jahrhunderts,* Basel, 1977, 242–253. See also Bruno Foucart, Introduction to *Débats et Polémiques, A Propos de l'Enseignement des Arts du Dessin,* Paris: Ecole Nationale Supérieure des Beaux-Arts, 1984.

30. Viollet-le-Duc, entry "Unité," *Dictionnaire,* vol. 9, 339.

31. Quatremère de Quincy, "Gothique (Architecture)," in *Dictionnaire méthodique,* Paris, 1832, vol. 1, 678.

32. Preface to vol. 1, xix–xx.

33. Preface, *op. cit.,* x.

34. *Dictionnaire,* vol. 10, n.p.

35. Ibid.

36. Ibid. "Elle [cette forme] nous a paru, précisement à cause de la multiplicité des exemples donnés, devoir être plus favorable aux études, mieux faire connaître les diverses parties compliquées, mais rigoureusement déduites des besoins, qui entrent dans la composition de nos monuments du moyen âge, puisqu'elle nous oblige pour ainsi dire à les disséquer séparément, tout en décrivant les fonctions, le but de ces diverses parties et les modifications qu'elles ont subies."

37. The only sustained consideration of Viollet-le-Duc's interest in Cuvier's comparative anatomy is the suggestive article by Bernard Thaon, "Viollet-le-Duc, Pensée Scientifique et Pensée Architecturale," in *Actes du Colloque International Viollet-le-Duc,* Paris, 1982, 131–142. On Cuvier, see most recently Dorinda Outram, *Georges Cuvier: Vocation, Science and Authority in Post-Revolutionary France,* Manchester, 1984. Semper's relationship to Cuvier has been outlined by Rosemarie Bletter, "Semper," in *Macmillan Encyclopedia of Architects,* vol. 4, New York, 1982, 25–33; by Harry Malgrave in the Introduction to *Gottfried Semper: The Four Elements of Architecture and Other Writings,* Cambridge University Press, 1989; and by Andreas Hauser, "Der 'Cuvier der Kunstwissenschaft': Klassifizierungsprobleme in Gottfried Sempers 'Vergleichender Baulehre,' " in Thomas Balt (ed.), *Grenzbereiche der Architektur,* Basel, 1985, 97–114. The possible influence of Cuvier's writings on other nineteenth-century architectural theorists, including the Americans Horatio Greenough and Leopold Eidlitz, is worthy of further investigation.

38. Marc-Antoine Laugier, *An Essay on Architecture* (translation of *Essai sur l'Architecture,* Paris, 2nd ed., 1755), Los Angeles, 1977. For the nineteenth-century writers, see N. Pevsner, *Some Architectural Writers of the Nineteenth Century,* Oxford, 1975.

39. Eugène-Emmanuel Viollet-le-Duc, *Le massif du Mont-Blanc, étude sur sa constitution géodesique et géologique, sur ses transformations et sur l'état ancien et modern de ses glaciers,* Paris, 1876. See Robin Middleton, "Viollet-le-Duc et les Alpes: la dispute du Mont-Blanc," in *Viollet-le-Duc, Centenaire de la Mort à Lausanne,* Lausanne: Musée historique de l'Ancien-Evêché, 1979, 100–110, and the catalogue edited by Pierre A. Frey, *E. Viollet-le-Duc et le Massif du Mont Blanc, 1868–1879,* Lausanne: Payot, 1988.

40. Ibid., Introduction.

41. Eugène-Emmanuel Viollet-le-Duc, *Histoire d'un dessinateur.* Paris, 1878, 302.

42. It is hinted at in an illustration in the entry "Architecture" in the *Dictionnaire* in which thin iron columns are slyly substituted for masonry supports in a nave elevation, a suggestion realized in 1864 by

Viollet-le-Duc's pupil Anatole de Baudot, in his parish church at Rambouillet.

43. *Dictionnaire,* vol. 9, 345.

44. Ibid.

Architecture

PAGES 31–101

1. G[eorgius] F[lorentius] Gregory, bishop of Tours, *Hist. ecclés. des Francs,* in 10 volumes, revised and collated from new manuscripts and translated into French by J. Guadet and Taranne, Paris, 1836; J. Renonard, vol. 1, p. 178. See the article "Eclaircissements et Observations."

2. Augustin Thierry, *Récits des temps mérovingiens,* vol. 1, p. 253, *Editions* Furne, Paris, 1846.

3. Mabillon, *Ann. Bén.,* vol. III, p. 330.

4. *Bibl. Clun.,* cols. 1, 2, 3, 4—*Cluny au XI*e *siècle,* by the abbé F. Cucherat, 1 vol., Lyons and Paris, 1851.

5. *Bull. Clun.,* pp. 1, 2, 3—Ibid.

6. Udalrici, *Antiq. consuet. Clun. mon.,* book III, chapters VIII and IX.

7. *Cluny au XI*e *siècle,* by the abbé F. Cucherat.

8. Udalrici, *Antiq. cons. Clun. mon.,* book II, chapter VIII *in fine*—Bernardi, *Cons. coenob. Clun.,* P I, chapter XXVII—the abbé Cucherat, p. 83.

9. *S. Anselme de Canterbury,* by M.C. Rémusat, Paris, 1833, p. 43.

10. The abbé Cucherat, p. 104.

11. See the entry "Architecture Monastique."

12. *Ann. Bénéd.,* vol. IV, pp. 207–208.

13. "*Inter praedictus cryptas et cellam novitiorum, posita sit alia cella ubi aurifices, inclusores et vitrei magistri operentur; quae cella habeat longitudinis* CXXV *pedes, latitudinis* XXV."

14. *Cluny au XIe siècle,* by the abbé Cucherat, pp. 106–107.

15. Augustin Thierry, *Lettres sur l'Histoire de France,* Paris, 1842, pp. 401–402.

16. Ibid., p. 412—Hug. Pictav. *Hist. Vezeliac monast., lib.* III, *apud* d'Achery, *Spicilegium,* t. II, pp. 533–535.

17. See the entry "Architecte."

18. See the entry "Architecture Monastique."

19. Ibid.

20. *Histoire des communes de France,* by Baron C.F.E. Dupin, Paris, 1834.

21. Ibid.

22. *Grégoire VII, Saint François d'Assises et Saint Thomas d'Aquin,* by J. Delécluze, Paris, 1844, vol. II, pp. 64–85—*Ouvrages inédits d'Abailard,* by M. Cousin, Introduction, pp. CLV ff.

23. *Abailard et Héloïse,* historical essay, by M. and Mme. Guizot, new edition entirely corrected, Paris, 1853.

24. Félix de Verneilh, *l'Architecture byzantine en France,* Paris, 1852.

25. See the entry "Architecture Religieuse."

26. *Op. cit.,* note 24.

27. See the entry "Construction."

28. See the article of Vitet, in the *Journal des Savants,* January–February and May 1853, on Félix de Verneilh's *l'Architecture byzantine en France,* note 24.

29. See the entries "Architecture Religieuse" and "Construction."

30. See the entry "Autel."

31. See the entries "Peinture" and "Sculpture."

32. The term *Romanesque architecture* is extremely vague, if not false. The "Romanic language," by contrast, was circumscribed within a territory with known limits, on both sides of the Loire. Can the same thing be said of the kind of architecture described as "Romanesque"? (See the article of Vitet cited in note 28, pp. 30–31, for a judicious critique of this term.)

34. See the entries "Architecture Religieuse," "Architecture Civile," and "Architecture Militaire."

34. See the entry "Construction."

35. See the entries "Construction" and "Voute."

36. See the entry "Arc."

37. See the entry "Pinacle."

38. See the entries "Arc" and "Construction."

39. See the entry "Construction."

40. See the demonstration for this in the entry "Flore."

41. See, for example, "Architecture Religieuse," "Architecture Monastique," "Architecture Civile," and "Architecture Militaire."

42. See the entries "Peinture" and "Vitraux."

43. See the entries "Cathédrale" and "Chapelle."

44. See the entries "Architecture Militaire" and "Château."

45. See the entry "Architecture Religieuse."

46. See the entries "Appareil" and "Construction."

47. See the entries "Meneau" and "Rose."

48. See the entry "Architecture Religieuse."

49. Letter from Luther to Ruhel.

50. See the entry "Architecte."

51. "Aliénation de l'hostel Saint-Paul, an. 1516," in *Histoire de la Ville de Paris* by D. Félibien, vol. III, *P. justif.*, p. 574.

52. *Essai sur l'histoire du tiers-état,* by M. A. Thierry, vol. I, p. 116, *éditions* Furne, 1853; *Recueil des anciennes lois françaises,* by M. Isambert, vols. XI and XII, *éditions de Villers-Cotterets,* August 1539.

53. See the entry "Architecture Religieuse."

54. See the entry "Architecture Civile."

Construction

Pages 103–191

1. See the entry "Architecture."
2. See the entry "Architecture Monastique."
3. See the entry "Chaînage."
4. See the entry "Architecture."
5. See the entry "Chapiteaux."
6. See the entry "Corniche."
7. See the entry "Architecture Religieuse."
8. See the entry "Ogive."
9. See the entry "Arc-Boutant."

Restoration

Pages 193–227

1. See the *Monographie de l'église de Notre Dame de Noyon,* by M. L. Vitet and Daniel Ramée, 1845.
2. Ibid., p. 38.
3. Ibid., p. 45.